Legal Frameworks for the Integration of Third-Country Nationals

Immigration and Asylum Law and Policy in Europe

VOLUME 18

Editors

Elspeth Guild
Kingsley Napley Solicitors, London
Centre for Migration Law, Radboud University Nijmegen

Jan Niessen
Migration Policy Group, Brussels

The Series is a venue for books on European immigration and asylum law and policies where academics, policy makers, law practitioners and others look to find detailed analysis of this dynamic field. Works in the series will start from a European perspective. The increased co-operation within the European Union and the Council of Europe on matters related to immigration and asylum requires the publication of theoretical and empirical research. The series will contribute to well-informed policy debates by analyzing and interpreting the evolving European legislation and its effects on national law and policies. The series brings together the various stakeholders in these policy debates: the legal profession, researchers, employers, trade unions, human rights and other civil society organizations.

Legal Frameworks for the Integration of Third-Country Nationals

Edited by

Jan Niessen and Thomas Huddleston

MARTINUS
NIJHOFF
PUBLISHERS

LEIDEN • BOSTON
2009

This book is printed on acid-free paper.

Library of Congress Cataloging-in-Publication Data

Legal frameworks for the integration of third-country nationals / Edited by Jan Niessen and Thomas Huddleston.
p. cm. — (Immigration and asylum law and policy in Europe ; v.18)
Includes index.
ISBN 978-90-04-17069-8 (hardback : alk. paper) 1. Aliens—Civil rights. 2. Emigration and immigration law. 3. Immigrants—Government policy. 4. Social integration—Government policy. 5. Immigrants—Cultural assimilation I. Niessen, Jan. II. Huddleston, Thomas.
K3274.L42 2009
342.08'3—dc22

2009016418

ISSN 1568–2749
ISBN 978 90 04 17069 8

PRINTED IN THE NETHERLANDS

Contents

Foreword

This book is about a comparative research project on the legal integration of third-country nationals, investigating six areas critical to a legally-resident third-country national's opportunities to participate in their country of residence: labour market access, family reunion, long-term residence, political participation, access to nationality, and anti-discrimination. The project compared legislation in 28 countries, the EU Member States (except Romania and Bulgaria), Canada, Norway and Switzerland on the basis of a set of 142 legal and policy indicators. Although comparing countries on the basis of various indicator types is common in the private sector and increasingly used in policy areas like development, good governance and equality, the exercise remains relatively new in justice and home affairs. A website dedicated to this project, now known as the MIPEX, contains all the research data. The research project's key findings for each country and for the areas of strength and weakness for the 25 EU Member States surveyed were published in the book, the Migrant Integration Policy Index. Policy indicators do not replace in-depth legal and policy research. Rather, MIPEX's quantitative and comparative results make integration policies in Europe more accessible to a wider range of stakeholders and provide a framework for more comprehensive investigations. As such this book's secondary analysis of the MIPEX results can offer a much richer description of the dynamics within integration laws and policies in Europe.

The first section of the book lays out the instruments used to construct the MIPEX (Chapter I) and then situates the study within current debates on integration indicators and policy evaluation (Chapter II). The following chapters consider what the study's key findings add to our understanding of the relationships not only within integration policymaking, but also between law, policies and the other factors at play in the integration process. Chapter III considers the MIPEX correlations within integration policies and with related policy areas, such as good governance, welfare policy, and gender equality. Chapter IV uses clustering to question the continued relevance of "models" for describing countries' integration policies. Chapter V highlights the relationships between the policy framework and the public opinion climate across Europe. The authors of the chapters VI–IX focus on their area of expertise to trace recent trends on anti-discrimination, naturalisation and citizenship, labour market access, and political participation.

Chapter 1

Construction of the Migrant Integration Policy Index

Jan Niessen

The Migrant Integration Policy Index (MIPEX) began as a pilot project in 2004 and expanded in 2007 to establish a reliable biannual standard-setting and monitoring tool for governmental integration policies. For that purpose the MIPEX authors designed policy indicators which enabled the comparison of the legal provisions in place across various European countries to promote the integration of third-country national migrant residents. The 2007 second edition examined a wide range of policy areas: labour market access, family reunion, long-term residence, political participation, access to nationality, and anti-discrimination law. Future editions may consider additional realms relevant to integration such as targeted migrant education policies. A country's policies can be compared against the highest European integration standards, to other countries and the EU average, and over time.

Although comparing and evaluating countries on the basis of indicators is commonly used in the private sector and increasingly in the public sector, the exercise remains a relatively new phenomenon for actors in the justice and home affairs field that are increasingly leading immigration and integration policies. This chapter briefly explains the construction of the MIPEX and its methodology. It specifies the adopted and proposed legal instruments that informed the selection of MIPEX strands, dimensions, indicators, and answer options. It explains how legal provisions were turned into numbers enabling quantitative comparisons by taking readers through the example of the family reunion policy strand.

A. *Valuing Legal Integration*

Legal integration, meaning an immigrant's legal status, residence rights, citizenship, and equal access to rights, goods, services, and resources, receives wide expert acceptance as the first step in promoting societal integration. Legal integration is a "key determinant" (Dayton-Johnson et al. 2007: Penninx and Martiniello 2004) and "the basis upon which expectations and obligations for the integration process are established."[1] It stands out as "a necessary prerequisite…[since] only when this issue has been successfully resolved that immigrants can go on to negotiate over other important."[2] Resolving legal integration also sets the terms for those later negotiations by creating a variety of incentives and "restrictions on decision-making, self-sufficiency, and the capacity of migrants to benefit from basic economic, political, social and cultural opportunities and services."[3] Groenendijk, Guild and Dogan 1998 argue that the importance of legal integration, especially residence rights, can hardly be overestimated as both "a firm base" for societal integration but also a "clear signal" committing public authorities to an inclusion agenda.

Realising immigrants' rights has a significant impact on immigrants' well-being and planning for the future, but is not the sole nor sufficient means for promoting societal integration. Those without full residence rights can still find ways to make significant economic and social contributions, while those with them are still in need of various other administrative and financial inputs to make societal integration successful (Spencer et al. 2006). That legal integration is the necessary but neither sole nor sufficient prerequisite for societal integration resurfaces in many studies and reaffirms the importance of policy indicators as the starting point in an integration policy evaluation chain (see Chapter 2).

B. *Equality Standards*

Many general human rights instruments and specific conventions on migration lay down the obligation of states to protect the rights of international migrants. These rights include those related to admission and residence status and that of migrant's family members, the right to receive equal treatment with nationals in terms of working and living conditions, and civic, social and cultural rights. International law also provides rules for the acquisition of nationality and offers protection against discrimination. These international instruments often form the basis of and inspire national migration and integration policies. The main idea underlying these policies is that the more time you legally stay in the territory

---

1 Alistair Ager and Alison Strang, *Indicators of integration: final report*, 4 (London, 2004). *See also* Jan Niessen, "Chapter 8: Monitoring and Measuring," in Council of Europe, *Diversity and Cohesion: new challenges for the integration of immigrants and minorities* (Strasbourg, 2000).

2 Feiwel Kupferberg "The Established and the newcomers: what makes immigrant and women entrepreneurs so special?" 90 (2003).

3 Integrating Ireland, *Getting on: from migration to integration*, 18 (2007).

of a host country, the more rights and responsibilities you acquire. Policies set favourable conditions as long as they tackle to access to the labour market, secure residence status, ensure family reunion, offer political participation, encourage acquisition of nationality, and prohibit discrimination. These six policy areas or "strands" form the core of the MIPEX.

The 1999 Tampere Presidency Conclusions confirmed that a non-EU citizen should enjoy a legal status and set of rights and obligations that is comparable to that of EU citizens. In addition, Tampere specified the policy realms that make up legal integration: all areas of residence rights like family reunion, long-term residence, and naturalisation as well as anti-discrimination, education, and employment. The Tampere vision recurs throughout EU binding and non-binding statements and policy documents on integration. Civil society also called for the implementation of equality and anti-discrimination principles in the field of migration and immigrant integration and has put forward concrete legislative proposals to that effect. Examples are the MPG/ILPA Amsterdam Proposals for EC "migration and integration" Directives and the Starting Line Proposals for Community anti-discrimination law. These proposals considerably influenced the drafting of the official Commission proposals for Community law which were presented to the Council of Ministers. Depending on the success of the subsequent negotiations in the Council, the final approved Directives have either come close to the equality vision through strict, comprehensive texts (with "Member States shall" clauses) that result in *à maxima* standards; or the texts ended up being removed from the equality vision as they have been watered down through various derogation clauses (with "Member States may" clauses) that result in *à minima* standards. In the latter case the Commission, civil society and possibly individual Member States may hope to renegotiate and level up these standards at a later stage. In the meantime, Member States are obligated to transpose into their national laws the adopted pieces of legislation.

The MIPEX is designed as a tool to assess to what extent equality principles are applied to integration policies. For that purpose an assessment framework has been developed. The MIPEX authors took as source proposals for Community law made by the European Commission and by non-governmental actors, European Council Conclusions and adopted Community law. In areas where the EU lacks legislative competence, MIPEX used two European Conventions, namely the European Convention on Nationality and European Convention on the participation of foreigners in public life at local level.

Table 1: Sources of MIPEX evaluation framework[4]

(1) Tampere European Council Presidency Conclusions, 15 and 16 October 1999
(2) Lisbon European Council Presidency Conclusions, 23 and 24 March 2000
(3) Immigration Law Practitioners' Association and the Migration Policy Group, The Amsterdam Proposals: Proposed Directive on Admission of migrants, 2000
(4) EC Directive on the right to family reunification, 2003/86 of 22 September 2003
(5) Immigration Law Practitioners' Association and the Migration Policy Group, The Amsterdam Proposals: Proposed Directive on family reunion, 2000
(6) EC Directive on the status of third-country nationals who are long-term residents, 2003/109 of 25 November 2003
(7) EC Directive on the right of citizens and their family members to move and reside freely within the territory of the Member States, 2004/38 of 29 April 2004
(8) Immigration Law Practitioners' Association and the Migration Policy Group, The Amsterdam Proposals: Proposed Directive on long-term residents, 2000
(9) Council of Europe, Convention on the participation of foreigners in public life at local level, 1992
(10) Council of Europe, European Convention on Nationality, 1997
(11) Directive implementing the principle of equal treatment between persons irrespective of racial or ethnic origin, 2000/43 of 29 June 2000
(12) Directive establishing a general framework for equal treatment in employment and occupation, 2000/78 or 27 November 2000
(13) Starting Line Group, Proposals for legislative measures to combat racism and to promote equal rights in the European Union, 1998

C. *Developing the Evalution Framework*

The rights of EU citizens living abroad in another EU Member State (free movement of persons) are the ultimate benchmarks (the highest standards) for third-country nationals living in the EU. These benchmarks enable policy actors to assess whether the rights and responsibilities of non-EU citizens are levelling up or down in each Member State and across the European Union as the result of domestic and European policy changes.

[4] *See* Niessen, Peiro, and Schibel, *Civic Citizenship and immigrant inclusion*, (Migration Policy Group, Brussels, 2005), http://www.migpolgroup.com/documents/2474.html.

1. *Strands, Dimensions and Indicators*

Policymakers consider policy options and make choices which may bring policies closer or more removed from equality principles. The evaluation framework captures options and choices. A total of 142 indicators were formulated which were aggregated in dimensions within each policy area (strands). They make up the MIPEX evaluation framework. For their conceptualisation and wording MIPEX drew on the sources listed in Table 1. Where Directives and Conventions only provide low minimum standards or allow numerous derogations, MIPEX drew on the higher standards from the proposals for EC directives as well as EC Presidency Conclusions or civil society proposals. The 142 indicators together illustrate to what extent integration policies provide the conditions for promoting legal integration and to what extent these conditions are closer to or further away from the highest equality standards.

Policies in relation to access to labour market usually tackle questions of eligibility, integration measures, security of employment and rights associated with it. Immigrants can, in varying degrees, benefit from equal access to employment or self-employment as EU nationals. Once employed, immigrants may be able to consolidate their worker status by, for example, being able to benefit from measures aimed at reducing unemployment of immigrants, training or language acquisition programmes. Their status can be secured by the renewal of work permits. The termination of an employment contract could or could not be made a ground for revoking or refusing the renewal of a permit. Immigrants are granted the right to change employer, job and industry as any other EU nationals or they are not granted this right. As a worker, immigrants are permitted to participate in trade-unions and representative negotiation bodies under the same or under different conditions as nationals.

Dimensions covering long-term residence, family reunion and acquisition of nationality include eligibility, conditions of acquisition, security of status and the rights associated with it. Legally resident immigrants can obtain a secure long-term residence status within a shorter or longer period of time, during which period they are allowed or not allowed to be absent for shorter or longer periods of time. After having settled down, immigrants could be given the right to bring together their family members, namely spouses, registered partners, minor children, or other dependent members in descending or ascending line. The conditions to acquire the status of long-term residence, for family reunion and for acquisition of nationality can be limited in number, simple in their application, proportionate in terms of the aims to be achieved and encouraging towards immigrants. Procedures can be short and may or may not entail more costs than for issuing identity cards. Immigrants may or may not be given access to judicial civil and administrative procedures so as to secure effective protection of their status and against discrimination. They may or may not be entitled to financial assistance to pursue complaints and sanctions for discriminatory behaviour, which could include compensation and restitution of rights. After a longer or shorter period of time, immigrants and their family members can gain access to full citizenship by acquiring nationality. It is an option to grant nationality to second and third generations automatically at birth on the basis of the ius soli principle. The acquisition of the host state's nationality may or may not preclude dual nationality.

Security of long-term residence status, family members' status and naturalised immigrants may in varying degrees be ensured. For example, the residence status could be valid for a long period of time and be renewable automatically or on request. Periods of absence may or may not cause the loss of that status. Grounds for withdrawal of status can be limited and expressly provided by law. They could include fraud in the acquisition of the status and a sentence condemning serious crimes, and/or immigrants' social and economic situation. Protection can also be offered against expulsion. Due account may then be taken of personal behaviour, age, duration of residence and links with society and country of origin. Legal redress may or may not be offered. As regards the rights associated, the residence status may or may not be lost after retirement for workers. Family members could obtain an autonomous status from their sponsor after a shorter or longer period of time, or not at all. Participation in economic life is considered to be key and in order to become attractive and competitive in the labour market, immigrants could be offered equal access to education and training. Similarly, they could or could not benefit from welfare state arrangements, from social security to maternity leave. Positive action programmes can be adopted promoting equality further.

Immigrants can be given the chance to participate in political life and policies related to political participation. This can cover four dimensions, namely formal political rights, informal politic rights, consultative and advice bodies and implementation policies. Immigrants can be given, after a certain number of years, the right to vote or to stand for elections, at local and other levels. Participation and membership to political parties can be encouraged and the right to association can or cannot be ensured. Consultative bodies of foreign residents can be established at local and national levels. Public funding can or cannot be allocated to immigrant associations. Active information campaigns to foreign residents may or may not be developed.

The grounds of anti-discrimination could include race and ethnicity, religion and belief, as well as national origin and nationality. Anti-discrimination law can cover employment, but also provision of public and private services and education and training. The law may or may not define and cover direct and indirect discrimination, discrimination by association and on the basis of assumed characteristics. Legislation may or may not apply to natural and legal persons and to both private and public sectors. Prohibitions concern public incitement to violence, hatred or discrimination, racial or religiously motivated public insults, threats or defamation, instigating, siding, abetting or attempting to commit such offences. Victims of discrimination may or may not be given access to judicial, civil, and administrative procedures. Sufficient enforcement and compensation arrangements can be laid out by national law. Entities defending victims may or may not be recognised. Equality agencies combating discrimination can be established by law.

2. *Turning Policies into Numbers*

The indicators were turned into questions with three answer options for each question, so as to do justice to the complexity of the realities in Member States. As with the strands and dimensions, the choice and wording of the options were inspired by (proposals for) EU legislation, international conventions and NGO proposals. Each option reflects the relative distance to the ultimate benchmark and is given a scoring number. Option 3 is based on favourable conditions laid down in NGO proposals or existing international legal instruments. Option 1 and 2 are rephrased versions of the more restrictive provisions of EC directives or national practice. In cases where a given country has no policies (i.e. no guarantee, no protection, no entitlement) on a specific indicator, it is given a default value of 1. Under the anti-discrimination strand the three options assess whether national law goes beyond EC Directive requirements.

This list of indicators was assembled into a questionnaire answered by a national correspondent and peer-reviewed by a second expert who assessed the national policies in terms of the three options. The correspondents best equipped to respond to the questionnaire are independent legal scholars and practitioners of a country's migration law. The MIPEX project used such experts not only because of their in-depth knowledge of the details of their national legal and regulatory provisions on integration policy, but because they have refined the ability to express their national provisions in a comparative vocabulary that can be applied across the European Union. It is relatively straightforward for these experts to document laws and policies, providing the necessary references to allow for possible questions of subjectivity and interpretation.

3. *Turning Numbers into Scores, Comparisons and Rankings*

Each indicator receives one of the three possible scores which can be translated into a 0–100 scale. Certain questions were aggregated together to create one indicator (i.e. integration measures, consultative bodies). Individual indicator scores can then be averaged together into one dimension and into one strand score. The average of the six strands in MIPEX II are averaged together to give an overall score for each country. Comparison and rankings can then be made on the basis of these scores as a means to provide a broad-brush overview for policy comparison. The meaning of the score in terms of its favourability for immigrant integration is described on the table below. These descriptions should be read as the "key" to the assessment of Member State performance – they give indications of what a country's integration policies look like:

Table 2: The score key for the second edition of MIPEX, October 2007

0	=	Critically unfavourable for promoting immigrant integration
1–20	=	Unfavourable
21–40	=	Slightly unfavourable
41–59	=	Halfway to best practice
60–79	=	Slightly favourable
80–99	=	Favourable
100	=	Best practice

The term "best practice" in this context refers to legal integration as a first step towards societal integration. In certain Member States where integration policy has, like immigration policies, become highly politicised and takes exception to EU principles of equality underpinning legal integration, the evaluation framework could alternatively be read as inclusive/exclusionary, liberal/restrictive, pro-/anti-migrant, and the like.

MIPEX's ambition is to provide, in a systematic way, a quantitative, comparative, and updated database for evaluating integration policy. At the national level, users can assess the success of government policies in meeting the MIPEX's evaluation framework for promoting integration. For instance, the labour market access strand in Sweden scores best practice (100%) since resident migrant workers have approximately equal access, security, and rights as Swedish workers, as well as possibilities to take up labour market integration measures. Comparisons can also be made between areas of policy strength and weakness to check for policy coherence. Luxembourg's policies score consistently halfway to best practice, except in the area of political participation where policies are found to be favourable for promoting integration. Published biannually the MIPEX has an additional longitudinal component to track policy changes over time. At the international level, a country's successful performance can be compared to those of its neighbours as well as to the "average" for the European Union as a whole, as well as for its "old" and "new" Member States. It is important to highlight that policy indicators do not replace in-depth research. Rather, MIPEX's quantitative and comparable results make integration policies in Europe more accessible to a wider range of stakeholders and provide a framework for more comprehensive investigations.

D. *Case Study on Family Reunion*

The strand on family reunion illustrates how MIPEX translates equality principles into an evaluation framework leading to a quantitative assessment of family reunion policy outcomes. The link between legal integration and societal integration has been affirmed by the EU Member States in the context of facilitating the legal right to family reunion: "It helps to create socio-cultural stability facilitating... integration... which also serves to promote economic and social cohesion."[5] For family reunion, this position corresponds to what EU citizens enjoy when they live abroad in another EU country. A country gets 1 or 2 points (0 or 50%) on each indicator if they opt for more restrictive policies and the minimum standards of EC Directives. For example, EU citizens can be joined by their spouse or unmarried partner living in a durable relationship. This was also the case in the EU Commission's initial proposal for a family reunion Directive. By the final version, Member States could choose not to include unmarried/ registered partners (Art.4§1(a)) and impose a min. age limit of up to 21 (Art.4§5). In total 26 indicators were drawn up on family reunion, each one with three options (Table 4).

Table 3: Constructing the MIPEX indicator on spouse/partner

	3 points (100%)	2 points (50%)	1 point (0%)
Eligibility for the sponsor's Spouse and registered partner	*Either**	*Spouse only* **	*Age limits apply****

*2003/86, Art. 4,§3. **2003/86, Art. 4,§1(a). ***2003/86, Art. 4,§5.

[5] Preamble (3)

Table 4: 26 MIPEX policy indicators on family reunion

Dimension 1: Eligibility

(1) How many years does a migrant need to wait to sponsor?

What family can he/she sponsor?

(2) A spouse or registered partner?
(3) Their minor children?
(4) Their dependent parents or grandparents?
(5) Their dependent adult children?

Dimension 2: Conditions for acquisition

To live together, does a family have to pass onerous conditions like:

(6–13) Integration/language measures? *(average of 9 indicators on tests/courses/study guides)*
(14) Accommodation requirements?
(15) Economic resource requirements?
(16–17) A long & costly procedure?

Dimension 3: Security of status

How secure are immigrant families in their status?

(18) Length of their permit
(19) Grounds to reject applications or withdraw statuses
(20) Personal factors that must be taken into account
(21) Legal guarantees & avenues for redress

Dimension 4: Rights associated

Do families have the same rights as their sponsor to:

(22–23) Autonomous residence permits?
(24) Access education & training?
(25) Work or become self-employed?
(26) Access social security/assistance, healthcare, & housing

As Table 5 shows below, the MIPEX evaluation framework on family reunion is 97% based on the right to family reunion of EU nationals, brought together in Directive 2004/38/EC. That is, a high-scoring national legislation on the MIPEX rubric upholds equal treatment and equal opportunity for third-country nationals (TCNs) and EU citizens. The MIPEX assesses whether domestic and European policy changes have the outcome of leveling up or leveling down the rights and responsibilities of non-EU citizens in each Member State and across the EU. The scores illustrate to what extent governments are providing the first step towards societal integration in law and policy, which they can then reinforce with the budgets, programmes, staff, and NGO partners that can help make integration work.

Table 5: MIPEX evaluation framework: family reunion

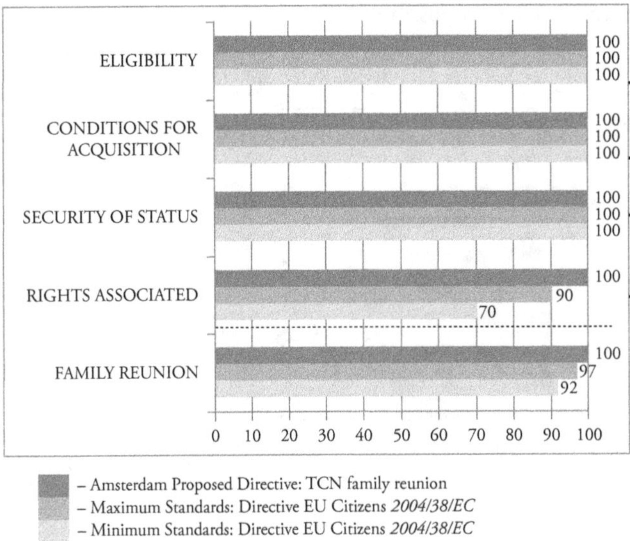

First 3 dimensions based entirely on rights/responsibilities of EU citizens.

They have the right to be joined quickly by their close family...

...Without onerous conditions...

.... & with relative security in their right to settle in the country.

MIPEX sets the bar slightly higher on rights associated. The maximum is higher because in countries like BE, CZ, FR, and NL, TCN family members have the right to an autonomous residence permit after 3 years—it's 5 years in the directive for EU citizens *2004/38/EC*. The directive allows some minimum standards here with a derogation clause stating that Member States can delay EU citizens' access to social assistance & financial aid for studies.

Using the MIPEX framework to evaluate the various proposals and Directives demonstrates to what extent the current EC legislation has achieved the Tampere vision. Comparing the Commission's 1999 proposal for a Directive for third-country nationals to the 2004 adopted Directive for EU citizens in Table 6 below, the high standards in the original proposal (overall score of 94) were hardly different from those for EU citizens (97).[6] The major difference was in terms of the use of derogation clauses to allow for minimum standards. While the Directive for EU citizens gives Member States very little room for manoeuvre (a difference of five points on the MIPEX matrix), the Commission's original proposal for third-country nationals for slightly more (19) in terms of security of status,[7] rights associated,[8] and most of all on conditions for acquisition.[9] Whereas Member States are required to provide EU citizens a very high basic right to family reunion that according to the MIPEX is favourable for promoting

[6] In cases of refusal or withdrawal, only the right to appeal was included in the original proposal. This was righted ten months later in the amended proposal with the addition of the right to a reasoned decision, leveling up the legal guarantees and avenue for redress for third country nationals to those currently enjoyed by EU citizens.

[7] Rather than receive a residence permit of a duration equal to that of their sponsor, the proposal included the derogation clause that Member States may limit the duration of the family member's first permit to one year.

[8] Member States were allowed to restrict access to education, vocational training, employment, and an autonomous residence permit for adult children and relatives in the ascending line.

[9] Third-country nationals could be asked to fulfill requirements for having accommodation "normal for a comparable family living in the same region" and for having economic resources: "stable and sufficient resources." The resources of EU Citizens need only be "sufficient."

Table 6: Bringing the EU citizen and non-EU immigrant's right to family reunion as near together as possible

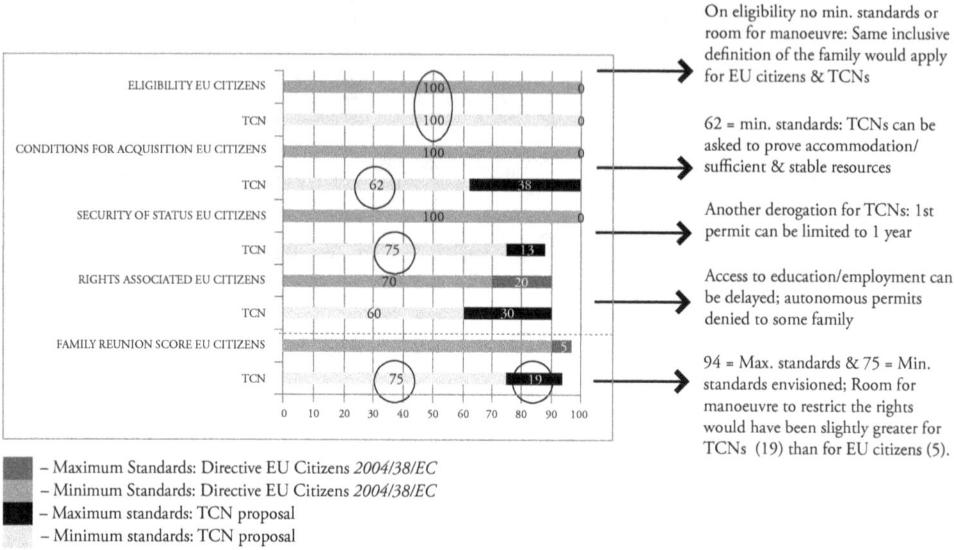

integration (92), the minimum standards in the Commission's proposal for third-country nationals would have been slightly favourable.

The negotiations of the Directive had the effect of watering down many of the minimum standards, leaving an enormous margin of appreciation for Member States to adopt restrictive policies unfavourable for promoting integration. The high standards are still present in the Directive and are better elaborated than in the Proposal, yet they have become optional. A MIPEX comparison of the 1999 Commission proposal with the 2003 adopted Council directive (Table 7) points to the numerous derogation clauses inserted on all four dimensions, even in areas where the Commission had not envisioned any possible derogations. The dimension on eligibility appears most striking in the MIPEX rubric. The Amsterdam proposals and the Commission proposal envisioned that a wide range of family members would be eligible. Under the Directive, Member States can choose to be so inclusive. Yet they can also choose to limit sponsors to those who, according to authorities, have "reasonable prospects of obtaining the right of permanent residence," exclude unmarried or registered partners, dependent adult children or direct relatives in the ascending line, and impose minimum age limits on sponsors and spouses and maximum age limits and integration conditions on minor children. These examples of eligibility are indicative of the room for manoeuvre and restrictionism introduced in the amendments and derogations in all four dimensions. As such, EC legislation unintentionally legitimated many national practices that were far from the Tampere standards.

Table 7: A final directive: Falling standards, wide room for manoeuvre

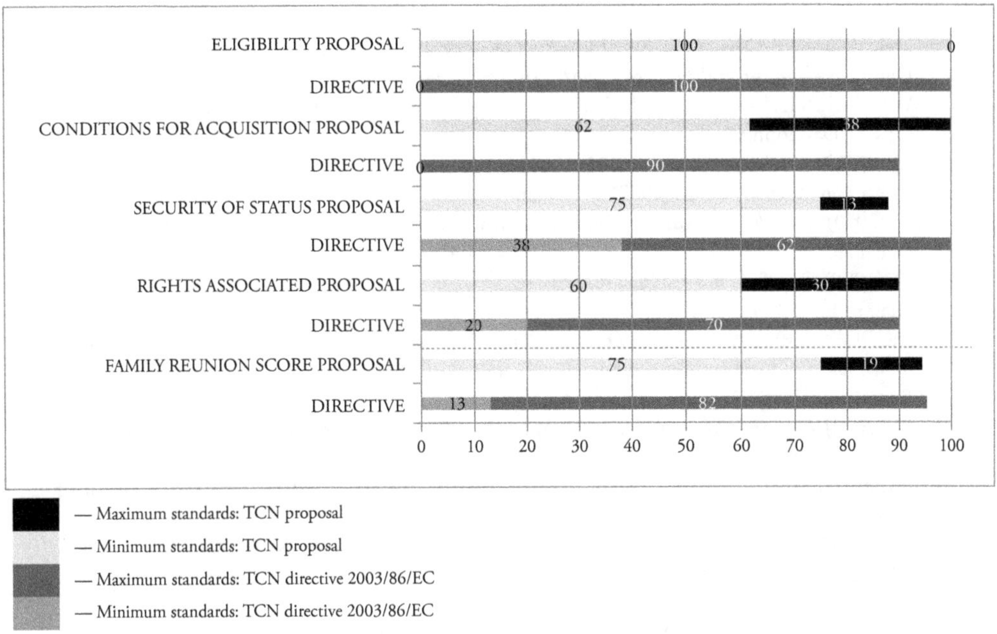

The MIPEX framework makes it possible to longitudinally monitor the impact of this European room for manoeuvre on the national legal framework. Although Member States could opt for the *à maxima* and not the *à minima* standards, the concern is that politically sensitive areas like immigration can often elicit a "race to the bottom" where "the exception becomes the rule." This trend was already observed between MIPEX I (October 2005) and MIPEX II (March 2007) in Austria and France, while the effect in Belgium was mixed. It cannot be forgotten that EC legislation is an ongoing story and as such the MIPEX normative framework enables prospective impact assessments of how future interpretations and modifications will bring the EU closer to or further from its vision on legal integration.

In conclusion, MIPEX can be used to monitor policy developments as a result of domestic change, the transposition of European directives, or ratification of international conventions, for pointing to the necessity to address important issues for immigrants and for bringing policies more in line with international human rights standards and equality principles.

List of References

AGER, A. & STRANG, A. (2004) Indicators of integration: final report, *United Kingdom Home Office Development and Practice Report*, http://www.homeoffice.gov.uk/rds/pdfs04/dpr28.pdf.

DAYTON-JOHNSON, J. ET AL. (2007) *Gaining from Migration: towards a new mobility system*, OECD Development Centre.

EUROPEAN COMMISSION (2002) *Amended proposal for a Council directive on the right to family reunification*, COM(2002) 225 final.

—— (2000) *Amended proposal for a Council directive on the right to family reunification*, COM(2000) 624 final.

—— (1999) *Proposal for a Council directive on the right to family reunification*, COM(1999) 638 final.

EUROPEAN COUNCIL (2004) *Directive 2004/38/EC of 29 April 2004 on the right of citizens of the Union and their family members to move and reside freely within the territory of the Member States*, O.J. L158/77.

—— (2003) *Directive 2003/86/EC of 22 September 2003 on the right to family reunification*, O.J. L 251, 12–18.

GROENENDIJK, K. ET AL. (1998) *Security of Residence of Long-Term Residents*, Council of Europe.

IMMIGRATION LAW PRACTITIONERS' ASSOCIATION & MIGRATION POLICY GROUP (2000) *The Amsterdam proposals: the ILPA/MPG proposed directives on immigration and asylum.*

INTEGRATING IRELAND (2007) *Getting On: From migration to integration.* http://www.immigrantcouncil.ie/images/5115_gettingon.pdf.

KUPFERBERG, F. (2003) "The Established and the newcomers: what makes immigrant and women entrepreneurs so special?" *In International Review of Sociology*, 13, 89–104.

NIESSEN, J., PEIRO, M. & SCHIBEL, Y. (2005) *Civic Citizenship and immigrant inclusion*, Migration Policy Group, http://www.migpolgroup.com/documents/2474.html.

PENNINX, R. & MARTINIELLO, M. (2004) Integration processes and policies. State of the art and lessons, In PENNINX ET AL. EDS. *Citizenship in European cities. Immigrants, local politics, and integration policies*, Aldershot, Ashgate, 139–164.

RUIZ, D.F.J. (2003) The relationship between legal status, rights and the social integration of the immigrants, *Working Paper 84*, Center for Comparative Immigration Studies, UCSD.

SPENCER, S. & COOPER, B. (2006) Social integration of migrants in Europe: a review of the European literature 2000–2006, *OECD*, http://www.compas.ox.ac.uk/publications/papers/Spencer%20Literature%20Review.pdf.

Chapter 2

On Using Indicators for Raising and Meeting Integration Standards

Jan Niessen and Thomas Huddleston

This chapter's introduction sets the Migrant Integration Policy Index (MIPEX) within the dynamic field of international cooperation on migration and integration in which indicators are increasingly being used as tools for policy evaluation. The first two sections of the chapter review current discussion about integration indicators as the outcome of two policymaking processes that came together at the turn of the 21st century: an emerging evidence-based approach to good governance and increased international cooperation on migration policy. They document the arrival of integration indicators and evaluation in the machinery of the European institutions and the state of play on the design and use of integration indicators. The second section clarifies how different types of indicators help to assess policies and policy outcomes and goes into depth on the strengths and challenges for the MIPEX policy indicators, which link principles to policies as a starting point for *ex ante* evaluations and as a feedback loop for ex post evaluations. The chapter concludes by outlining how MIPEX could be linked to the development of the other indicator types that follow in the evaluation chain.

A. *Introduction: Where International Cooperation meets Comparative Research*

Countries are working together when they face the same types of challenges and when they are confronted with common challenges. They can learn from each other's answers to international problems which play out nationally and they can adopt common solutions where national approaches alone do not suffice. Many examples of both can be given for international co-operation on migration and immigrant integration. The form and intensity of cooperation depend on such factors as the number of migrants and of countries of origin and destination involved. The economic, social, and human rights interests at stake determine to a great extent the priority that will be given to these matters. Bilateral and multilateral forms of cooperation on migration exist side by side.

Scientific research is used in various stages of policy-making, from needs assessments, policy design (prospective impact assessments) and policy implementation, to monitoring and evaluation (retrospective impact assessments). The importance of research is echoed in the call for evidence-based policies. In order to keep their policy relevancy, researchers will be asked to accommodate the needs of their users, be they policymakers, for example the executive and legislative branches of government; or policy beneficiaries, for example, interests groups of citizens. This accommodation should not affect the way research is conducted for which scientific criteria strictly apply, but it will influence research agendas and has an impact on how research results are presented.

The need for both scientifically-robust and policy-relevant research raises some pertinent questions. Are those setting the policy agenda also those setting the research agenda and is research only expected to deliver the desired evidence? What room is left for scientific research to find facts and to provide analysis independently from the "powers that be" and the interests that prevail? This is not the place to offer answers to these questions, except to plea for not only full respect of scientific methods, but also for being very open about research's fundamental assumptions. For the purpose of their use in policy debates, research results should be presented in a clear and concise way. Executive summaries, illustrations such as charts tables and rankings, and indeed indicators are means to that end. The use of indicators in the migration debates is rather new and seems to be limited to immigrant integration. It originated in the Council of Europe some ten years ago, became connected with debates on modern policy-making that took place in the OECD and is gaining importance in EU debates on social inclusion and immigrant integration.

On the face of it, integration indicators sound like straightforward measurements of immigrants' social outcomes that are meant to answer one deceptively simple question about success that can either set off or silence policy debates: "do we know if immigrants are integrated?" The question sometimes goes so far as "are they integrate-able?" Yet when searching for "the" definition of integration, the literature tends to treat the concept as a fashionable, catch-all buzz-word for what are multi-dimensional, long-term and non-linear processes of immigrant establishment (usually called immigrant integration) and societal cohesion in increasingly diverse societies (often called societal integration). These processes lie at the intersection of many personal and societal factors and of divergent policy realms, public attitudes, and public interests. As such there is no homogenous immigrant or native population, no uniform integration process, and no prevailing understanding of the impact of policies on processes (Penninx 2007;

Spencer and Cooper 2006). When searching for "the" definition of indicators, the literature on good governance tends to treat them as rather blunt, imperfect proxies for what are complex concepts that policy actors intend to "objectively" capture. There are many data gaps and non-measurable components, no one type of indicator, and no given hierarchy or casual relationship between them (World Bank 2007).

When indicators are then applied to integration, they need to counter the risk of becoming blunt tools for a catch-all concept. They must provide measurements of the different steps in policy development and in societal processes that are meant to answer a lot of highly specific questions about success: "Are policies upholding certain principles?" "Are they well implemented?" "Are they producing results?" "Have these results impacted on trends in immigrant and societal integration?" It is not surprising that policy actors have confronted immense conceptual challenges in designing and using a full set of indictors to build an evaluation framework for assessing integration processes and the impact of policies and programmes.

Despite this tall order, European policy debates continue to call for integration indicators to improve policy/programme evaluation, at a time when integration has been shooting up the political agenda of a Europe seduced by the evidence-based approach. Policymakers, be they local, regional, national, or European, are mostly the ones driving this call by making political statements on the basis of indicators. This use of indicators originated and finds its most forceful expression in longstanding countries of immigration that experienced significant populist movements peddling the perception that "integration has failed." Where this hypothesis has become an unavoidable part of the policy debate, governments have tried to promise an entirely different or more "effective" approach, with the aim of getting out of this perceived failed situation and this doomed-to-fail policy attitude. The call has a more positive echo in recent countries of immigration that have not experienced significant immigration flows or integration policy development. Governments in Southern and to a certain extent Central Eastern Europe have tried to learn from "best practices" or "models of success," with the expectation of getting their policies right from the start.

Increased political commitments on migration at the many levels of governance have made integration indicators part of Europe's policymaking and academic landscape. The need for indicators and an overall framework has reinforced the call for greater cooperation on migration (between data users and producers and between politicians, experts, statisticians, and civil society) and greater comparability, benchmarking, and mutual learning (though not harmonisation) between European countries and between their regions and cities. Debates and projects on indicators have emerged from within intergovernmental or civil society networks, particularly in connection with the European institutions.

The greater political weight given to these measuring instruments raises its own challenges for the design of a conceptual framework because the call for indicators cannot be disassociated from the increased politicisation of integration and citizenship (Bauböck et al. 2006; Givens and Luedtke 2005). Political priorities come from/with greater public expectations for results. The targeted policies and programmes that are evaluated should demonstrate that they are "managing" integration by reaffirming certain principles and by having a certain measurable impact on these complex processes. Not far behind the question most interesting to academics "do we know if our immigrants or societies are integrated?" lies the questions most interesting for policy actors: "have integration policies succeeded or failed?" or the more extreme "do integration policies even matter?" With a public seen as quick-to-judge, the governments behind these calls may, not surprisingly, want to see results in a limited period of time – between two elections, for example. Within this political and demand-driven context and in lieu of a comprehensive conceptual framework, governments will be tempted to use whatever type of indicator results are developed as their evidence-base not simply to monitor the integration situation, but most of all to judge the success (or failure) of their (or another's) immigration and integration policies.

Those wishing to contribute to building an evaluation framework must therefore work out the primary conceptual challenges within the reality of increasingly politicized in certain countries of immigration and ever closer cooperation within the EU. Indeed, the MIPEX generated such media coverage and political debate precisely because they provided the first European-wide comparative dataset based on integration policy indicators. The MIPEX publishers, the British Council and the Migration Policy Group, aimed for this data to be used as a starting-point for European multi-stakeholder debate and partnership on an overall evaluation framework for measuring integration policy success, with a strong focus on legal policy instruments. This chapter addresses some of the conceptual challenges by incorporating MIPEX into a proposed conceptual framework for measuring integration policy success.

B. *The State of Play*

1. *The Emergence of an Evidence-Based Approach to Migration Policies in Europe*

The paradigm called an evidence-based approach to good governance – integrating expertise, research, and evaluation on policies to improve decision-making and accountability – is a recent arrival in most fields. Although many West European and Scandinavian countries developed certain policy evaluation and audit systems in the postwar period, the call for an evidence base and indicators picked up steam in national and international policy circles in the late 1990s.

Australia, an often-cited international best practice for policy evaluation, shifted under the Howard government towards output and outcome indicators as the basis for annual reporting (Ellis 2007). A performance-driven approach can also be identified at the turn of the 21st century in the United Kingdom, the Netherlands, and Denmark as well as in international institutions. Furthermore the European Commission has been obliged since 2001 to conduct systematic evaluations for nearly all programmes. Indicators have become engrained in the European Commission's 2001 Laeken indicators on poverty and social exclusion, the World Bank's work on good governance and the fight against corruption, and the UN's work on development.

Integration indicators only moved up policymakers' agendas in Europe once migration moved from low to high salience and from national to international politics. In the 1970s and 1980s, migration was a low priority of the national sort that did not receive the same degree of government evaluation as other fields like development, health, education, or the environment (Bonin et al. 2008). The period produced a slim body of comparative European research that was largely commissioned by policymakers at the different of levels of governance, with at least the intention of being policy-relevant (Ireland 2004). At the international level, migration was largely left to expert organisations, from NGOs to international organisations. Two enduring examples from the period are the Organisation for Economic Cooperation and Development (OECD), with its Working Party on Migration and its 30-year-running annual report known today as SOPEMI, and the Council of Europe, with its Committee on Migration.

The emergence of migration as a top priority for international and European cooperation coincided with the new fascination with an evidence-based approach and good governance. Beginning in the early 1990s, new waves of extra-EC immigration flows brought migration policy to the fore in international fora. The OECD turned its SOPEMI report into a flagship publication in 1992 and by 2001 the OECD Council at Ministerial Level made international migration one of the organisation's top priorities. Immigrant integration policies figure in their current reviews on labour market integration and on migrant education. The Intergovernmental Consultations on Asylum, Refugee, and Migration Policies in Europe, North America, and Australia (IGC), as an off-spring of the UNHCR and IOM, first discussed asylum and return policy in 1990/1, before taking up family reunion in the late 1990s and labour immigration since 2001. The Council of Europe launched its community relations programme and published its reports on demography and on migration trends. The EU also entered the field more openly and prominently through a mix of intergovernmental cooperation between its members and supranational cooperation (Guild and Niessen 1996; Peers and Rogers 2006). In particular, the EU started to act against discrimination on many grounds, with race, ethnicity and religion and belief being important for those working on immigrant integration (Niessen and Chopin 2004).

The initial purpose of international cooperation was simply to enhance mutual understanding of international phenomena and the current situation in different countries. The first calls were for greater availability/comparability of statistics and greater rigor in government data collection. The increasing body of internationally-funded, policy-relevant research was preoccupied with comparative definitions of key concepts and quantitative statistics. The OECD, the IGC, and the Council of Europe's work programmes pushed for international data collection and comparative analysis on policies and the socio-economic situation of non-national or foreign-born residents. However the conceptual link between this international evidence-base and government evaluation was not far off. Comparative statistics can easily be interpreted as outcome indicators, targets, or benchmarks for the evaluation of government policy, for instance using the employment situation of immigrants.[1] Comparative statistics would later serve as the building blocks for the call for indicators and evidence-based evaluation.

At the European level, the link between indicators for policy evaluation and international cooperation on integration first emerged and received the greatest attention at the Council of Europe. A 1997 report provided a conceptual framework defining indicators and integration. Three key types of indicators (policy, outcome, and attitude) were distinguished and later extensively elaborated into various dimensions,[2] a stockpile of common indicator examples,[3] and checklists for the implementation of integration policies and actions.[4] The Council of Europe has made a considerable contribution to the form and content of comparative integration indicators, which in recent years has been mainstreamed into and incorporated in its work on social cohesion, where migrants are considered as one specific vulnerable social group out of many.

The main accomplishment of the EU institutions with regard to integration indicators has been agenda-setting, moving in the opposite direction of the Council of Europe from mainstreamed social cohesion indicators to immigrant integration. Integration emerged in the context of the outcome indicators on poverty and social cohesion at the 2001 Laeken conference (Atkinson et al. 2002). Evaluation was introduced as a specific priority for the EU's agenda on Justice and Home Affairs in the 2004–2009 Hague Programme. The aim of the evaluation framework was in the words of the 2004 European Council

---

[1] OECD, *International migration outlook: SOPEMI 2008*, 74–77 (Paris, 2008).

[2] Jan Niessen, "Chapter 8: Monitoring and Measuring," in Council of Europe, *Diversity and Cohesion: new challenges for the integration of immigrants and minorities*, (Strasbourg) 2000.

[3] Council of Europe, *Proposed Indicators for Measuring Integration of Immigrants and Minorities with a View to Equal Rights and Opportunities for All*, MG-IN 7 (Strasbourg, 2003).

[4] Council of Europe, *Concerted Development of Social Cohesion Indicators: Methodological Guide*, (Strasbourg 2005) 70 and Mary Coussey, "Section 9: Monitoring and Evaluation," in Council of Europe, *Framework of Integration Policies* (Strasbourg, 2000).

Conclusions to "respond to the real expectations of European citizens."[5] In those conclusions, the 11 Common Basic Principles for Immigrant Integration Policy in the European Union (CBPs) provide a specific definition of the purpose of evaluation and indicators for migration and integration policy. These good governance principles are supposed to be used by EU actors as a framework for cooperation and by national actors as a simple guide for the evaluation of government policy. An evidence-based approach was introduced with CBP 11, which calls for the development "of indicators and evaluation mechanisms to adjust policy, evaluate progress and make the exchange of information more effective." The Commission's interpretation of Common Basic Principle 11 can be characterised[6] as the need for tools and yardsticks to enhance government's capacity to evaluate the relevance, efficiency, effectiveness, sustainability, and impact of policies and practices, which were adopted as criteria for the selection of best practices in its Handbooks on Integration.[7] The European Commission continues to press for a *de facto* Open Method of Coordination in the form of a "common methodology" linked to multi-annual objectives and guidelines.[8] The overall vision on integration indicators that emerges from the EU agenda is one of varied instruments that together constitute a framework for an evidence-based and publicly-available evaluation. The design of indicators is repeatedly emphasized as one of the many priorities for EU Member States that can be facilitated by European cooperation and a potential common framework.

These increasing calls have also been linked to new EU funding opportunities on comparative indicators and evaluation frameworks. Over the past fifteen years, half a dozen or so research projects addressing various forms of integration indicators have been funded through the European Commission's research framework programmes, the INTI fund, and sources in various DGs. Feasibility studies for the development of a common EU benchmarking framework on integration were commissioned on integration by DG Justice and Home Affairs (Entzinger and Biezeveld 2003) and the European Parliament (Niessen and Huddleston 2007) and on anti-discrimination by DG Employment and Social Affairs (Dahan et al. 2008). The 825 million euro Community and national Funds for the Integration of Third-country nationals 2007–2013 will continue

[5] *The Hague Programme*, Annex 1 to the Presidency conclusions of the Brussels European Council, November 2004.

[6] European Commission, *Communication on a Common Agenda for Integration: Framework for the Integration of Third-Country Nationals in the European Union*, 11–12 (Brussels, 2005) COM/2005/0389 final.

[7] "Annex 1: Praxis-based policies – the translation of practices into policies" in European Commission, *Handbook on Integration for policymakers and practitioners: second edition*, 89–91 (Brussels, May 2007).

[8] COM(2008) 359 final.

to support the design of indicators, benchmarking and common frameworks for evaluation. The EU will continue to fund models and recommendations for the different types of common indicators to be developed by governmental and non-governmental actors.

Furthermore, the national Funds will require EC-funded projects and programmes to carry out ongoing monitoring and evaluation to ensure the quality and effectiveness of implementation.[9] In some EU Member States, the national Integration Fund will be the key national instrument for setting up an integration public infrastructure. The EC obligation for evaluation may thus have a considerable direct impact on the development of an evidence-based approach for measuring project/programme inputs, outputs, and outcomes in the cities, regions, and civil society organisations that benefit from these funds.

2. *State of Play: Integration Indicators and their Critiques*

The development of different types of comparative integration indicators is still considered avant-garde in a European debate on integration policy evaluation that is only a decade-old. Besides funding projects, the EC has been less successful in designing and using common integration indicators within its own work. The closest the EC comes to using integration indicators is in *ex ante* and *ex post* evaluations of EC legislation. The European Commission's Green Papers and Impact Assessments draw on comparative statistics and legal/policy mappings, but without the explicit intention of benchmarking or evaluation. Monitoring exercises on the transposition of EC directives into national laws often provide qualitative output indicators based on expert reports (Bell et al. 2007; Odysseus Network 2007; Bell et al. 2006; Bell and Cormack 2005). These reports highlight areas where transposition is correct, incorrect, or incomplete. The latter two scores lead recalcitrant Member States down the long road towards infringement proceedings. Transposition monitoring does not tend to benchmark the different Member States' performance or consider the outcome or impact of these national changes in achieving the overall objectives and principles set out in the EC directives (Bonin et al. 2008).

The European Commission has also been less successful in winning over Member States to the idea of adopting common integration indicators within the EU's various cooperation structures. The Handbook on Integration, a product of close cooperation between the National Contact Points on Integration and the European Commission, chose not to propose common indicators or an overall framework in its chapter on Indicators. Rather, the Handbook clarified the various

[9] European Commission, *Communication establishing a framework programme on Solidarity and the Management of Migration Flows for the period 2007–2013*, (Brussels, 2005) COM/2005/0123 final.

types of indicators necessary for policy evaluation and provided conclusions about their design and use. The European Union has called for common indicators for immigrant integration policy tied to the Lisbon Strategy's social, economic and educational indicators. Yet few have been developed by the Member States to set targets or measure progress (Niessen and Huddleston 2007). Immigrants have been repeatedly identified as a target group in the Open Methods of Cooperation on Employment and Social Protection/Social Inclusion. However the number of common integration indicators adopted stands at two. The pair is limited to outcomes in the labour market: the comparative employment and unemployment rates for third-country nationals. Current efforts at the EU level to adopt common integration indicators have so far produced weak analytical tools, modest Member State implementation, and light benchmarking.

Outside the EU machinery, the greatest progress on comparative integration indicators at the international level has been made on policy indicators. The MIPEX (Niessen et al. 2007; Niessen et al. 2005) produced the first EU-wide dataset on a wide range of integration policies, while drawing on the experience of earlier proposals and pilot studies by independent scholars (Howard 2005; Medda-Windischer et al. 2003; Çinar, Davy, and Waldrauch 1999; Coussey and Christiensen 1997). Other projects often funded by the European Commission or the Council of Europe have designed several lists of common indicators, mostly of the outcome sort, in various areas of life: the labour market, housing, health, citizenship, and so on. They are likely to go unused insofar as enormous data availability and comparability gaps frustrate the provision of an EU-wide data on inputs, outputs, or outcomes (MITI 2008; III 2008; Entzinger and Biezeveld 2003). Beyond outcomes, the Council of Europe 2005 and 2003 developed more comprehensive, web-accessible bundles of indicators on the inputs, outputs, outcomes, and impact of immigrant integration policy. The European Commission's DG Employment and Social Affairs has commissioned similar exercises on government equality policies (Dahan et al. 2008) and company diversity policies (CSES 2003).

Comparative indicators for regions and cities across Europe have also been proposed (Zincone and Caponio 2005) – by and large in terms of output or outcome indicators (MITI 2008). A few national governments have invested in monitoring systems, bringing together these indicators with the aim of measuring the situation of immigrants and benchmarking municipal performance and outcomes (Husted and Heinesen 2007; Gregori 2006). The Commission's third annual report on migration and integration observed that governments are increasingly aware of the need for tools and indicators, comparative or not, to improve their integration policy evaluation. A wide spread of non-comparative indicators have been designed as part of ambitious integration plans (CBS 2006, also Estonia, Spain, Portugal, Berlin, Wiesbaden and most recently Vienna) or as one-off commissioned reports (Spoonley et al. 2008, Baldwin-Edwards 2005,

Reichwein & Vogel 2004, Ager and Strang 2004). Within the EU's OMC on Social Protection/Social Inclusion, just a handful of leading benchmarker countries in Western and Southern Europe have put forward their own non-comparative indicators. Here government preferences lean more towards "results" indicators (outcomes/output) than "process" indicators (policy/input) (Bijl 2008). On the basis of various reports of the National Contact Points on Integration to the European Commission, it appears that Member State governments tend to report on input and output indicators and target outcomes when asked to provide updates on actions related to Common Basic Principle 11.

However there is a significant discrepancy between so-called "awareness" and the actual use of integration indicators for policy evaluation. The Commission's third annual report, after acknowledging this greater awareness, goes on to state diplomatically that in practice "further progress is necessary."[10] Reviews of European practices have concluded that there is a startling inconsistency between public discourses on the usefulness of various integration indicators for policy evaluation and the sparse use of indicators, let alone of an evaluation framework (IOM/Eurasylum 2008; Spencer and Cooper 2006). Indeed, the "evidence base" most often used by migration policymakers is seldom based on research and systemic evaluation.

At the heart of these meagre, fragmented developments on integration indicators are what the World Bank Institute's Director of Global Governance Daniel Kaufman calls "false dichotomies;" "Too often discussions of indicators over-emphasize distinctions between types of indicators with insufficient regard for the strong complementarities between them."[11] Three features of these false dichotomies in the field of integration often drown out the recognition of the added value and the usefulness of each indicator type within an overall evaluation framework. First there is in-fighting between indicator designers over what indicator should be given the most weight by funders and by actors in policy debates. The principal weapon used is an artificial hierarchy of policy needs. What does it mean for instance that "the first condition used for drawing up a common list of indicators *must* be results indicators?" (III 2008). Why would indicators at one level of governance, such as the national, be more or less meaningful for integration policy impact than those at another, such as the local or regional/state? These attempts to establish "the" definitive type of indicator are often linked to what the stakeholder has the mandate/capacity to provide or what the government/funder has an interest to see.

---

[10] European Commission, *Third Annual Report on Migration and Integration*, 9 (Brussels, September 2007) COM/2007/512.

[11] Daniel Kaufman and Aart Kraay, "Governance indicators: where are we, where should we be going?" 24 (2008).

These false dichotomies often confuse more than clarify what are indeed ambiguous terms in the integration debate. How does the meaning of "best practice" change when it refers to policy principles on promoting integration, the implementation of policies, the outcomes of policies, or the living situation of migrants and of society as a whole? Do outcome indicators measure integration policy's impact or do they just measure the socio-economic position of immigrants? This confusion of terms can lead to the misinterpretation of indicator results; policy indicators can be taken for outcome indicators (Hanssen 2007) and poor outcomes can be taken as failed policy outputs or as the origin of social conflict (Ireland 2007).

A third related feature concerns casual relationships that jump over different time-periods, generations, groups, steps in policy delivery, and types of indicators (Dronkers 2007). Can one directly compare policies and outcomes to test for correlations? Behind such outcome-driven analyses lay the assumption that targeted policies are the major factors that influence migrants' social realities. To take one example, if a country is found to have high policy principles but migrants have less favourable societal outcomes, this logic "allows for only one conclusion: [that] policy has failed miserably. In fact it looks like [the country] would have been better off without it."[12] These false dichotomies obscure the complementary, complex links between the different types of indicators. They deflect evaluation from its main purpose: providing a robust evidence-base for this controversial policy field. Not only does this impede the joining-up of a necessary evaluation framework to measure integration policy success as a whole, but it also confuses the purpose of each type of indicator in the first place.

C. *Building an Evaluation Chain on Integration Policy*

1. *So What are Indicators Good for?*

Indicators are most useful if policy actors want to see whether or not certain policies stimulate societal change. Governments and non-governmental organisations have an interest in providing evidence for their theories of change. Moreover, the public, in a liberal democracy, expects this sort of accountability. Indicators can only be developed once there is an agreed vision of the direction of change – the impact that policy aims to have on social realities. This vision is stated and reset with changes in government, and policy proposals. Evaluations operationalise this vision of change. In the *ex ante* evaluations (prospective

[12] Ruud Koopmans, "Good intentions sometimes make bad policy: a comparison of Dutch and German integration policies," (2003) 3.

impact assessments) that sometimes accompany policy formulation, policymakers start out with the results they want to achieve and work backwards. They use their vision of change to fix targets for results and then fix the resources and policies. In *ex post* evaluation (retrospective impact assessments), the order is reversed; evaluators begin with the policies and inputs provided, before moving on to assess their results.

To determine whether a policy has helped bring about the desired change, evaluation frameworks must look at **intermediate indicators** and **results indicators**. With intermediate indicators, evaluators are looking for the policies, inputs, and outputs provided to achieve that change. Indicators measure the quantity and quality of policies, resources, and activities provided by government. With results indicators, evaluators are looking at the societal effects of their policies, resources, and activities. Indicators measure outcome and impact again relative to the vision of change.

Both sets of indicators are vital for *ex ante* and *ex post* evaluation. Policymakers developing evaluation frameworks tend to neglect intermediate indicators, known as the "missing middle," due to a discomfort with enforcement/oversight mechanisms and a preference for measures of their impact and achievement. NGOs may fear that these indicators lead to sterile and self-satisfied tick-the-box exercises to the detriment of a focus on results and practice. It will not be possible for stakeholders and the public to understand the ends of policy without understanding its means, since intermediate indicators are most susceptible to government action and describe the conditions for achieving the results that are supposed to bring about change.

The table below demonstrates how intermediate and results indicators are broken down into five **main indicator** types in a link along the evaluation chain from **policy and input, to output, outcome, and impact**. To the extent that *ex post* evaluation establishes that there was causality in the chain, each of these indicators is linked together sequentially; the outputs of one are the inputs of another. The scope of policy action determines the scope of the administrative and financial inputs, which determines the scope for outputs, and so on. Skipping one link in the chain would be to neglect one potentially significant explanatory factor and give a misleading interpretation of integration policy performance. These main types of intermediate and results indicators are linked together by linkages that are called **performance (also known as efficacy) indicators**. Performance or efficacy indicators measure how well outputs on the first link in the chain translate into outputs at the next link. How efficient are policies and inputs in producing outputs? How effective are outputs in changing outcomes? Did outcomes have a sustainable impact? Together these main and efficacy indicators allow for an evaluation of policy success at each link towards the overall vision.

But where does one draw the line between intermediate and results indicators? The line is roughly between output indicators, measuring the provision of deliverables, and outcome indicators, measuring the effect of those deliverables on the lives of participants and target groups. In practice this line is blurred by policy actors who publically speak about output indicators as if they were outcome indicators. For example, the fact that 2,000 immigrants have passed a test at the end of a language course does not necessarily mean that their language skills, or that their overall employability has improved, or that the course was responsible for such changes. This confusion may come from an assumption that deliverables have a societal impact in and of themselves (as if the only impact that integration policies intend to have is making immigrants spend three hours a day sitting in a classroom). This confusion may also come from a simple lack of data on the short and medium-term outcomes of their policies.

Table 1: Indicators for an evaluation framework of social change

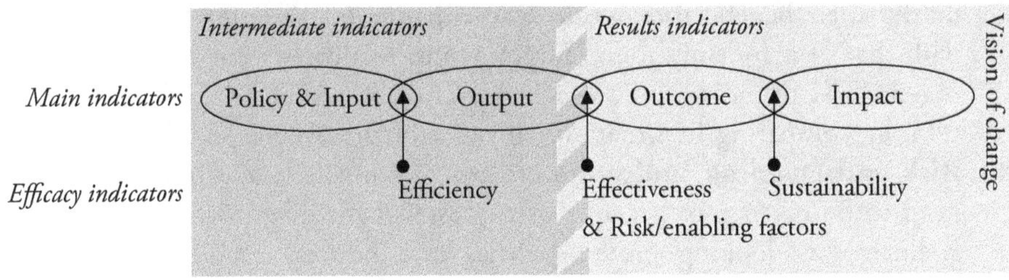

(1) **Policy indicators** measure whether the normative principles that make up a vision of change have been translated into concrete laws and policies. Policies are a major resource in policymakers' toolbox to set the conditions for government action and the later allocation of financial and administrative resources. Policies are deemed successful (or best practice is achieved on policies) when its various components are found coherently favourable for promoting the desired change.

(2) **Input indicators** measure whether implementing actors are equipped with the supporting resources to properly deliver on agreed policies. They measure the quantity and quality of administrative support (i.e. implementing agreements, structures, programmes, evaluation mechanisms, et cetera) and material support (i.e. funds, human resources, training, equipment, materials, et cetera). Best practice is achieved on inputs when they meet the demands of the normative vision and certain good governance benchmarks. **Performance or process indicators** are a series of benchmarks in the process of producing the targeted inputs.

(3) **Output indicators** measure whether implementing actors are producing the deliverables as promised in the implementation of policy and the provision

of inputs. They measure the quantity and quality of deliverables (goods and services) in terms of the target group's access, uptake, and satisfaction. Best practice on outputs occurs when the deliverables have reached the target levels that policymakers have theorised will stimulate the desired change in the target group's situation.

(4) **Efficiency indicators** are performance/efficacy indicators that measure the ratio of inputs needed per unit of output produced (in terms of financial and administrative support). Policies are deemed efficient when a few key inputs produce major outputs.

(5) **Outcome indicators** measure whether these deliverables are changing the situation of a target group in the short-term. A **monitoring system** (also known as **relevance or contextual indicators**) on the comparable situation of the target group and the whole population provides the background statistical information needed to construct possible outcome indicators. **Participant indicators** are designed at the **micro level** to measure the effect on the direct beneficiaries, ideally by comparing the situation of participants with that of a control group. **Target group indicators** are designed at the **macro level** to measure the wider impact on a specific part of the population, by comparing its situation with that of the overall population.

(6) **Risk and enabling indicators** are performance/efficacy indicators that need to be taken into account in any assessment of outcomes or impact. Evaluators are looking to see if policies have induced changes in outcomes in the desired direction, knowing that change depends on many external factors. Policymakers would hope that these external factors have a favourable or at least a negligible influence on policy performance, but many are beyond government control. This stage of analysis must measure the status of the exogenous factors assumed to have a direct and significant influence on outcomes. Outcomes for participants or for the wider target group are deemed successful when analysis of the risk and enabling indicators finds that there is still a strong casual link between policy outputs and "desirable" changes in the situation.

(7) **Effectiveness indicators** are performance/efficacy indicators that measure the ratio of outputs per unit of project outcome (or in other words the degree to which policy outputs affect outcomes). Policies are deemed effective when a few key outputs lead to major improvements in the outcomes of the target group on the ground. Again risk and enabling indicators should inform this calculation.

(8) **Impact indicators** measure whether these deliverables and targeted outcomes have had the desired results on the medium and long-term well-being of the overall population. Again this analysis must take into account risk and enabling factors including the target group's share, position, and relationships with the overall population. Best practice is attained here when the changes

in participant and target group outcomes have had the desired change on society in general.

(9) **Sustainability indicators** are performance/efficacy indicators that can be thought of as longitudinal outcome indicators, following the same participants or target group over time. They measure whether gains attained in the short-term are sustained in the long-term, particularly when funding ends and the external factors change. Monitoring systems and longitudinal surveys are two statistical instruments that help link explanations of short and long-term outcomes, target group outcomes, and the wider societal impact.

This evaluation framework can be applied to immigrant integration policies. For example, policymakers in an increasingly diverse society want to improve political participation and make politics more representative. They can pursue this overall vision in many policy domains. In terms of their integration policy, they can aim to improve opportunities for migrant participation in politics and/or facilitate their access to nationality. Their *ex ante* evaluation can assess various target groups (EU citizens, third-country nationals, naturalised citizens, ethnic minorities born in the country, *et cetera*). For the sake of argument, let's say policymakers focus on the political participation of third-country nationals, perhaps with reference to the 1992 Council of Europe Convention on the participation of foreigners in public life at local level. In the long-term, they would like to see equal participation and proportional representation rates for third-country nationals as for nationals or EU nationals. In the short-term they want to see a movement towards equal participation by opening various opportunities for political participation and developing support programmes in partnership with relevant stakeholders.

Ex post evaluation tests whether political participation policies to promote integration are creating more equitable and greater participation. **Policy indicators** could measure whether third-country nationals have access to various forms of political participation: electoral rights, political party and NGO membership, and consultative bodies. In this case government action could have focused on granting local active and passive electoral rights. **Input indicators** consider the financial and administrative resources like the design of information, voter registration, and political party outreach campaigns. **Output indicators** could be the number of, and satisfaction with, the campaigns completed, the number of political parties conducting outreach activities, and the numbers of third-country nationals reached and voters registered. An **efficiency indicator** could be how much money was spent on political party outreach per migrant candidate who eventually stood for election. **Participant outcome indicators** could be the number and experience of new migrant voters, party members, candidates standing for election, and elected representatives. An **effectiveness**

indicator could compare the number of migrant residents registered with the number voting in the election.

It is interesting to note that the World Bank does not require its projects to go beyond the measurement of participant outcomes, acknowledging that it is extremely difficult to attribute larger target group outcomes to specific policies or programmes. For instance, in the Commission's Second Annual Report on Migration and Integration, the Netherlands, one of the countries with the most developed integration evaluation tools, stated that "in general terms, it is often difficult to quantify the effective results of integration programmes, as mutual understanding or acceptance can hardly be measured." If policy evaluation was so ambitious in this case, **target group outcome indicators** could be comparative participation rates of eligible third-country nationals and nationals/EU citizens in terms of voting and political party membership rates. These indicators could also measure whether third-country nationals' demographic representation in elected positions is proportional to their share of the local population. They would take into account **risk and enabling factors** like age, level of education, socio-economic background, years of residence, country of origin, and previous activist experience. **Sustainability indicators** can track movements in participation and representation rates after the date that electoral rights were granted and the first information and outreach campaigns were launched. It can also follow the careers of migrant politicians and the voting patterns of migrants before and after naturalisation. **Impact indicators** can measure whether greater political participation among migrants has led to greater overall political participation rates, and whether greater demographic representation among politicians has improved substantive representation in decision-making.

2. *Key Features for Evaluation in Integration Policy*

Have all of these indicator types been recognised in the current integration literature? And what specific challenges do designers of different types of indicators face in the development of this evaluation chain that is still to be completed?

The various indicator types appear here and there in lists, categories, and groupings in the current literature. The literature agrees that indicators should make integration policy evaluation operational. Spoonley et al. 2006 criticise the use of **monitoring systems** of outcomes in lieu of multi-indicator type evaluation frameworks; "An analysis framework that makes sense of such changes is required, especially given the complex nature of immigration impacts and community processes."[13] The indicator types may go unnamed in many contributions, but

[13] Paul Spoonley et al., "Social cohesion: a policy and indicator framework for assessing immigrant and host outcomes," *Social Policy Journal of New Zealand*, 106 (March 2005).

can be recognized by descriptions of the function indicators are supposed to play for policy evaluation. Ager and Strang 2004 and Bijl 2008 lay out descriptions of nearly all the types in their explanation of indicators' goals. Spencer and Cooper 2006 add a few more "to investigate the factors which contribute to integration outcomes **[risk and enabling]**, to monitor change **[sustainability]**" before summing up the overall purpose of evaluations; "so that there is an authoritative evidence base for policy development."[14] Ager and Strang 2004 assess the greatest use of an indicator framework as being a basis for public dialogue on the successes and failures of integration policy and practice.

However these indicator types have rarely been linked together in a coherent, comprehensive evaluation chain. The Council of Europe's social cohesion indicators provide one overall **impact indicator** (a society's ability to ensure the long-term well-being of all its members) and then suggest three catalogues including all the indicator types on the vulnerable situation of migrants. Evaluators are invited to pick and choose from this catalogue to construct their own evaluation chain. Saad 2006 sorts out the mix of indicators suggested in the European Commission's Handbook on Integration, linking inputs, outputs, outcomes, and inputs and distinguishing "objective" quality of life indicators from "subjective" well-being indicators. Niessen and Huddleston 2007 touched on these various indictor types and laid out the evaluation when applying private sector benchmarking to integration policies. The CSES 2003 developed a rather coherent evaluation chain for measuring the cost effectiveness of diversity policies in companies.

The authors that piece together the parts of an evaluation chain see integration indicators as the very concrete building blocks of *ex ante* and *ex post* policy evaluation mechanisms. Lewis and Naqvi 2008 illustrate the *ex ante* and *ex post* evaluation chains with an EU example of the adoption and transposition of an EC asylum Directive. European Commission assessments of social, economic, and environmental impact function like **policy indicators** by demonstrating how European principles are translated into the design and negotiation of EC Directives. The Commission often takes care of intermediate monitoring (**inputs**) through the creation of structures for Member State exchange of information, funding programmes, monitoring and evaluation mechanisms, and scoreboards to track transposition. The outputs measured in *ex post* evaluations are often whether or not Member States have properly transposed the EC directive into national laws. Lewis and Naqvi suggest these evaluations could go further to measure **outcomes** (i.e. whether Member States have seen improved levels of

[14] Sarah Spencer and Betsy Cooper, *Social integration of migrants in Europe: a review of the European literature 2000–2006*, 67 (Oxford, 2006).

protection for asylum seekers and a reduction in fictitious claims) as well as **impact** (whether the EU has guaranteed minimum levels of protection across all Member States).

Although this evaluation chain is only starting to be developed, the integration literature has already provided a few essential words of caution for evaluations in the integration field. Evaluators should not overvalue the importance of policies for integration and social cohesion processes. Frameworks that begin with **policy indicators** provide a policy-oriented narrative based on the premise that states are able to define, manage, and structure integration processes. Ireland 2004 and Favell 2003 recall that individual integration processes often take different pathways (sometimes around) the models laid out in state policies and regulation. These different pathways are particularly true for different target groups of immigrants, be they legally resident third-country nationals, or EU citizens, asylum seekers, refugees, or unauthorised migrants. The host population is an equally important, though critically neglected, target group if integration is to be taken seriously as a two-way process.

Evaluations must capture integration as a multi-dimensional process revealing strengths and weaknesses across policy domains and areas of life. Many authors challenge the primacy of economic indicators which cannot tell the full story of integration (Spoonley et al. 2006). Spencer and Cooper 2006 note that migrants can have strong transnational links and be well integrated into the host society. They can also be well integrated into one sphere like intermarriage but not in another sphere like education. Though few indicator reports reduce integration to one key domain, none of them can claim to capture them all. The criterion for inclusion is usually based on widely agreed expert assessment that the given area of attainment is a critical factor for integration and social cohesion. Entzinger and Biezveld 2003's benchmarking report for the European Commission classifies its indicators into four dimensions, the III 2008 INTI project found eleven, and Ager and Strang 2004 arrange their ten into a convenient pyramid. Designers of these multidimensional frameworks either try to be comprehensive, leading to ambiguity, overlap, and serious data collection challenges; or they choose to be pragmatic, subordinating their analysis to the limits of data sources or political will. For statistical bodies working for government, the 2008 Conference of European Statisticians concluded on this point that "users [i.e. politicians and other funders] will determine the relative priority given to migration's various demographic, economic, and social impacts in their work programme."[15] A pragmatic approach leads Ireland 2004 to call these studies

[15] UN Economic Commission for Europe, Draft Conclusions: Seminar on "Measuring population movement and immigration in a globalized world," Conference of European Statisticians (2008).

highly subjective and political. Whatever the proper interpretation may be, it is clear that the dimensions of integration are not static, as shown by MIPEX's successive expansion from five, six and now possibly seven policy strands as a function of the increasing scope of Europeanisation.

Determining the proper level of analysis is also a challenge for each type of integration indicator. The bulk of the **legal policy framework** on migration, integration, and citizenship is determined at the national level. Local policies on access to education, housing, and health, for instance can vary considerably. Furthermore, national policies are often delivered through **inputs** and **outputs** at the local level. Cross-city comparison within the same country can investigate the local level's degree of autonomy in integration policy and the degree of divergence between local and national policy approaches (Poppelaars and Scholten 2008). These comparisons can then assess the coordination mechanisms between local and national policies and inputs. Many authors agree that social cohesion is specific to local contexts, dynamics, and opportunities, making **outcome** and **impact indicators** most reliable and meaningful at the local level. Local investigations allow for qualitative and ethnographic dimensions to measure how the same policy may produce strikingly different outcomes for different migrant groups and generations.

The time dimension is also critical for evaluation in the field of integration and social cohesion. Each indicator is linked to its own timetable: the period between adoption and entry into force for **policy indicators**, the funding cycles for **input indicators**, and the implementation phase for **output indicators**. **Outcome and impact indicators** have even longer timescales. What's more, achievements in integration are far from linear and irreversible. These indicators need to be monitored for reversals over time with changes in political will, funding resources, administrative discretion, and changes in the overall economic, political and even security or foreign policy situation. For instance, outcome indicators portray convergences between immigrant and overall participation rates as a fixed figure at a given moment in time. Yet the immigration population, as one of several traditionally vulnerable groups, can be harder hit by economic downturns (the "last in, first out" principles), causing divergences to widen. Like all societal processes, integration is arguably never finished. Different criteria for success can apply at each stage of settlement, involving new challenges and opportunities. Integration is not only a long-term but also a multi-generational process, sometimes taking two if not three generations. What constitutes success for one generation would be an inappropriate standard for another. Longitudinal surveys and a life-cycle approach to integration can follow immigrants and their descendents, disaggregated by age and generation, as they move from one stage in their life to another.

3. *The Challenges for Policy Indicators*

One challenge endemic to benchmarking and policy indicators is that evaluation frameworks are by definition based on expert assumptions as to the principles and policies that best promote the overall goal, in this case immigrant integration. This good governance approach addresses the manner in which policymakers exercise their authority to shape law and provide public goods and services (World Bank 2008). To some extent the MIPEX policy indicators could be interpreted as a "state integration-willingness barometer" (Kleres 2005) classifying a government's level of activity on legal integration. In some countries the normative framework may not correspond on every point to the public philosophy, priorities, and activities of the current government. Here the term integration is aptly described as "word used by many but understood differently by most" (Robinson 1998) and policies are "controversial and hotly debated." (Castles et al. 2001). Therefore these principles are translated into laws and policies to varying degrees, especially given the EU Member States' increasing politicisation of immigration, the different historical and political traditions, and the piecemeal creation of integration policies.

In this context, MIPEX's normative framework outlined in Chapter 1 calls attention to the fact that policies deviating from these principles of equality and comparable rights run the risk of obstructing rather than facilitating integration processes. The onus is then upon governments to provide and then to prove reasonable and proportionate arguments as to how these digressions will ultimately serve best as a tool for facilitating integration. In this light, MIPEX follows the suggestion of the Commission Handbook to adopt a transparent and explicit interpretation where users can easily identify which direction of change represents progress. The fact that the project has brought a normative framework to the realm of integration clarifies the terms in the debate and facilitates reflection on the policy intentions and actions of governments;[16] What principles lay behind different national integration policies? What justifications are made for changes in law? What are policies intended to achieve? And what policy coherence has been attained?

What policy indicators can do best are *ex ante* evaluations by holding a mirror up to EU Member States for stakeholders to use in the evaluation of new law and policy proposals. In practice, Ardittis and Laczko 2008 found frequent implementation evaluations but little to no *ex ante* evaluation in countries of immigration. Publically available evaluations are even rarer. For Joanne van

[16] Spencer and Cooper 67 (2006); Wetenschappelijk onderzoek en documentatiecentrum, *Immigrant integration indicators* 17 (2008).

Selm 2008 the reason that *ex ante* evaluations are avoided is that they carry the greatest policy influence:

> An *ex ante* evaluation assesses the potential impact and seeks to demonstrate weaknesses as well as strengths in the proposed policy instrument and the capacity to meet the stated objectives. It is also the point at which questions can still be raised concerning the objectives, and whether realization is both reasonable and viable given a particular context. 96.

The underdevelopment of *ex ante* evaluations means that evaluations in integration policy tend to privilege efficiency and effectiveness over vision and principles. This discrepancy favours recommendations to toughen, reinforce, or improve current measures and therefore rules out policy alternatives. As noted by Dahlström 2007 in the Swedish case on immigrant integration; "the conclusions for policymakers were, therefore, that they were doing the right thing, but just not enough."[17] The European Commission's second edition of the Handbook on Integration observes that exclusively implementation evaluations will not capture problems with the overall strategic direction and use of integration standards. In that sense policy indicators are also useful in *ex post* evaluations when evaluating new directions and higher normative standards for unsuccessful policy approaches.

What policy indicators have difficulty doing is making recommendations for change. Certainly, the normative content of the MIPEX indicators draws attention to areas of policy weakness and strength. On the basis of policy indicator scores alone, it is difficult for governments, with their limited political capital and many tradeoffs and lags, to know which policies to reform when and in what order.[18] Kaufman and Kraay further caution against "teaching to the test" or "reform illusion" where, in the international development field, rules are changed in isolation on easily "actionable" indicators with the aim of climbing higher on donor's scorecards. The same could be said for the transposition of EC directives where Member States may adopt a "copy out" strategy by lifting the minimum requirements and wording from the directive in a new national law that goes unenforced. Here the government's aim would be ticking-the-box on Commission scorecards and avoiding infringement proceedings. Coming back to the hypothesis that legal integration is the necessary but not sufficient first step, it holds that policy indicators must be complemented with the other indicator types in the evaluation chain. This joined-up approach will capture the poorly understood casual links between policies, outcomes, and the other

---

[17] Dahlström, Carl, "Rhetorical Objectives and Program Efficiency in Swedish Policy about Immigrants," *Journal of Public Policy*, (Cambridge University Press; 27, Cambridge, 2007) 319–340.

[18] Kaufman and Kraay 8 (2008).

parts in the "missing middle." These assessments can then give weight to policy indicators found to have a significant effect on outcomes and inform policy recommendations for change. A diverse set of other integration actors must step up with complementary indicator types in order to evaluate which actionable MIPEX indicators are also "action worthy," meaning changes in these policies will translate into real progress on meeting integration principles.

4. *Linking up MIPEX Policy Indicators in the Evaluation Chain of Integration Policy*

This last section will consider how the methodological merits and limits change moving down the evaluation chain from the MIPEX policy indicators to the design of further input, output, outcome, impact, and risk and enabling indicators. It will highlight which policy actors (from government to civil society) are best equipped to be responsible for, and to partner in, the construction of these various indicators. It will also suggest where MIPEX could continue to develop in support of this joined-up approach to a more informed and effective integration policymaking.

Table 2: From integration principles to policy impact: linking MIPEX with the other indicators in the evaluation chain

Step 1	**From principles to policies**
Question	What are the principles behind integration policies? How do they compare across Europe?
Tool	MIPEX policy indicators
Partnership	Independent legal experts and practitioners National NGO partners
Evaluation framework	European legal standards for promoting integration
Challenge	Debating norms & recommendations for change

Step 2	**From policies to practice**
Question	To what extent are governments equipped to deliver on national policies?
Tool	Input and output indicators
Partnership	Project managers, Ombudsmen, equality bodies, legal practitioners, NGO service-providers, migrant representatives
Evaluation framework	Fair and equal access, participation, and satisfaction for services
Challenge	Setting the bar for success

Table 2 (*cont.*)

Step 3	**From implementation to results**
Question	Are the results impacting on immigrant and societal integration?
Tool	Outcome and impact indicators
Partnership	Policymakers, statistical bureaus, relevant stakeholders
Evaluation framework	Convergence of outcomes and positive impact
Challenge	Irresistible urge to link outputs and outcomes

Step 4	**Weighing the other factors at play**
Question	What factors mitigate the link between policies and outcomes? Public and migrant perceptions, migrant's background, levels of discrimination, other policy areas, et cetera.
Tool	Risk and enabling indicators as well as public opinion polls, longitudinal surveys, multivariate analysis, et cetera.
Partnership	Researchers, scholars
Evaluation framework	Facilitators of, or obstacles to, integration
Challenge	Nascent field, scarcity of quantifiable data

a. *Efficient policies: input, output, and measuring the implementation process*

Comparisons between a country's scores on MIPEX and on input and output indicators can identify problems in the implementation of legal provisions based on the perceptions and satisfaction rates of both service providers and service users (Constant et al. 2008). The MIPEX can continue to build on its input indicators that currently capture procedural time delays and fees, enforcement mechanisms, and measures to limit administrative discretion. Nevertheless, only government can overcome the current poor state of development of government evaluation of immigration policies by requiring itself and its implementation partners to conduct regular and publicly available evaluations of administrative and financial inputs and their outputs. Input and output indicators require a partnership beyond the MIPEX legal experts to include the relevant state and non-state actors involved in policy implementation, such as ombudsmen, equality bodies, migrant NGOs, and legal practitioners. The challenge is constructing an evaluation framework for input and outputs indicators, namely setting the bar for successful implementation. Here the evaluation framework can be built on the principle of "fair and equal service delivery and outcomes." Fairness can be understood as the transparent implementation of government commitments "on paper" into mainstream services or targeted measures. Equality can be understood as comparable per capita and per GDP services for migrants as for a comparable segment of the rest of the population (i.e. in terms of socio-economic profile or living conditions). Output indicators can check if a favourable access to services has translated into an equally favourable participation in and satisfaction with services.

b. *Integration, social cohesion, and sustainable policies: the difference between outcome and impact*

Measurements of policy outcomes for immigrants and the impact for a diverse society can provide statistics on the relevant areas of integration that policies aim to influence. The evaluation framework can be derived from the principle of equal outcomes for migrant residents as for the segment of the overall population with the same socio-economic profile. These indicators measure convergence over time and over generation – in other words, the sometimes lengthy movement towards equality. They can compare how quickly or slowly immigrants and societies are integrating compared to times past (Vigdor 2008) or to other countries (Hawthorne 2008). The most critical partners in identifying outcome and impact indicators are statistical bureaus and the state actors with the budgets and sources of data to make them possible. Indicators need to be developed in cooperation with the other relevant partners like colleagues from various ministries, civil society organisations, and migrant representatives. Should local or national outcome indicators become sufficiently comparable at the European level, the MIPEX partners could agree on outcome indicators that directly correspond to the MIPEX policy indicators, for instance the extent to which labour markets have benefited from migrants' full employment potential or to which extent political systems have benefited from their active participation.

c. *Enabling and risk factors: weighing the factors at play in the integration process*

The risk in adopting outcome indicators is the irresistible urge to draw parallels between input and outcome indicators. One must keep in mind that government policy is only one of a number of factors that impacts on integration processes, meaning that successful integration outcomes may or may not be attributable to government policy interventions. Before policymakers begin to hold input indicators directly responsible for outcome indicators, they need to weigh the influence of various factors on outcomes, among them public perceptions, migrants' experiences and capacities, levels of discrimination, and a country's general labour market, societal, and political structures.

An evaluation framework should consider how certain factors serve as a facilitator of, or obstacle to, desired integration outcomes in a particular societal context. For example, certain Member States have adopted integration and citizenship tests with the rationale that they act as integration incentives to learn the language and basic knowledge necessary for daily life and political participation. Other Member States have removed or simplified such tests, viewing them as legal obstacles to migrant participation that serve policy goals other than integration. A number of factors can be evaluated to determine whether and for whom certain policies constitute an incentive or an obstacle for promoting integration.

The most appropriate actors are researchers and scholars from a wide range of academic disciplines. Relying on literature reviews, stakeholder interviews, and ultimately their own expert opinion, researchers often adopt theoretical or qualitative approaches with the aim of identifying possible factors.[19] Yet they can increasingly draw on more quantitative tools to weigh the influence of these factors on outcomes and construct the causal links from policies to societal realities. Academics have begun to make basic comparisons between a few integration factors through multivariate analysis involving the MIPEX results.[20] The methodologies of such quantitative studies of integration factors merit further debate in this rather nascent field. Attitudes can also be measured through indicators depending upon the availability of standardised, reliable, and genuinely comparable quantitative public opinion data. Recent analysis of Eurobarometer surveys and national polls among migrants have revealed some of the individual factors, including policies, which influence and can in the future change attitudes.[21] These "subjective" indicators can not only be used as output, outcome, and impact indicators, but also as an evidence base for recommendations for policy change.

5. *Conclusion: The Current and Future Uses of MIPEX in a Joined-up Evaluation Chain*

This chapter has complicated what for many policymakers are seductively simple: integration indicators. The assumption that constructing indicators of immigrants'

---

[19] *See* OECD, *Jobs for Immigrants: Labour market integration in Australia, Denmark, Germany and Sweden*, 2007.

[20] *See* Fenella Fleischmann and Jaap Dronkers, "The Effects of Social and Labour Market Policies of EU-countries on the Socio-Economic Integration of First and Second Generation Immigrants from Different Countries of Origin," (ISA, 2007) and Ruud Koopmans, "Tradeoffs between Equality and Difference: Immigrant Integration, Multiculturalism and the Welfare State," (Berlin, 2008).

[21] For instance in terms of EU-wide polls, for migrant attitudes, *See* EUMC, *Migrants' experiences of racism and xenophobia in 12 EU Member States: pilot study*, (Vienna, May 2006); For public attitudes, *See* EUMC, *Attitudes towards migrants and minorities in Europe: Key findings from the Eurobarometer and the European Social Survey*, (Vienna, March 2005); And for comparable attitudes, *See* Jan van Dijk et al., European Crime and Safety Survey EU ICS (January 2007).

socio-economic outcomes is the key to policy evaluation is undone by the fact that these results speak to the "successfulness" of integration in certain areas of life and speak nothing to the successfulness of integration policy. This chapter has also clarified that those in the integration indicator debate do not need to reinvent the wheel in order to construct indicator-based evaluation mechanisms. They can draw on the host of indicator types produced in the fields of good governance, development, and human rights. Rather than constructing false dichotomies, they should consider how each indicator type, with its individual merits and limits, can support each other in an evaluation chain.

This vision for evaluating integration success can guide those with a stake in informing policymaking in finding their place in the process of developing indicators. The road to successful integration leads from principles to the comparison of policies and other governmental inputs, and from there to the more complicated measurements of outputs, outcomes, and impact. It is a bumpy road with many challenges, yet indicators and analytical tools can illuminate where policies match high principles, are efficient and effective, produce clear results and have an impact on the convergence of outcomes despite the various other factors at play. Realistically speaking, this joined-up approach requires significant time and investment from its partners in addition to favourable policymaking conditions, timing, and political will. Piecemeal progress has been achieved through contributions like the MIPEX in various local, national, and European circumstances.

Without MIPEX, stakeholders and the public would have little access to knowledge about how their legal position as nationals or EU citizens differs from non-EU migrants and what governments are doing across Europe to promote their legal integration. Only "knowledge insiders" like national governments, international institutions, academics, and think-tanks would be party to the discussion about what should be the EU's normative framework, and what should be done at the national and European level to address the areas of policy strength and weakness. National governments are particularly responsible for instrumentalising this information gap. By taking a few examples from other countries, they argue that their vision of integration is no different from the rest of Europe and that new legislation fully meets European standards.

Notwithstanding its accomplishments on policy indicators, the MIPEX team hopes to, in their own way, to facilitate new partnerships in this joined-up evaluation framework as part of its mandate to enhance European cooperation between and amongst governmental agencies, civil society organisations, and the private sector. In future editions, MIPEX's policy indicators could include other political issues like education and further input indicators on procedures and good governance mechanisms. The project could also link up with indicator-based evaluation projects among equality bodies, NGOs, and governmental implementing bodies, with monitoring systems initiated by statistical bureaus, and with migrants themselves through representative surveys.

List of References

AGER, A. & STRANG, A. (2004) Indicators of integration: final report, *United Kingdom Home Office Development and Practice Report*, http://www.homeoffice.gov.uk/rds/pdfs04/dpr28.pdf.

ATKINSON, T. ET AL. (2002) *Social indicators: the EU and social inclusion*, Oxford University Press.

BALDWIN-EDWARDS, M. (2005) The Integration of immigrants in Athens: developing indicators and statistical measures, *MMO Working Papers*, http://www.mmo.gr/pdf/publications/mmo_working_papers/Migrants_in_Greece_Report_Eng.pdf.

BAUBÖCK, R. ET AL. (2005) *Acquisition and Loss of Nationality: Policies and Trends in 15 European Countries*, Amsterdam University Press.

BELL, M. ET AL. (2007) *Developing anti-discrimination law in Europe: the 25 EU Member States compared*, European Commission, http://www.migpolgroup.com/documents/3949.html.

BERRY, J. ET AL. (2006) *Immigrant youth in cultural transition: Acculturation, identity, and adaptation across national contexts*, Lawrence Erlbaum Associates.

BIJL, R. (2008) Evaluating the social integration of immigrants: how to measure successes and failures? *The Netherlands Institute for Social Research.*

CASTLES, S. ED. (2001) *Assessment of research reports carried out under the European Commission targeted socio-economic research (TSER) programme*, European Commission, ftp://ftp.cordis.lu/pub/citizens/docs/migration_report.pdf.

CBS (2006) Integratiekaart 2006, http://www.cbs.nl/NR/rdonlyres/4336C8A9-8E06-46BE-B1C0-CB0B21AD1AD4/0/2006integratiekaartpub.pdf.

CENTRE FOR SOCIAL INNOVATION (2006) Immigrants and ethnic minorities in European cities: life-courses and quality of life in a world of limitations LIMITS.

CENTRE FOR STRATEGY AND EVALUATION SERVICES – CSES (2003) *Methods and indicators to measure the cost-effectiveness of diversity policies in enterprises*, European Commission, http://ec.europa.eu/employment_social/news/2003/jan/diversityinterimreprev_en.pdf.

ÇINAR, D., DAVY, U. & WALDRAUCH, H. (1999) Comparing the rights of non-citizens in Western Europe, *Research Perspectives on Migration*, Washington D.C., Carnegie Endowment for International Peace, 8–11.

CNEL (2004) *Immigrazione in Italia. Indici di inserimento territoriale. III Rapporto*, Rome.

CONSTANT, A. ET AL. (2008) Attitudes towards immigrants, other integration barriers, and their veracity, *IZA Discussion Paper Series*, IZA DP No. 3650, http://ftp.iza.org/dp3650.pdf.

COUNCIL OF EUROPE (2003) *Proposed Indicators for Measuring Integration of Immigrants and Minorities with a View to Equal Rights and Opportunities for All*, MG-IN, Strasbourg.

—— (2005) *Concerted Development of Social Cohesion Indicators: Methodological Guide*, Strasbourg.

COUSSEY, M. & CHRISTENSEN, E. (1997) Indicators of integration, In *Measurement and indicators of integration*, Council of Europe, 15–22, http://www.coe.int/t/dg3/migration/Documentation/Series_Community_Relations/Measurement_indicators_integration_en.pdf.

COUSSEY, M. (2000) Section 9: Monitoring and Evaluation, In COUNCIL OF EUROPE, *Framework of Integration Policies*, Strasbourg.

CRAWLEY, H. (2005) Evidence on attitudes to asylum and immigration: what we know, don't know, and need to know, *Working paper 23*, Oxford, Centre on Migration, Policy and Society.

DAHAN, J. ET AL. (2008) *How to measure progress in combating discrimination and promoting equality? Final report* European Commission, http://ec.europa.eu/employment_social/fundamental_rights/pdf/pubst/stud/meaprosum08_en.pdf.

DAHLSTRÖM, C. (2007) Rhetorical objectives and program efficiency in Swedish policy about immigrants, *Journal of Public Policy*, 27, Cambridge University Press, 319–340.

DEPARTMENT OF IMMIGRATION AND CITIZENSHIP (2005) The Longitudinal survey of immigrant to Australia, http://www.immi.gov.au/media/research/lsia/index.htm.

DIJK, J. (2007) *The burden of crime in the EU: a comparative analysis of the European Crime and Safety Survey 2005*, http://www.gallup-europe.be/euics/Xz38/downloads/EUICS%20-%20The%20Burden%20of%20Crime%20in%20the%20EU.pdf.

ELLIS, P. (2007) The 'Deregulation of evaluation,' http://webdiary.com.au/cms/?q=node/2144.

ENTZINGER, H. & BIEZEVELD (2003) *Benchmarking in immigrant integration*, European Commission, http://publishing.eur.nl/ir/repub/asset/1180/SOC-2003-011.pdf.

EUMC (2005) *Attitudes towards migrants and minorities in Europe: Key findings from the Eurobarometer and the European Social Survey*, Vienna, http://fra.europa.eu/fra/index.php?fuseaction=content.dsp_cat_content&catid=3fb38ad3e22bb&contentid=42369ad95426f.

—— (2006) *Migrants' experiences of racism and xenophobia in 12 EU Member States: pilot study*, Vienna, http://www.libertysecurity.org/IMG/pdf_Migrants-Experiences-web.pdf.

EUROPEAN COMMISSION (2004) *Handbook on Integration for policymakers and practitioners: first edition.*

—— (2005) *Communication establishing a framework programme on Solidarity and the Management of Migration Flows for the period 2007–2013*, COM/2005/0123 final.

—— (2007) *Handbook on Integration for policymakers and practitioners: second edition.*

—— (2007) *Third Annual Report on Migration and Integration*, COM(2007) 512 final.

—— (2008) *A Common Immigration Policy for Europe: Principles, Actions and Tools*, COM (2008) 359 final, http://eur-lex.europa.eu/LexUriServ/LexUriServ.do?uri=COM:2008:0359:FIN:EN:PDF.

EUROPEAN COUNCIL (2004) *Conclusions on the establishment of Common Basic Principles for immigrant integration policy in the European Union*, 13973/04 MIGR 96.

—— (2004) *The Hague Programme, Annex 1 to the Presidency conclusions*, Brussels.

FAVELL, A. (2003) Integration nations: the nation-state and research on immigrants in Western Europe, *Comparative Social Research*, 22, 13–42.

FLEISCHMANN, F. & DRONKERS, J. (2007) The Effects of Social and Labour Market Policies of EU-countries on the Socio-Economic Integration of First and Second Generation Immigrants from Different Countries of Origin, *ISA Research Committee conference paper.*

GESEMANN, F. (2006) Indicators of integration in education, *Office of the Commissioner for Integration and Migration of the Berlin Senate.*

GIVENS, T. & LUEDTKE, A. (2005) European immigration policies in comparative perspective: issue salience, partisanship, and immigrant rights, *Comparative European Politics*, 3, 1–22.

GREGORI, E. (2006) Indicators of migrants' socio-professional integration, *FEEM Working Paper*, 56.

GROENENDIJK, K. ET AL. (1998) *Security of Residence of Long-Term Residents*, Council of Europe.

GUILD, E. & NIESSEN, J. (1996) *The developing immigration and asylum policies of the European Union: adopted conventions, resolutions, recommendations, decisions and conclusions*, Martinus Nijhoff.

HANSSEN, B. (2007) http://www.regjeringen.no/en/dep/aid/Whats-new/News/2007/Successful-Norwegian-integration.html?id=485748.

HOWARD, M.M. (2005) Variation in Dual Citizenship Policies in the Countries of the EU, *International Migration Review*, 39, 697–720.

HAWTHRONE, L. (2008) The Impact of economic selection policy on labour market outcomes for degree-qualified migrants in Canada and Australia, *IRPP Choices*, 14, 5, http://www.irpp.org/choices/archive/vol14no5.pdf.

HUSTED, L. & HEINESEN, E. (2007) Benchmarking analysis of Danish municipalities' integration policies in the period 1999–2004, http://www.akf.dk/udgivelser_en/container/2007/udgivelse_2330/

INTEGRATION FOUNDATION (2008) Integration Foundation Strategy 2008–2013, http://www.meis.ee/eng/Foundation/strategy.

IOM/EURASYLUM (2008) Assessing the costs and impacts of migration policy: an international comparison.

IRELAND, P. (2007) Immigration, integration, and everyday life in Europe's neighborhoods, LSE Workshop Paper "Everyday Life in World Policies and Economics," http://www.lse.ac.uk/collections/CIS/papers/Ireland_Immigration.pdf.

KAPPHAN, A. (2006) Indicators of immigrant integration in urban development and housing.

KAUFMAN, D. (2004) Human rights and governance: the empirical challenge, *Discussion paper for Conference on human rights and development: towards mutual reinforcement*, http://siteresources.worldbank.org/EXTWBIGOVANTCOR/Resources/HumanRights2.pdf.

KAUFMAN, D. & KRAAY, A. (2008) Governance indicators: where are we, where should we be going?, *MPRA Paper*, 8212, http://mpra.ub.uni-muenchen.de/8212.

KLERES, J. (2005) Selected indicators of social integration of migrants, minorities, and asylum seekers, *www.undp.org.pl/poverty/Selected_Indicators.pdf.*

KOOPMANS, R. (2008) Tradeoffs between Equality and Difference: Immigrant Integration, Multiculturalism and the Welfare State, *Wissenschaftszentrum Berlin für Sozialforschung.*

—— (2003) Good intentions sometimes make bad policy: a comparison of Dutch and German integration policies, http://www.wz-berlin.de/zkd/zcm/pdf/koopmans_good_intentions.pdf.

LANDESHAUPTSTADT WIESBADEN EINWOHNER- UND INTEGRATIONSAMT ED. (2004) *Integrationskonzept für die Landeshauptstadt Wiesbaden*, 2004.

MEDDA-WINDISCHER, R. (2003) *Legal indicators for social inclusion of new minorities generated by immigration* (LISI).

MICHEL, J. (2008) Migration: Welcoming the stranger is not optional, says WCC, *Standard Newswire*, http://www.standardnewswire.com/news/625792576.html.

MIDDLESEX UNIVERSITY (2008) *Migrants Integration Territorial Index.*

MINISTERIO DE TRABAJO Y ASUNTOS SOCIALES (2007) Plan Estratégico de Ciudadanía e Integración 2007–2010, http://www.carm.es/ctra/cendoc/doc-pdf/pub/ciudadania.pdf.

MPG & EUROCITIES (2008) Benchmarking Integration Governance in Europe's Cities: Lessons drawn from the INTI-Cities project, www.inticities.eu.

NIESSEN, J. & CHOPIN, I. (2004) *The Development of legal instruments to combat racism in a diverse Europe,* Immigration and Asylum Law and Policy in Europe, Martinus Nijhoff.

NIESSEN, J. & HUDDLESTON, T. (2007) *Setting up a system of benchmarking to measure the success of integration policies in Europe*, European Parliament, http://www.migpolgroup.com/multiattachments/3669/DocumentName/Benchmarking_Integration_EN.pdf.

NIESSEN, J. (2000) Chapter 8: Monitoring and Measuring, In COUNCIL OF EUROPE, *Diversity and Cohesion: new challenges for the integration of immigrants and minorities*, Strasbourg.

NIESSEN, J. ET AL. (2005) *Civic Citizenship and Immigrant Inclusion Index*, British Council and Migration Policy Group.

—— (2007) *Migrant Integration Policy Index*, British Council and Migration Policy Group.

NIESSEN, J., PEIRO, M. & SCHIBEL, Y. (2005) *Civic Citizenship and immigrant inclusion*, Migration Policy Group, http://www.migpolgroup.com/documents/2474.html.

ODYSSEUS NETWORK (2007), *Comparative study on the implementation of 10 EU directives in the field of immigration and asylum*, not yet publicly available.

OECD (2008) *International migration outlook: SOPEMI 2008*, Paris.

—— (2007) *Jobs for Immigrants: Labour market integration in Australia, Denmark, Germany and Sweden.*

PECKHAM, D. ET AL. (2004) *The impact of Home Office funded services for refugees*, Home Office Online Report 45/04, http://www.homeoffice.gov.uk/rds/pdfs04/rdsolr4504.pdf.

PENNINX, R. ET AL. (2008) *Migration and Integration in Europe: the State of Research*, Norface, http://www.norface.org/files/migration-COMPAS-report.pdf.

POPPELAARS, C. & SCHOLTEN, P. (2008) Two worlds apart. The Divergence of national and local immigrant integration policies in the Netherlands, *Administration & Society*, 40, 335–357.

REICHWEIN, A. & VOGEL, S. (2004) *Integrationsarbeit effektiv organisiert: Ein Handbuch für Kommunen*, Auftrag des Ministeriums, Gesundheit, Soziales, Frauen und Familie des Landes Nordrhein-Westfalen, Düsseldorf.

ROBINSON, V. (1998) Defining and measuring successful refugee integration, In ECRE, *Report of conference on integration of refugees in Europe.*

RUNNYMEDE TRUST (2008) Written consultation response to the Path to Citizenship: the next steps in reforming the immigration system, http://www.runnymedetrust.org/uploads/policy Responses/PathToCitizenship.pdf.

SAAD, H. (2006) Integration of immigrants: an overview, http://www.qec-eran.org/projects/ lapsraps_PREW.htm.

SPENCER, S. & COOPER, B. (2006) Social integration of migrants in Europe: a review of the European literature 2000–2006, *OECD*, http://www.compas.ox.ac.uk/publications/papers/ Spencer%20Literature%20Review.pdf.

SPOONLEY, P., CHAPMAN, J. & YOUNG, G. (2005) Social cohesion: a policy and indicator framework for assessing immigrant and host outcomes, *Social Policy Journal of New Zealand*, 24.

STATISTICS CANADA (2001) Longitudinal survey of immigrants to Canada: Process, progress, and prospects, http://www.statcan.ca/english/freepub/89-611-XIE/89-611-XIE2003001.pdf.

UNITED NATIONS ECONOMIC COMMISSION FOR EUROPE (2008) Draft Conclusions: Seminar on "Measuring population movement and immigration in a globalized world," *Conference of European Statisticians.*

VIGDOR, J. (2008) Measuring immigrant assimilation in the United States, Civic Report, 53, Manhattan Institute,http://www.manhattan-institute.org/pdf/cr_53.pdf.

WETENSCHAPPELIJK ONDERZOEK EN DOCUMENTATIECENTRUM (2008) *Immigrant integration indicators (III).*

WOOD, P. & LANDRY, C. (2007) *The Intercultural city: Planning for diversity advantage*, London, Earthscan.

WORLD BANK (2008) Types of performance indicators, http://www.worldbank.org/html/opr/ pmi/maintxl1.html.

ZINCONE, G. & CAPONIO, T. (2005) The Multilevel governance of migration, In PENNINX ET AL. *The Dynamics of international migration and settlement in Europe. A State of the art*, Amsterdam University Press, 269–304.

Chapter 3

Correlations within Integration Policies in Europe: Internal Dynamics Across National Contexts

Thomas Huddleston and Frida Borang

The main innovation that the Migrant Integration Policy Index (MIPEX) has brought to integration policy research is its comparative and quantitative approach, resulting in a vast database counting 142 policy indicators, 24 composite dimensions, six composite strands, and the one composite score. Comparison between indicator, dimension, and strand scores is facilitated through the application across all indicators of a consistent normative framework based on the principles of equality of opportunity and active participation. This normative framework turns "policies into numbers" and scores that can be understood at the EU level as favourable/unfavourable for promoting the EU principles on legal integration, enshrined at Tampere as near-equal rights and responsibilities for non-EU nationals as compared to EU nationals. MIPEX makes European-wide assessments operational through the overarching legal context of soft and hard Europeanisation of integration policies and norms. One additional added value for researchers is the database's monitoring of policy change over time. The pilot version in 2004 and the future updates on a biannual basis allow for a longitudinal assessment of MIPEX's set of unchanged indicators as well as fresh assessments of newly included indicators, strands, or countries.

These longitudinal, quantitative, and European-wide features are especially welcome within an academic literature on integration policy that is relatively recent in nature, fragmented across disciplines, and limited in comparative scope (Penninx et al. 2006; Spencer and Cooper 2007). Comparisons of policy realities are often made within a national context, while conclusions on the European context tend to be generalised from case studies of a smattering of countries (often in Northwest Europe), theoretical models, policy statements, or negotiating positions within EU institutions. Researchers tend to specialise in one area, like citizenship or labour market integration, or tackle one area at a time through distinct projects. This disciplinary focus makes comparisons rare between these different areas that make up this multidimensional policy field. Given the significant demands on expertise and research budgets, systematic datasets and European-wide analyses are remarkably few, although integration policy research and networks like IMISCOE are going in that direction (see Penninx et al. 2006; Bell, Chopin, and Palmer 2007, NATAC 2006).

What are the dynamics within and between integration policy areas? National policymakers are faced with certain choices in the design and adjustment of policy, before these new initiatives are then wrapped in the official discourses, statements, and theoretical models on promoting integration that have been the usual level of analysis among researchers. The question concerns how laws, policies, and state programmes intervene in integration processes; What conditions do non-EU migrant residents have to fulfil to access the labour market, family reunion, long-term residence, and nationality? Does the state play a role in labour market integration programmes and equality policies? Are opportunities for political participation provided by granting passive and active voting rights to non-EU migrants and/or by facilitating their access to nationality? Since the MIPEX measures the translation of inclusion/exclusion principles into integration policies, it is possible to evaluate whether national policymakers react to these choices in similar liberalising or restrictionist ways by applying similar logics and intentions across their different policy areas: promoting opportunities for integration, reducing migration flows, prioritising national security, protecting the labour market, reassuring anxieties within public opinion, or playing party politics.

This chapter intends to provide a deeper understanding of what the MIPEX quantitative policy database has done to fill gaps and identify the links within integration policymaking. This introductory analysis searches through the 142 indicators, 24 dimensions, and six strands for correlations that are statistically significant across the EU Member States. The chapter will identify correlations first between the dimensions within a MIPEX strand score and then between the MIPEX strand scores. It also intends to investigate to what extent integration policies are parts of broader policy contexts on competition, welfare policy, good governance, etc. Therefore, we also compare countries' performance when it comes to integration policy making with their performance in other policy areas, measured with similar comparative indices. It would not be sensible for this introductory analysis to use these correlations as the basis for strong conclusions about the design and use of integration laws and policies. Instead, the chapter considers to what extent these significant correlations may indicate trends in national policy performance in Europe. The chapter combs the very broad and fragmented literature on contemporary European immigration policymaking to see whether the two policy elements identified in a correlation may be linked together by certain intentions or unavoidable logics that tend to arise in their design and use by governments as instruments for inclusion or exclusion. The chapter brings out these correlations as "food for thought" and hypotheses for further research by area and national specialists.

We investigate the relationships between different strands and dimensions of the MIPEX, as well as between MIPEX and various other country indices, using the Pearson product-moment correlation coefficient. To make the most out of the information gathered, we choose to use the Pearson's on the country scores, rather than for example the Spearman rank order correlation on the country rankings. A positive relationship between two areas means that the more favourable a score is in one area, the more likely it is to be more favourable in another – and vice-versa. For the sake of coherence, the findings tend to be presented with the more favourable example, although the world could easily be replaced with unfavourable or the other MIPEX terms. Although we make statements about the strength of correlations, it is always difficult to determine what should be considered a "strong" or a "weak" correlation. What is most interesting is therefore the relative strength of relationships between pairs of strands and dimensions – and in some cases a glaring lack of correlation is of most interest. If not stated otherwise, by "significant" we mean a p-value less than 0.05.

We chose to use a symmetric measure of covariance rather than for example regression analysis, since in many cases the direction of a potential causal relationship is difficult to determine. Even if there are cases where it seems clear which of the variables, if any, would be the independent variable, we do not do the necessary controls to draw reliable conclusions about causality (i.e. a more favourable score in first area directly leads to a more favourable score in the second). For that reason when an example is presented (the more favourable A, the more favourable B), the reader should know that the construction "and vice-versa" could always be added. If these are in fact also causal relationships is a question for future analyses.

Since the number of cases is small and sometimes very small (ranging from 28 countries where the non-EU countries are included to only 8 countries when only the EU-8 is considered) it can sometimes be more informative to look at the graphs, where the cases are visible, than to look at correlation coefficients. The graphs show clusters of countries as well as outliers. They might also give the reader an idea about what controls would be necessary to add in future analyses. In many cases, results are therefore shown in graphs as well.

A. *Correlations within each Integration Policy Strand*

We first explore correlations within each of the six MIPEX II policy strands: labour market access, family reunion, long-term residence, political participation, access to nationality, and anti-discrimination. The MIPEX breaks down each strand into four dimensions, each of which considers one distinct policy element. By way of example, the strand on labour market access addresses the overall legal integration question of whether non-EU migrant residents, including those with temporary work permits, enjoy equal access to the labour market like EU citizens. The indicators in the first dimension consider a non-EU migrant's "eligibility" for various jobs and sectors. The second dimension maps a wide range of "labour market integration measures" adopted by the state to help migrants adjust to the demands of the labour market. The set of indicators on "security of employment" address how easy the law makes it for non-EU migrants to lose their right to work, while the set on "rights associated" addresses their right to join trade unions and change jobs.

The theoretical links between dimensions are not evident. In this case, the state may exclude non-EU migrants from employment in certain sectors while adopting integration measures to encourage their employment in others. Likewise, non-EU migrants may be entitled to access trade unions on work permits that are nevertheless temporary in nature and non-renewable. This section identifies where these dimensions are critically related to one together in national integration policymaking in Europe.

1. *(Un)equal Labour Market Access/(Non)Existent State Programmes*

The highest correlation for the EU-25 within the labour market strand emerges between eligibility and integration measures (r=0.497, p-value=0.011). Countries that do not impose legal obstacles to non-EU national's equal access to employment and entrepreneurship tend to adopt positive measures and programmes to promote employment, training, profession-based language training, and the recognition of skills and qualifications obtained outside the EU. This finding indicates that removing obstacles in labour laws and adopting positive state programmes might be used in equal measure by national policymakers (Ray 2004). Their scores on both dimensions may depend on the extent to which policymakers wish to encourage entry and professional development of all non-EU nationals in the labour market, as either employees or entrepreneurs (Bommes and Kolb 2006). On the one end of the scale, countries that treat non-EU labour migration as a permanent and welcome feature of the labour market tend to ensure that labour laws and state programmes facilitate the active involvement of a wide range of non-EU nationals, regardless of the temporary nature of their residence or work status. On the other end of the scale, those countries that treat it as temporary or unwelcome (the guest worker or zero migration model) do not adapt their labour laws or adopt new programmes that encourage an active, long-term contribution from those non-EU workers on their territory (Cholewinski 2005). In between these extremes lay legal and policy frameworks that promote the active involvement of some, but not all, migrant workers; for instance only those that are unemployed, permanent residents, or nationals.

2. *The Right to Sponsor One's Family (of a Certain Size and Capacity)*

26 indicators consider to what extent governments facilitate family reunion as a means of integration of non-EU migrant sponsors and their family members. The first two dimensions, "eligibility" and "conditions for acquisition," map which migrants can be joined by which family members and under what additional conditions. The second two dimensions, "security of status" and "rights associated," consider the procedures and safeguards in cases of refusals of applications or withdrawals and the social and residence rights enjoyed by family members. The highest, and the only statistically significant, correlation for family reunion is between eligibility and conditions for acquisition (r=0.541, p-value=0.005). Countries with more inclusive definitions of the family are also unlikely to impose significant conditions upon a migrant sponsor. Alternatively, countries that increasingly restrict the definition of the family tend to impose increasingly higher conditions upon sponsors.

The correlation between these two dimensions addresses how discretionary and conditional a government chooses to make the right to family reunion – tipping the balance between the individual right to preserving family life and state projections of migration control. The eligibility and conditions for family reunion set the prerequisites not only for promoting the integration of the sponsor, but also for the immigration of family members. They determine which families (i.e. those whose sponsor has a certain income) and which family members (i.e. spouses, parents, those who speak the language of the country) have the right to immigrate. Expansions and restrictions on these indicators can have a significant impact on immigration flows, particularly for most EU countries for whom family reunion is largest category of entry.

In the migration control context, policy change may affect both dimensions in the form of optional restrictions for "unselected" immigrant families and more favourable treatment for selected families. A government may for economic policy reasons may introduce an economic resource requirement for non-EU residents wishing to live with their family (conditions) and restrict their right to sponsor their dependent parents (eligibility). They may on the other hand grant highly-skilled workers an immediate and unconditional right to reunion with a wide range of family members. Therefore eligibility provisions and conditions for acquisition are both equally critically important regardless of whether the primary goal of a state's family reunion policies is to promote integration or to increase (or in most cases decrease) the size of family migration flows. This finding confirms that states tend to use adjustments in definitions, waiting periods, and conditions for a similar policy goal: promoting immigrant integration or responding to changes in the country's demographics, economic needs, welfare system and public opinion.

In the EU legal context, many national governments have agreed in the negotiation of the EC directive to certain bare minimum standards on the security and rights of family members while fighting to retain a great deal of discretion on eligibility and conditions (Cholewinski 2004). This stance allows Member States to maintain control over which and thus how many family migrants can enter and settle in their territory – playing with the supposed trade-off in immigration policy between numbers vs. rights (Ruhs and Martin 2008). The Directive's subsequent derogation clauses allowing this difference of interpretation have served as examples for other Member States to copy, since Member States are free to go both ways on the MIPEX scale in the absence of a standstill clause (Groenendijk et al. 2007).

One cannot attribute this correlation only to migration control and EU minimum standards, since these two dimensions have been the site of a conflict between two camps at either side of the MIPEX scales regarding how family reunion policies promote integration. The traditional hypothesis on family reunion is that the facilitation of eligibility provisions and conditions is a means to promote the integration of migrant residents. Bringing families together can give them a sense of social and cultural stability in socio-economic life and help build stable diverse societies. This normative approach is upheld in the stated aims and discourses of the various European institutions, many national governments, and diverse civil society and private sector stakeholders. Gross (2005) observes that "the integration argument switched sides" during the negotiation of EC directive of family reunion, with countries like Austria and Denmark arguing that family reunion should be used as a reward for integrated migrant sponsors or "integrate-able" families. Eligibility and conditions should be made more restrictive despite the consequences for migrant's fundamental rights (Schibel 2004; Carrera and Apap 2004). Age limits, economic, housing, and language conditions, and a greater sense of insecurity would serve as disincentives for sponsors and their family members to become burdens on public services. In this way granting the right to live together only to "integrate-able" families is also linked to the ill-defined concept of a state's "reception capacity." Our findings confirm that eligibility provisions and conditions go hand-in-hand in this unsettled challenge to a rights-based approach to family reunion. The evaluation of the impact of these new restrictions on migrant's life choices and integration processes will be a much needed long-term undertaking for the research community.

3. *Long-term Residence: A Significant Insignificance*

The construction of the long-term residence strand resembles that of family reunion. The 30 indicators consider which migrant residents are "eligible" and under what "conditions" to obtain a long-term residence permit granting certain residence "security" and equal social and social, economic, and mobility "rights" like nationals. The most significant finding for this strand is that all correlations between dimensions are small and non-significant. Indeed the various conditions required for long-term residence are entirely unrelated to government facilitation of residence eligibility (r=0.003, p-value=0.989) or the security of status (r=-0.0271, p-value=0.898).

This significant lack of coherence between the dimensions reinforces the idea that the legal arrangements on long-term residence across Europe are filled with integration contradictions. In some countries these statuses are the vestiges of quasi-citizenship or denizen statuses that emerged during transitional periods of nation-building or decolonisation (Groenendijk 2006). In others, long-term residence is a very recent invention required by EC directive 2003/109/EC. In either case, the EC directive allows countries to keep their various bilateral agreements, more favourable legislation in the EC directive 2003/109/EC, and restrictions on rights for all or some groups of non-EU nationals.

This wide scope for interpretation points to the severe limitations of the final EC directive in guaranteeing a homogenous European statute (Carrera 2005). Due to a similar watering down process as for the EC directive on family reunion, the policy direction for long-term residence in Europe is made up of a multiplicity of binding inclusive elements (i.e. rules on eligibility) and optional exclusionary elements (i.e. conditions for acquisition, restrictions on rights). These integration contradictions are evident in the recent policy shifts spurred by transposition. The Member States leveled up standards through the five-year residence requirement to qualify for the status, while several scaled down standards through optional conditions and grounds for withdrawal that make the status harder to obtain and easier to lose (Groenendijk 2006). As a consequence, many of the similarities and differences observed at the beginning of the millennium (Groenendijk et al. 2001) remain in the patchwork of national legal frameworks, while efforts towards harmonization have produced both convergence and divergence from the established thinking on integration.

4. *The Building Blocks of Political Participation*

The 18 indicators on this strand capture four dimensions often employed by national governments to promote opportunities for the participation of non-EU residents in political life: electoral rights, political liberties (the right to form associations and join political parties), consultative bodies, and implementation policies (information campaigns and funding opportunities for migrant associations). The consultative bodies' correlations with political liberties (r=0.443, p-value=0.026) and implementation policies (r=0.713, p=0.000) are analysed in detail in chapter nine.

5. *Dual Nationality,* ius soli, *and a Civic Concept of the Nation*

The 26 indicators comprising the access to nationality strand consider to what extent governments facilitate viable pathways to nationality for non-nationals with genuine and effective links to their country of residence. The first dimension on "eligibility" maps the residence period for first-generation migrants and spouses/partners of nationals and the use of *ius soli* for the second- and third-generation. The second considers whether eligible migrants must fulfil "conditions for acquisition" over and above the residence period and a simple criminal background check for serious convictions. "Security of status" examines the procedures and safeguards in cases of refusals of applications or withdrawals of nationality. The final dimension addresses the tolerance of "multiple/dual nationality" for naturalising migrants and their children born in the country.

Like long-term residence, access to nationality reveals little correlations between the four dimensions. The only significant finding between the four dimensions is the strong link between eligibility provisions and dual nationality (r=0.673, p-value=0.000); a country that facilitates naturalisation and recognises *ius soli* is also likely to tolerate dual nationality. More specifically, countries applying some form of *ius soli*, for instance automatically at birth or upon simple application or declaration, also tend to tolerate dual nationality for those born in the country. Facilitated residence requirements and acceptance of dual citizenship have been presented as closely-related (Howard 2005), path-dependant (Faist 2007) components of naturalisation policies in old and new countries of immigration. Both are considered as means for facilitating integration (Mazzolari 2006) in states moving away from ethnic to more civic concepts of the nation (Dahlin and Hironajka 2008).

6. *Anti-discrimination: Applying the Definitions, Enforcing Laws and Policies*

The 25 indicators on anti-discrimination address to what extent migrants and their descendents are guaranteed effective protection against racial, ethnic, religious, and nationality discrimination. The first two dimensions consider how the forms and grounds of discrimination are "defined" and "applied" in the law, while the second two dimensions compare how the law is "enforced" in judicial proceedings, the roles accorded to "equality" bodies, and state equality actions. Two strongly significant correlations emerged between the two sets of dimensions. Countries with broader definitions of the forms and grounds of discrimination were more likely to apply them to many areas of life (r=0.532, p-value=0.006).

States with more rigorous enforcement mechanisms to support victims in judicial proceedings are more likely to empower equality bodies and to actively promote equality at the state level (r=0.517, p-value=0.008). In chapter six, Mark Bell sees that the basic definitions and fields are often related to the European legal benchmark, while enforcement and equality policies are more related to the wider framework of national judicial and equality practices.

It is also striking that relatively strong positive correlations emerged between each and every of the four dimensions on anti-discrimination, which could imply that all dimensions in one country are linked to similar overall national logics and impulses on anti-discrimination. This web of significant links is likely shaped by the transposition of the EC directives on Racial Equality and Employment Equality which have had an immense impact on Europe's provision of legal protection against discrimination on many grounds (Bell, Chopin, and Palmer 2007). One should keep in mind that anti-discrimination and equality extends far beyond immigrant integration to cover diversity, vulnerable groups, and social inclusion in terms of age, disability, and sexual orientation. Nevertheless, discussions around Community law have stimulated a new elite consensus on the role anti-discrimination laws in integration policy (Joppke 2007) by reason of its salience in many national agendas, its consistency with established international norms, and its coherence with EU free movement principles (Lavenex 2006). Further research may also wish to compare typologies of equality models (Schutter 2006) with the MIPEX scores on anti-discrimination and especially equality policies.

B. *Between Integration Policy Strands and Dimensions*

The second section analyses the correlations between different MIPEX strands and the like-dimensions within them. All six MIPEX strands address how the legal framework regulates access to residence statuses and to opportunities for participation in the life of the country of residence. Each strand responds to the same normative framework on equality of opportunity and inclusion, even though national interpretations of what is favourable for integration may come and go with successive governments. The common legal approach and normative framework that binds these six strands together enable the identification of correlations at the level of strand scores and dimension scores. We expected many relationships at the strand level. For instance, labour market access, family reunion, long-term residence, and nationality all provide migrants with a certain level of residence rights and security; do national legal frameworks make it equally easy or hard to acquire them? We also expected to come across significant relationships between like-dimensions, such as the conditions for family reunion, for long-term residence, and for access to nationality. However, we did not rule out possible correlations between unlike-dimensions that may find possible resonance with policy debates and our literature review.

1. *The Web of Links between Integration Policies*

As demonstrated in Table 1, many significant and at times unforeseen correlations emerged from comparisons between the six strands for the 28 countries surveyed in the MIPEX second edition's measure of legal frameworks on integration. The highly significant correlations are in bold, while the most significant relationship for each strand is underlined. This section links some of these connections with the existing literature on comparative integration policies and recommends areas for further investigation. The relationship between access to nationality and political participation will be investigated in this volume by Jacobs and Herman.

The composite score (the average of the six strands) are not surprisingly strongly and positively correlated to each of the six strands. All strands are at least slightly positively correlated to one another, but there is a lot of variation. For example, whereas labour market access and family reunion is highly correlated, the correlation between nationality and long term residence is low and not significant. Comparable like-dimensions within those strands (for example, family reunion eligibility and long-term residence eligibility) are significantly correlated.

The various correlations identified for the 28 were the same if not slightly stronger when only considering the EU-15 countries, many of which have significant third-country national populations. The EU-10, however, show a significantly more scattered picture. For the countries of the Eastern Mediterranean and Central Eastern Europe, the links between the six integration policy areas are generally weaker and often non-existent. The policies on nationality, anti-discrimination, political participation, and labour market access are found to be generally unrelated to one another in the EU-10. Although one should not discount the fact that a smaller number of cases will make it more difficult to obtain significant results, it seems clear that the relationships between different migration policy areas are weaker in these countries. There is only one strong correlation within the EU-10 integration policy strands; namely between family reunion and long-term residence (r=0.657, p-value=0.039) which will be discussed in this section.

2. *Which Policy Area was most Determinate for MIPEX Success?*

Labour market access stands out as the most determinate strand for the composite score (r=0.832, p-value=0.000). It is the only strand to be strongly correlated with the five other strands,[1] although it is also the smallest in terms of

[1] Anti-discrimination is a possible exception to these strong correlations (r=0.377, p-value=0.048), but the correlation is still significant at the 95% level.

Table 1: Correlations between strands, and between strands and composite score, MIPEX-28

	Long term residence	Family reunion	Nationality	Anti-discrimination	Political participation	Labour market status
Family reunion	**0.5955**					
	0.0008					
Nationality	0.2489	**0.4939**				
	0.2015	*0.0076*				
Anti-discrimination	0.2266	0.4753	**0.6392**			
	0.2462	*0.0106*	*0.0003*			
Political participation	0.3351	0.3669	**0.4924**	0.3766		
	0.0813	*0.0548*	*0.0078*	*0.0482*		
Labour market status	**0.4903**	**0.6461**	**0.5259**	0.4423	**0.5714**	
	0.0081	*0.0002*	*0.0041*	*0.0184*	*0.0015*	
Composite score	**0.5705**	**0.7596**	**0.7637**	**0.7288**	**0.7638**	**0.8322**
	0.0015	*0.0000*	*0.0000*	*0.0000*	*0.0000*	*0.0000*

Correlation between strand averages, using Pearson correlation coefficients. Significance levels in italics. Highly significant correlations ($p<0.01$) in bold. The most significant relationship for each strand is underlined.

number of indicators. A country that facilitated a non-EU migrant's access to the labour market is most likely to have implemented favourable integration policies composite and in other policy areas. Policies on labour market access have been viewed as central to Member States' actions in developing broader national integration strategies (European Commission 2004 Annual Report; RAXEN 2003). Integration policy has been historically built around the labour market flexibility and requirements for migrant residents (Hansen 2005). To what extent do labour market policies confine non-EU nationals into the temporary and rotational logic as guest workers that impede the development of other integration policies? To what extent do they treat migrant workers as integrating residents who are encouraged to pursue greater opportunities on the labour market and in other areas of life? (Cholewinski 2005). A number of scholars have also discussed whether socio-economic integration serves a first step or precondition for wider integration (OECD 2007, UK Cabinet Office 2003, Waldenrauch 2001), noting that a migrant's position in the labour market tends to have the greatest impact on the other dimensions of integration as well as on public perceptions (Spencer and Cooper 2007).

The least determining factor behind a high MIPEX score was long-term residence, which received the highest average score for the 28 countries surveyed. More than on any other strand, a country was likely to do well on long-term residence without doing well overall on integration policies. An analysis of the countries whose long-term residence score diverge significantly with their composite and other strand scores suggests two potential explanations. Countries in Eastern and Southern Europe like the Czech Republic, Greece, Malta, Poland, and Slovakia may have made literal transpositions of the EC directive (also known as the copy-out option). Significantly higher scores on long-term residence in comparison to the other five strands could be interpreted as a sign of strategy on EU compliance rather than on integration. Alternatively a secure residence status for non-EU nationals may genuinely be as a restrictive legal framework's major contribution to promoting integration, as in Austria, Estonia, or Latvia, or in contrast as one of an inclusive one's major shortcomings, as in Ireland.

3. *Imposing Conditions on the Security of Residence*

The three strands on family reunion, long-term residence, and access to nationality are built around a similar structure to measure government facilitation of access to residence in terms of the eligibility provisions, conditions for acquisition, security of status, and rights associated. The three statuses cannot be viewed as one in the same, with each resting on very different international instruments and philosophical/moral arguments. And yet all three regulate the security of residence for immigrant residents with a long-term prospective in the country. Security of residence is one of the essential conditions for integration whose importance can hardly be overestimated in the legal framework (Groenendijk 1998).

Table 2: Imposing conditions on the right to residence

Conditions for family reunion and long-term residence
r=0.708, p-value=0.000
Conditions for family reunion and access to nationality
r=0.5146, p-value=0.009
Conditions for long-term residence and access to nationality
r=0.492, p-value=0.012

The one strong positive correlation that appeared between three strands was on conditions for acquisition (see Table 2). The more unfavourable conditions a country imposes on one status, the more it is likely to impose on the other two. Indeed, the conditions and procedural cost/time limits for one status are often the same as those imposed for the others. This finding reinforces the general claim by Hansen and Weil (2001) that "throughout Europe the politics of immigration have become the politics of nationality" in so far as similar conditions for family reunion, long-term residence, and naturalisation respond to similar policy impulses – promoting integration, selective/gate-keeping immigration (Green 2007), or otherwise. Further research could investigate whether adopting conditions for one status, such as family reunion, "sets the bar for gate-keeping" and puts pressure on policymakers to introduce similar conditions for the other statuses. There is a corollary link between the eligibility provisions for family reunion and the conditions for naturalisation (r=0.546, p-value=0.005), though not for long-term residence. Since the previous section already identified the relationship between eligibility and conditions for the acquisition of family reunion, it is not surprising that the countries imposing more restrictive the definitions of the family tend to impose more restrictive conditions on family reunion and access to nationality.

4. *Family Reunion and Labour Market Access: Both Part of an* "integration choisie?"

The strand with which labour market access had the highest significant correlation was family reunion (r=0.646, p-value=0.000). Even though opening labour market access for migrant residents and opening family reunion channels are opposed in public discourses on imposed/selective immigration, our findings demonstrate that the more a country restricts family reunion, the more it tends to restrict access to the labour market. Or conversely, the more a country opens legal access to the labour market for non-EU migrant residents, the more it opens opportunities for them to be reunited with their families. Among the similar dimensions of the two strands, eligibility and security of status show strong correlations (r=0.502, p-value=0.011, r=0.534, p-value=0.006).

5. *Family Reunion and Long-Term Residence: The Same Set of Choices*

The most significant relationship for the strands on family reunion and long-term residence was with each other (r=0.595, p-value=0.001). Countries that facilitate the reunification of sponsors with family members are more likely to facilitate acquisition of a long-term residence status. The significant outlier frameworks are found in Denmark, where slightly favourable long-term residence policies come with much less favourable policies on family reunion, and Ireland, where less favourable strand score stems from the non-existence of a long-term residence status.

Although facilitating eligibility for long-term residence is little related to that for family reunion, correlations were strongest for the conditions for acquisition (r=0.708, p-value=0.000), significant for security of status (r=0.571, p-value=0.003) and slightly significant for rights associated (r=0.4419, p-value=

0.027). Countries appear to use acquisition conditions and procedural safeguards in equal measure for family reunion and for long-term residence. The application of similar conditions, procedures, and safeguards to family reunion and long-term residence may indicate general national practices concerning residence rights and services for non-EU nationals. These correlations may also be partly explained by further monitoring and analysis of the transposition of the EC directives on family reunion (2003/86/EC) and on long-term residence (2003/109/EC). The directives, negotiated and transposed at nearly the same time, both rely on basic principles, minimum requirements, and various derogation clauses (Niessen and Huddleston 2007; Groenendijk 2006; Gross 2005; Schibel 2004). The potential influence of these similar "minimum standards" directives is strengthened by the fact that the correlation between family reunion and long-term residence is the only significant one in the EU-10, where governments tend to deny the "country of immigration" label and be inactive on integration unless otherwise obligated by the European institutions.

6. *Becoming a Long-Term Resident or a National: What's the Difference?*

The correlation between long-term residence and access to nationality is weak and non-significant (r=0.249, p-value=0.201). A country may have favourable policies for migrants becoming long-term residents, but that has little to do with whether or not it facilitates their becoming full national citizens. Yet the lack of an overall correlation between national approaches to long-term residence and access to nationality belies significant relationships between the strands' like-dimensions. There is a significant relationship between the two strands on security of status (r=0.558, p-value=0.004) as there was on conditions: the greater the conditions or insecurity imposed on long-term residents, the greater the one or the other is for naturalising migrants.

The major difference between the two strands lies with eligibility. In fact, comparing all 24 MIPEX dimensions to one another, the only significant negative correlation that arises is between eligibility for long-term residence and eligibility for nationality (r=-0.397, p-value=0.050). The countries that facilitate the ordinary eligibility provisions for long-term residence are slightly less likely to do so for ordinary access to nationality.[2] The previous statement could be applied to the majority of EU Member States, since the EU on average receives its lowest dimension score eligibility for access to nationality. This finding could be interpreted as a mark of European cooperation, which has introduced minimum

[2] It should be noted that MIPEX compares ordinary procedures for long-term residence and access to nationality. A number of the countries that facilitate eligibility for long-term residents do the same for access to nationality for preferential ethnic or national categories of immigrants, as in Hungary or Spain, or descendents of emigrants, as in Italy.

standards for long-term residence like the five-year residence period but not for access to nationality, a purely national competence. It also could bolster the claim made around the time of the negotiations of the EC directive that long-term residence will be used by policymakers and perceived by migrants as "second-class citizenship" – a stand-in for facilitating naturalisation (Groenendijk 2006). Although national governments tend to impose similar conditions, procedures, and safeguards for both long-term residence and naturalisation, they tend to use inverse logics when facilitating access to one over the other.

7. *Is there a (Non)discriminatory Approach to Turning Migrants into Citizens?*

The most significant relationship for access to nationality policies and for anti-discrimination law is with each other (r=.639, p-value=0.000). A country with wide-ranging anti-discrimination legislation and equality policies tends to facilitate access to nationality for migrants and their descendents. At first glance the idea of a link between anti-discrimination and nationality laws seems counter-intuitive. Much of the international cooperation that has led to improvements in national anti-discrimination legal frameworks, these processes has explicitly excluded ordinary naturalisation procedures or nationality discrimination. The 1965 UN Convention on Racial Discrimination, one of the keystone international legal instruments, goes so far as to state in Article 1.3 that "nothing in this Convention may be interpreted as affecting in any way the legal provisions of states parties concerning nationality, citizenship, or naturalisation, provided that such provisions do not discriminate against any particular nationality." As a matter of fact many European governments are not uncomfortable in maintaining more favourable naturalisation procedures for certain nationalities based on historical, cultural, ethnic ties or membership in the European Union. Furthermore, governments and scholars often conceive of naturalisation as a by nature discriminatory procedure, especially through the adoption of conditions intended to determine the individual's "genuine link" (Hailbronner 2006) like economic resource requirements (Bauböck 2006). Why then would countries end up with related scores on anti-discrimination and access to nationality?

An investigation of the correlations between the dimensions points to the hidden links between the two strands. First, there is not even a slightly significant correlation between the conditions for the acquisition of nationality and any of the four anti-discrimination dimensions. The MIPEX results confirm arguments in the literature that countries impose various economic, language, and integration conditions for naturalisation without clear link to their anti-discrimination frameworks. The dimension where nationality laws are most likely to depart from their overall (non)discriminatory approach is on the conditions set for acquisition.

The MIPEX results do reveal a relatively strong correlation between definitions and concepts and security of nationality (r=0.512, p-value=0.009). The broader the definitions and concepts are for racial, ethnic, religious, and particularly nationality discrimination, the more procedural guarantees and avenues for redress in the acquisition and loss of nationality. This link is suggested by Tóth in chapter seven to the extent that prohibitions on discrimination in the UN Covenant of Civil and Political Rights and European Convention on Nationality may be generally applicable in matters of distinctions between the security and rights of nationals by birth and nationals by acquisition in terms of withdrawal.

A pattern of slight correlations emerges between the two dimensions, dual nationality and eligibility, and the three anti-discrimination dimensions, definitions and concepts, fields of application, and equality policies. Countries that tolerate dual nationality and facilitate the residence requirement for migrants and their descendents are slightly more likely to outlaw nationality discrimination in many areas of life, empower equality bodies, and take state action on promoting equality. It would be difficult to dismiss these slightly significant correlations as mere coincidence. The European trends of increasing tolerance of dual nationality and the introduction of various forms of *ius soli* (NATAC 2006) have occurred simultaneous to national transpositions of the EC Racial and Employment Equality Directives. The circumstances could be read as states responding to different pressures (one internal, one European) – that is, if nationality discrimination, equality policies, and many powers of equality bodies were not, like naturalisation policies, left up to the decision of individual Member States.

An underlying logic may draw access to nationality and anti-discrimination together. The countries that score favourably on both sets of dimensions may ground access to rights and opportunities on residence criteria rather than nationality. This non-discriminatory and individual rights-based approach also underlies the European Institutions' concept of "civic citizenship," which according to a 2003 report from the European Parliament, "implies that citizenship requirements are non-discriminatory."[3] This links means that certain rights and responsibilities cannot be denied by states to non-EU nationals solely on the basis of their nationality. The longer the period of residence, the more equal a migrant's rights, access, and treatment. Further analysis should investigate the concepts that may tie together state actions on anti-discrimination with policies in the area of integration like civic citizenship and access to nationality.

[3] European Parliament, Report on Communication from Commission on immigration, integration, and employment, A5-0445/2003, Article 32 (December 1, 2003).

8. *Is there Policy Coherence in Integration Policy?*

Policy coherence is a legally obligatory framework for the European Union's development policies that many argue could be taken up in the EU's Global Approach to Migration (ENAR 2006; IOM 2005). According to the concept, the various components of a country's foreigners' law should support, and not undermine, the government's targeted goals on promoting integration. Governments may be unaware of both the negative and positive "spill-over" effects that frustrate or enhance their targeted and overall integration goals, arising from a lack of information, institutional constraints, or diverging interests among stakeholders in different fields. This lack of coherence affects not only state policy goals, but more importantly the lives and well-being of migrants and their local communities. The logic of policy coherence fuels many governments' mainstreaming efforts to develop an overall integration agenda, enhance interministerial cooperation, and review existing and proposed policy interventions for their impact on integration and anti-discrimination.

The MIPEX normative framework provides a good starting point for measuring policy coherence across the 28 countries surveyed. Measurements of the standard deviation from the composite score demonstrate to what extent a country's legal framework on integration applies the principles of equality of opportunity and active participation in equal measure across all six policy strands. We also identify areas of relative strength and weakness which may have spill-over effects in other policy areas. By way of example, France's favourable anti-discrimination laws must be paired with its critically unfavourable score for eligibility for labour market access; the law protects non-EU nationals from racial, ethnic, religious, and nationality discrimination in employment while excluding them from a considerable number of private and public sector jobs. The MIPEX normative framework thus identifies those countries whose policies in these six areas are most structurally coherent and those with major asymmetries between policy strengths and weaknesses.

Of the ten most coherent policy frameworks illustrated in Table 3, six are among the highest-scoring on MIPEX (Belgium, Netherlands, Sweden, Finland, and Portugal, and the United Kingdom). The four others in this table are coherently "middle of the road" as in the Czech Republic and Germany or coherently slightly unfavourable as in Austria. The other high-scoring frameworks do not appear in this top ten due to a particular area of strength (political participation in Norway, labour market access in Spain) or weakness (access to nationality in Italy, political participation in Canada). Indeed Canada, Italy, and Spain figure among the ten least coherent, along with Greece and seven of the EU-10 countries.

Table 3: First calculation of composite score and standard deviations (calculated from the different strand scores for each country)[4]

	Mean (Composite score)	Standard Deviation
Belgium	69	7.24
Ireland	53	7.62
Portugal	79	8.52
Germany	53	8.76
Great Britain	63	10.21
Austria	39	10.21
Sweden	88	10.32
Netherlands	68	10.80
Finland	67	11.61
Czech Republic	48	11.72
France	55	11.97
Denmark	44	12.78
Cyprus	39	12.83
Slovakia	40	13.13
Switzerland	50	13.15
Latvia	30	13.36
Luxembourg	55	13.68
Norway	64	14.74
Greece	40	16.26
Spain	61	16.30
Italy	65	16.90
Canada	67	17.39
Lithuania	45	17.43
Hungary	48	17.95
Malta	41	18.07
Poland	44	19.46
Estonia	46	20.40
Slovenia	55	21.13

Since the standard deviation has to be understood in the context of the mean of the data, using only this measure can make comparisons between high-scoring countries and low-scoring countries misleading. Therefore we also look at the coefficient of variation (the ratio of the standard deviation to the mean). In this analysis (see Annex) the gap between the EU-15 and EU-10 becomes even more striking, with the EU-10 occupying the ten lowest positions. These two calculations lead to the initial conclusion that the newer EU Member States tend to

[4] Formula for the standard deviation:

$$\sqrt{\frac{\sum(x-\bar{x})^2}{n}}$$

have less coherent policies across the integration strands. Their scores come closer to the EU average in areas of European cooperation like long-term residence and family reunion, but diverge significantly on political participation.

Given the glaring disproportionate effect of political participation across the EU-10 and on otherwise well-scoring countries like Canada, the strand was removed to test a third calculation of policy coherence. On this third measure, Canada's policies are found to be among the most coherent, along with coherently middle of the road Cyprus and Lithuania. For the rest of the EU-10, only Malta, Hungary, Poland, and Estonia remain among the most incoherent, joined by Denmark, France, Switzerland, Spain, and Italy.

C. *Correlation between Integration and Other Policies: MIPEX Compared to Other Indices*

The MIPEX's indexing of legal integration is modest in scope, covering targeted policy measures for non-EU nationals. However integration as a multi-dimensional policy issue is developed by policymakers in conjunction with their policies on social inclusion/cohesion, employment, demography, competitiveness, and the list goes on. In order to put the phenomenon of integration policymaking in context, it is useful to explore possible comparisons between the MIPEX and frequently used indices of good governance and socio-economic policies that are regularly used by international institutions or scholars.

This introductory analysis checks whether a government's integration policies for its non-EU residents are part of its good governance framework for its citizens or whether they are worlds apart. In other words, does a government's approach to promoting equal opportunities through targeted integration policies complement its other policy efforts to promote good governance, social justice, and economic competitiveness? As was the case with the correlations within the MIPEX, we do not attempt to make inferences about causal relationships, but rather to compare the MIPEX composite score and certain dimension and strand scores with those of relevant indices.

A disclaimer should be made about the use of the MIPEX composite score, which is nothing more than the non-weighted average of the six strands. Although the project asserts that these six encompass critical areas that shape a migrant's journey to full citizenship, it also states its ambition to cover a widening range of policy areas. These missing components could have an effect on the strength of correlations with other indices. The MIPEX could consider expansion into more soft integration policy areas like access to health, education, housing, and social services. The MIPEX composite score should thus be understood as six parts of a larger whole or a rich, multidimensional, but not complete picture of integration policy.

In this section, we attempted as much as possible to compare the MIPEX with other indices comprised of policy and input indicators. The complicated links between integration policy, input, output, outcome, and impact would make a direct comparison of target integration policies and mainstream policy outcomes far too simplistic. MIPEX assesses the favourability of targeted policies for promoting immigrant integration. It does not assess the favourability of the mainstream labour market or education system for the integration of outsiders. For instance, a country may have favourable targeted policies for non-EU migrant's access into a labour market that is itself structurally unfavourable to outsiders in terms of unemployment benefits, the tax wedge, and labour market dualism (Causa and Jean 2006). The MIPEX also does not assess the impact of immigration flows and policies which determine the skills, needs, and legal statuses (or lack thereof) of the non-EU migrant population that is affected by targeted integration policies. For instance, the legal framework may make full labour market access available to the non-EU immigrant population, which may be made up mostly of refugees and asylum seekers who did not come for economic reasons. Given the questionable ability to link integration policies and outcomes, we only used indices comprised of outcome indicators when their designers, unlike those of the MIPEX, made a strong case for the link in their domain between policies and outcomes. One should also note that many of these other indices are based on expert assessments of the policy climate, as opposed to the rather straightforward legalistic questions in MIPEX on the presence or absence of various legal and policy elements.

So, which indices are used, and why? This section compares the MIPEX to the Bertelsmann Transformation Index, the World Bank Governance Indicators, the Expected Benefits Index, the UNDP's Gender Empowerment Measure and Gender-related Development Index, the Global Competitiveness Index and the Lisbon Review. Each section explains the scope and methodology of the specific Index as well as the possible links between this wider policy area and the integration policies measured in MIPEX. The findings are then linked with arguments and trends in the literature which could serve as the basis for further analysis.

1. *Is Integration Policy Part and Parcel of a Good Governance Approach?*

Are policies on immigrant integration linked to or disconnected from a government's overall good governance framework? The European institutions and international expert organisations have used a good governance framework on migration and integration (sometimes called rights-based or citizens-centred) to promote local and national efforts that they argue set the conditions for inclusion (Niessen and Huddleston 2007). The World Bank has used aggregate indicators since the mid-1990s to monitor good governance and anti-corruption efforts that it argues set favourable conditions for poverty reduction. The good governance indicators are divided into six dimensions, including Voice and Accountability, Government Effectiveness, Rule of Law, and Control of Corruption. Several hundred representative and non-representative data sources measuring governance assessments by a wide range of stakeholders are aggregated into indicators, whose weighted average provide the dimension score. A positive correlation was hypothesized between the MIPEX and corresponding World Bank good governance dimensions. The hypothesis was that countries with more favourable integration policies would also be those that grant citizens wide freedoms and avenues to participate in government (Voice and Accountability), provide quality, transparent and efficient public services and well-implemented policies (Government Effectiveness), have well enforced and independent judiciaries, police systems, and implementing bodies (Rule of Law), and combat corruption in decision-making and service-delivery (Control of Corruption).

Table 4: Good governance and integration policy

GI: Dimension Voice and Accountability: – MIPEX Composite Score

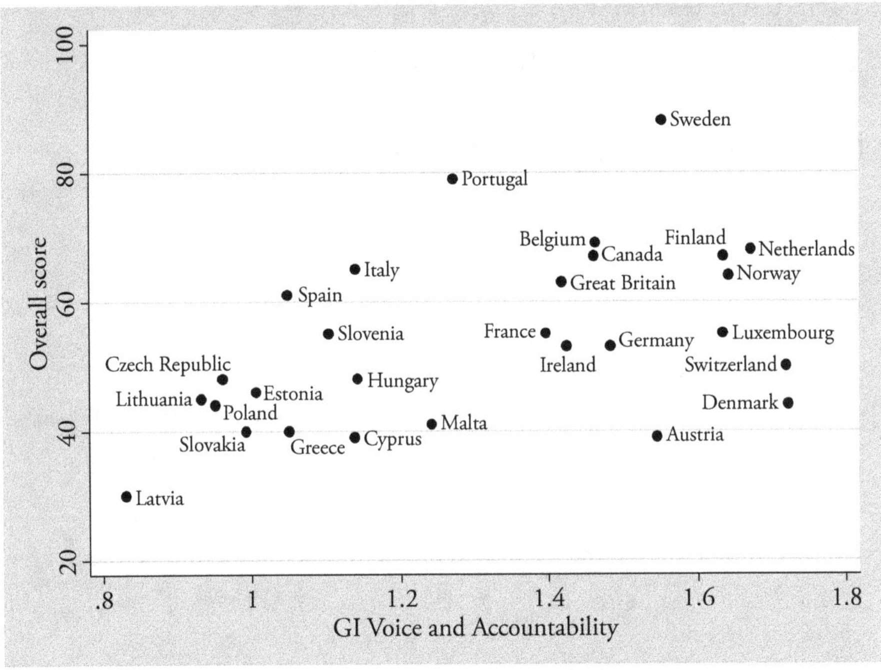

GI: Dimension Government Effectiveness: – MIPEX Composite Score

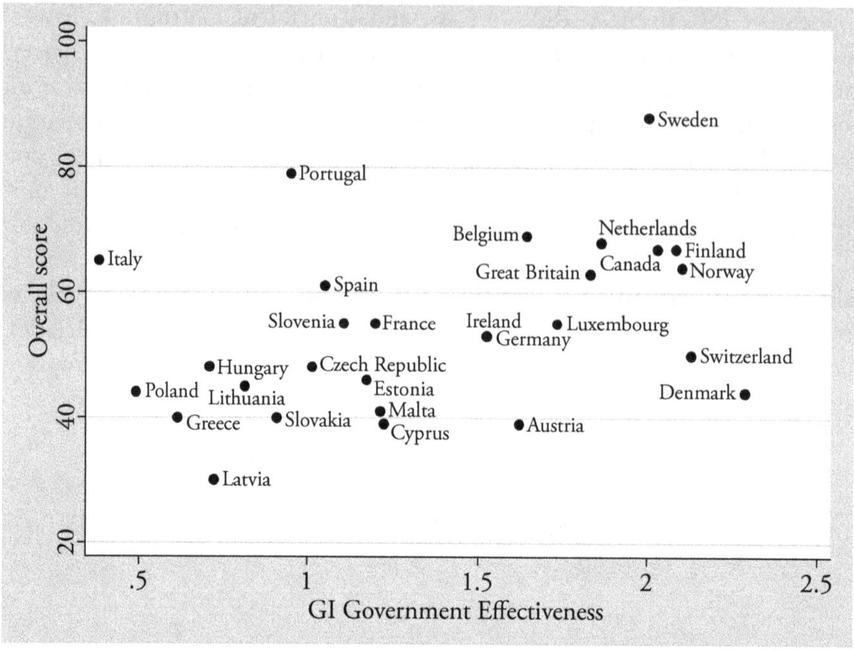

GI: Dimension Rule of Law: – MIPEX Composite Score

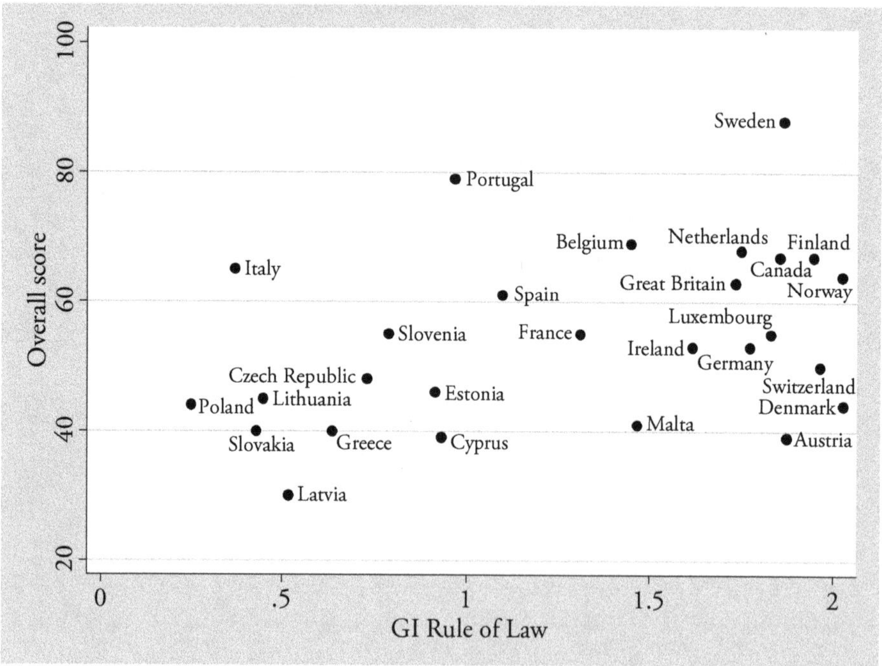

A relatively strong positive correlation between the MIPEX composite score and the dimension Voice and Accountability (r=0.469, p-value=0.012) demonstrates that the greater voice a country grants to its citizens in decision-making, the more likely it is to promote legal equality for non-EU migrant residents. A similar set of correlations emerge with control of corruption (r=0.47, p-value=0.011), while government effectiveness (r=0.395, p-value=0.037), and rule of law (r=0.398, p-value=0.038) show weaker correlations. As the graphs shows for all these correlations, there remains a lot of variation. For example, Sweden and Austria have similarly high levels of voice and accountability for its citizens, while their respective MIPEX scores on the integration of non-EU citizens differ significantly. The outlier policy frameworks across all three correlations are Italy, Portugal, and Spain, whose policies on integration surpass their ratings on overall good governance. Another clustering of outliers are Austria, Denmark, Switzerland and to a certain extent Germany and Luxembourg, whose high World Bank scores on accountability, effectiveness, and rule of law for the general population are not matched with high MIPEX scores on targeted integration policies for immigrants. A final cluster of Cyprus, Malta, and Latvia are slightly less favourable than the trend in the EU on both good governance and integration policies.

A final set of significant correlations point to a link between government effectiveness/the rule of law/control of corruption and the security of long-term residence and nationality status. Countries with poorly functioning, excessive bureaucracies and justice systems tend to grant a low security of status for long-term residents and naturalising migrants. It is interesting to observe that security of status for family reunion is little related to government effectiveness and the rule of law scores. The outliers on family reunion are the Czech Republic, Hungary, Poland, and Slovenia, whose policies on the books on security of status score significantly better than the effectiveness, rule of law, or control of corruption in public administration. Whereas in Germany, Austria, Luxembourg, the opposite occurs: a lower level of security for the family reunion status is delivered through more effective, orderly, and law-abiding bureaucracies.

Control for corruption's relatively strong correlation is with the strand on political participation (r=0.73, p-value=0.00), and in particular with electoral rights (r=0.53, p-value=0.00). The countries most active on combating corruption in decision-making and service-delivery are those most likely to open political opportunities to migrants such as local passive and active voting rights. This correlation complements findings based on multilevel regression model on 2004 ESS data that generalized trust levels are significantly higher in countries where non-EU migrants can exercise local and regional electoral rights, even rendering the effect of the stock of foreigners non-significant in explaining trust levels.[5]

[5] Tim Reeskens, Dietland Stolle, Marc Hooghe, Integration Policies and Social Cohesion Indicators in Europe. A Multilevel Test on 19 Countries, *Migration and Immigrant Incorporation Workshop* 19 (Harvard University, 2008).

Table 5: GI: Control of Corruption – MIPEX Political participation strand

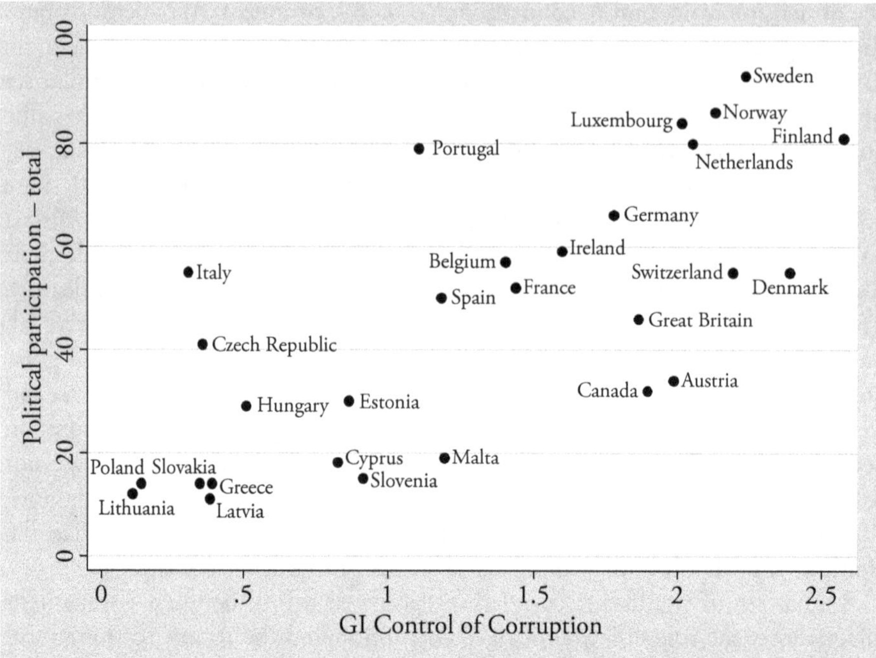

Chapter nine finds a similarly significant relationship between policies enabling political participation of third-country nationals and the public's assessment of whether the national parliament should contain more MPs of foreign origin. Our finding suggests that a country's political participation policies have links not only to public perceptions and trust, but also to a government's general anti-corruption policies.

2. *Integration Frameworks for Countries in Transition: Central Eastern Europe*

Given the stark contrast between the average MIPEX scores for Western Europe and Eastern Europe and the formers' poor scores on policy coherence, the explanations behind the EU-8's MIPEX scores may be linked to processes other than migration and integration. National governments in the region do not tend to recognise their nation as a present or future country of immigration. Since flows are new, small and often ethnic/kin-related or seasonal/cross-border, these countries often do not adopt comprehensive integration strategies for non-EU nationals. The political dynamics and left-right opposition that is observed in Western Europe does not apply in most of Central Eastern Europe (Howard 2009).

What then explains the inclusiveness/exclusiveness of Central Eastern European legal frameworks in areas like nationality, political participation, and anti-discrimination? Scholars have taken note of a largely "ethnic" interpretation of nationality (Bauböck et al. 2007) linked to traditional 19th and 20th century concepts of nationhood that have been reasserted in the post-communist era: "the fragility of statehood in East Central Europe drives all these countries in the direction of a state-reinforcing overcompensation."[6] Although the particular cultural, social, political and psychological reasons differ country-by-country, an overall link has been hypothesized between a post-Communist country's process of transition and its position in typologies on citizenship, the market economy, legal systems, and national and minority coexistence (Klicperová-Baker 1999). We investigate the hypothesis that the EU-8 countries whose policies scored highest for having the greatest potential on immigrant integration are those that have resolved past issues of sovereignty and progressed the furthest in the transition to a liberal democracy that could be welcoming to foreign residents and a market economy that could be responsive to domestic immigration needs (Akule eds. 2008). In contrast, those countries whose policies according to MIPEX could have an exclusionary effect on foreign residents would tend to be those in earlier stages of agreement on citizenship and adjustments to the market economy. The link between integration policies and democratic and economic development is therefore assumed to be positive and strongly significant.

The biannual, composite Bertelsmann Transformation Index (BTI) compares the current state of transition to liberal democracy and the market economy in 125 countries, including the EU-8 countries. Both a domestic and an international expert assess legal, political, and social performance using a 1–10 grading scale on 32 "Status" questions, which are aggregated into five dimensions in the section "Status of Democratic Development" and seven dimensions in the section "Status of Economic Development." In these analyses the number of cases is very small which is why the graphs might speak louder than the correlation coefficient. One should also take note of the rather small variation in this measure between the EU-8 countries. This case is illustrative of a challenge confronted in a number of our analyses. There may be a lack of variation between countries for the different indicators; many indices are intended for world-wide comparisons and the MIPEX countries tend to fall into the same group of high-scoring nations.

A very strong correlation emerged between the MIPEX composite score and the BTI overall "Status of Democratic Development" score for the EU-8 countries ($r=0.825$, p-value=0.012). The more favourable a country's democratic, judicial, and nation-state structures scored in the transition to liberal democracy, the more favourable its policies scored in the six MIPEX areas. Comparisons of like-strands and dimensions between the two indices revealed further strong correlations for Central Eastern Europe. Countries with greater agreement on the state's founding principles and citizenship arrangements tend to grant more favourable policies on access to nationality ($r=0.754$, p-value=0.03). Countries

[6] Andre Liebich, Altneuländer or the Vicissitudes of Citizenship in the New EU States, in *Citizenship Policies in the New Europe*, 18 (Amsterdam University Press, 2007).

with more favourable frameworks on the rule of law and on the representation of interests and civic culture were more likely to have favourable integration policies. Furthermore, the countries that made the greatest progress towards the market economy according to BTI tend to be those that provide a fair and equal access to the labour market for non-EU migrant residents (r=0.766, p-value=0.027). One outlier with very high scores on Market Economy Status, but more modest scores on labour market access is the Czech Republic, which has nevertheless developed a number of labour migration pilot projects with the IOM.

These correlations reinforce the hypothesized link between paths to economic and democratic transition in Central Eastern European countries and their actual legal and policy framework on integration, particularly access to nationality, political participation, labour market access, and the security of residence. The initial agreement (or lack thereof) on national concepts of citizenship, the status of national minorities, and societal integration concepts may have a strong impact on the principles that these countries generally apply to immigrant integration (Cholewinski 2005). It may also determine their readiness to adapt these policy areas in response to societal changes and to migrant newcomers. In this policy change promoting integration may be best promoted not through the introduction of targeted measures, but through greater reflection within the receiving society on the global competitiveness of the labour market and the inclusiveness of social and democratic structures.

Table 6: Integration Policies in Central Eastern Europe

SI Democracy Status – MIPEX Composite Score

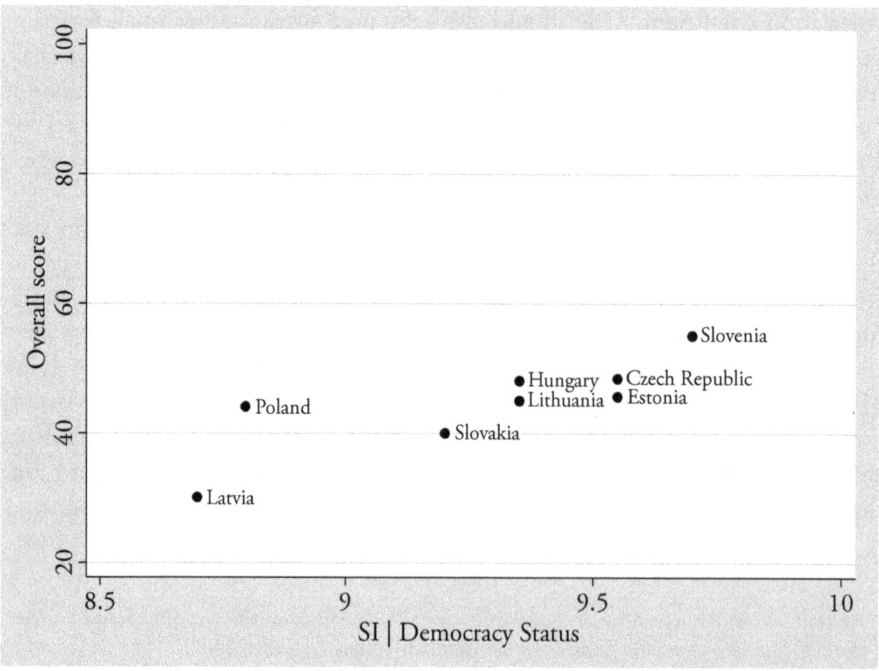

Stateness (dimension Q1) – Nationality Strand Score

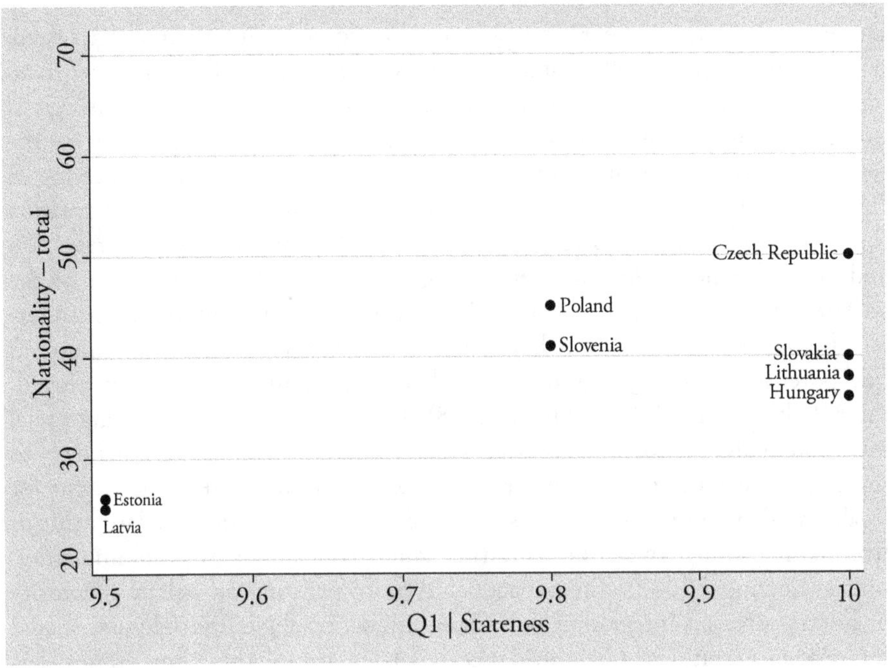

Market Economy Status (SII) – Labour Market Strand Score

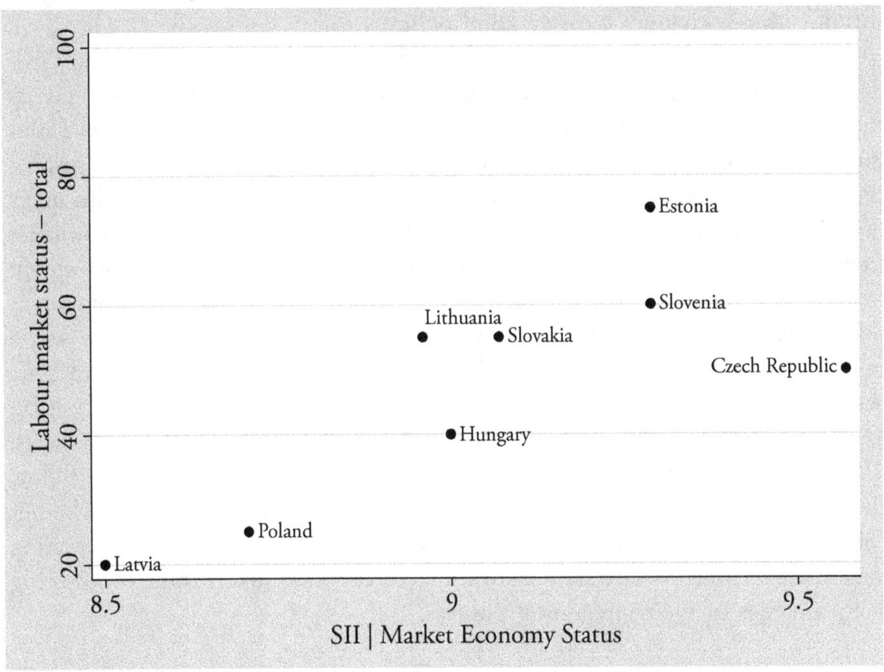

3. *Integration Policy and the Welfare State Paradigm*

Do countries adopt integration policies that square with their welfare state policy? Are stronger welfare states more likely to use the legal framework to remove obstacles to participation and codify positive state obligations? Or is the state following a different logic when it takes action in its legislation on the residence status and rights of third-country nationals? Although the meeting of "insider" welfare states with "outsider" immigration presents a general paradox for European nations (Brochmann 1999), the relationship between integration and welfare policy is less apparent. Integration policy has been a part of the welfare state's core equality business in post-war Western Europe. Humanitarian discourses on integration have tended to portray non-EU immigrants as one potential vulnerable group in need of help, alongside the unemployed, the elderly, and the infirm (Freitas 2008). In the context of overarching social inclusion goals, the logic of securing social rights to vulnerable groups does to some extent extend to securing various social, political, and residence rights for legally-resident immigrants. It is speculated that this traditional relationship is fragmenting and high-scoring countries could take four new accommodation routes (Entzinger 2007). The impact could be lower scores on welfare generosity or lower scores on integration policy conditions, or eligibility/rights associated for residence statuses. Little evidence has been found that immigration has shrunk welfare state generosity (Banting and Kymlicka 2004), leading to the hypothesis that it is inclusive capacity of the welfare state that is most likely to shrink through changes to integration policy.

This analysis follows one of the concluding suggestions in Bommes and Geddes (2000) to focus on the structure of immigrant policies as a means to clarify the interaction between migration and welfare. The Expected Benefits Index (Scruggs 2006) compares the generosity of welfare states based on their institutional commitments, rather than the programme spending ratios traditionally used in international comparisons. 2002 OECD data, covering 13 countries from the 2007 MIPEX sample, is used to determine the income replacement rate and coverage rate for three major forms of social insurance: unemployment insurance, sick-pay insurance, public old-age pensions. Our hypothesis was a positive and significant correlation between welfare state generosity and state action on promoting integration; in general the more generous a country is on expected institutional benefits, the higher it scores for its integration policies. The degree of significance could test if integration and the welfare state follow the same road across Europe's diverse social models. It can also test whether certain outlier countries have elected to take the less likely route of lowering generosity of their welfare state institutions or the more likely route of lowering the principles of their integration policies.

The correlation between the MIPEX composite score and the Expected Benefits Index score was positive, though, despite expectations, rather weak, and not significant (r=0.319, p-value=0.267). There is only a slight tendency for countries with more generous welfare structures to apply principles of equality across all their integration policy areas. Sweden appears as an outlier with a proportionally higher score on integration policy. The other two major outliers are Austria and Denmark, whose integration policies measured in 2007 score significantly lower than their welfare state generosity measured in 2002. This gap may be understood in the context of the important immigration and integration restrictions introduced in both countries since 2002, pointing to a discursive shift away from the application of a "welfare" paradigm in integration policy (Torfing 2003).

Drilling down from the composite score, relatively strong correlations were found between the Expected Benefits Index and the strands on long-term residence and political participation. The countries with more generous welfare structures are more likely to facilitate access to a secure long-term residence status for non-EU immigrants (r=0.551, p-value: 0.041). One important outlier policy framework is the United Kingdom's. For scoring so low as a "liberal" welfare state, the UK still comes out high on securing opportunities for long-term residence based postcolonial arrangements. The relatively significant correlation between the Expected Benefits Index and political participation (r=0.499, p-value=0.0695) indicates that the higher a country scores on the generosity of its welfare structures, the higher it scores on granting opportunities for the political participation of non-EU migrant residents. Sharing access to political rights appears partly linked to welfare state generosity. For what the counties scores on expected benefits, Finland, Sweden, and the Netherlands score notably more favourable on political participation, while Austria and Canada score notably less favourable. This analysis suggests that the greatest link between a country's welfare state infrastructure and its integration legal and policy framework is observed in the extension of political rights and in the granting of permanent residence and the accompanying near-equal social rights.

Table 7: Welfare and integration

Expected Benefit Index (Scruggs 2006) – MIPEX composite score

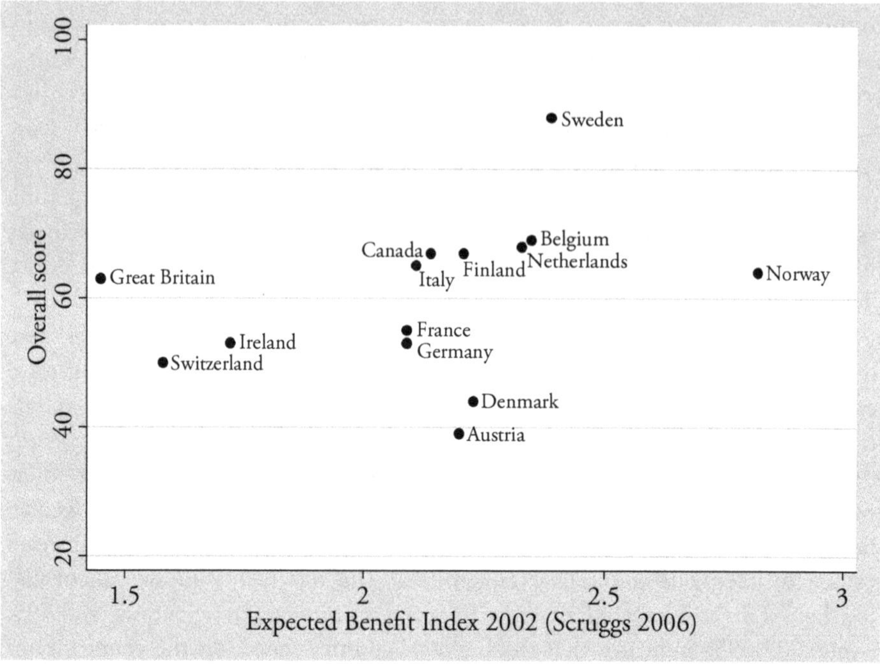

Expected Benefit Index (Scruggs 2006) – MIPEX Long-term Residence

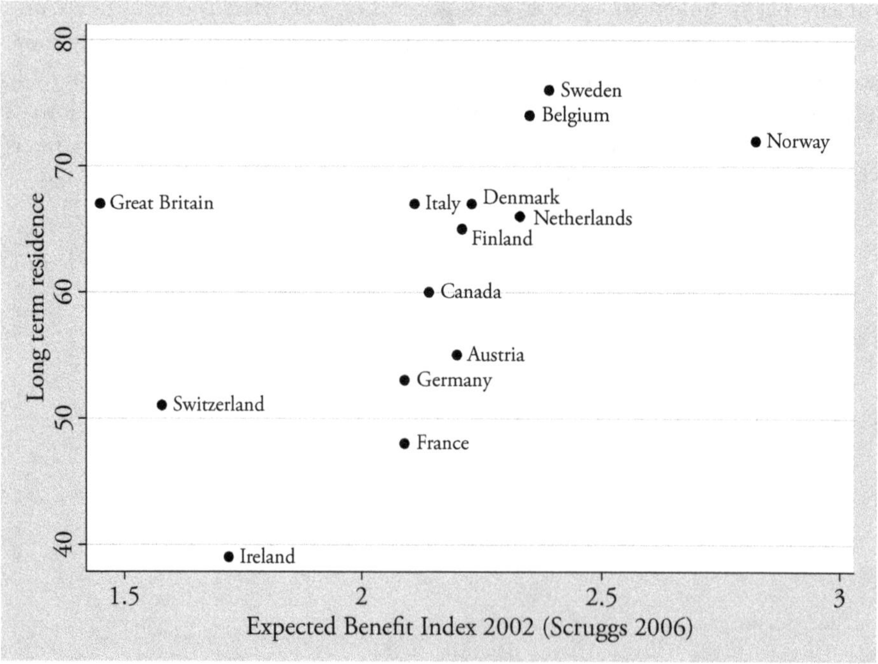

Expected Benefit Index (Scruggs 2006) – MIPEX Political Participation

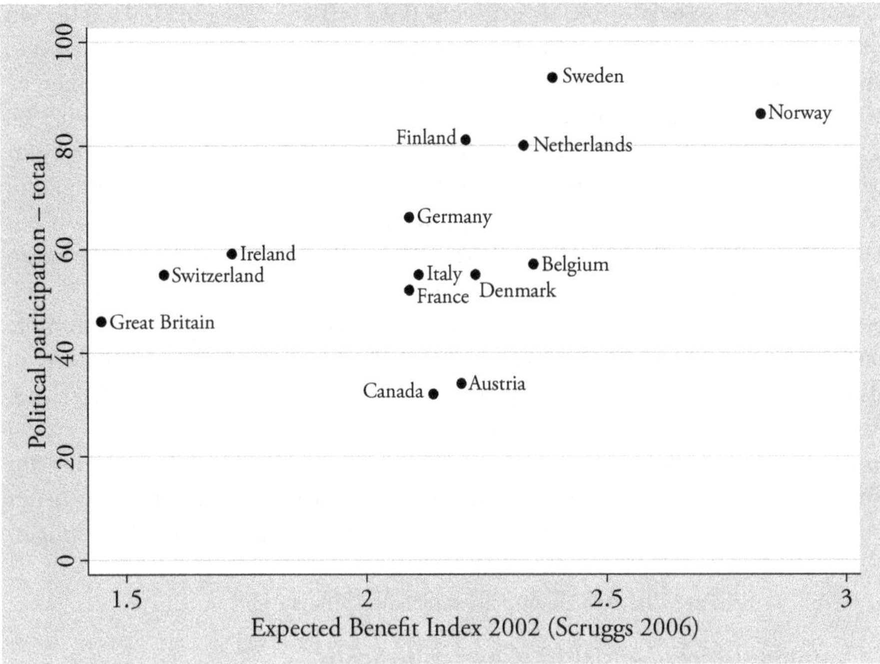

4. *Integration Policies and Economic Competitiveness*

Integration policies and anti-discrimination law have been integrated into the EU's approach to competitiveness as one of the key priorities in the implementation of the Lisbon Strategy and the EU's Open Method of Coordination on Social Protection and Social Inclusion. The European Commission repeatedly mentions a government's efforts to improve competitiveness in the context of the adoption of a legal policy framework on integration.

The World Economic Forum has adopted two similar indices for measuring global and European economic competitiveness. The Global Competitiveness Index measures a country's largely outcome-related performance on economic competitiveness. The Index relies on twelve dimensions, including an assessment of the legal and governmental framework. The second Index, the Lisbon Review, only applies to the EU Member States and measures their performance in meeting the specific Lisbon strategy's goals on competition and innovation, competitive, social inclusion, and sustainable development. Both measures combine publicly-available hard data and qualitative assessments from top CEOs and executives contained in the annual World Economic Forum's Executive Opinion Survey. A positive correlation was expected between MIPEX and the two indices, since policy changes to promote immigration and integration are often justified in the name of economic competitiveness.

The overall correlations with the Global Competitiveness Index and the Lisbon Review were positive, as expected (GC r=0.462, p-value=0.013, Lisbon r=0.476, p-value=0.016). Countries with more favourable MIPEX scores tend to obtain more favourable competitiveness scores. Somewhat weaker links emerged between the MIPEX labour market access strand and the indices (GC r=0.383, p-value=0.044, Lisbon r=0.318, p-value=0.120). Countries that promote competitive economies are slightly more likely to remove legal obstacles to migrant's access to the labour market and adopt workplace integration measures – but a lot of variation remains. A more telling correlation was observed between the MIPEX composite score and the GC dimension on institutions (r=0.399, p-value=0.035). Countries with legal and policy structures in place to promote the Lisbon agenda and the economic competitiveness were slightly more likely to also adopt favourable policies on promoting integration. Germany, Switzerland, Austria and Denmark represent one cluster of outlier countries, with high-scoring institutional frameworks for promoting competitiveness but lower-scoring for immigrant integration, whereas Italy, Spain, Portugal score significantly better on their integration policies than on their competition framework. The strongest

Table 8: Competitiveness and integration

GC composite score – MIPEX Composite Score

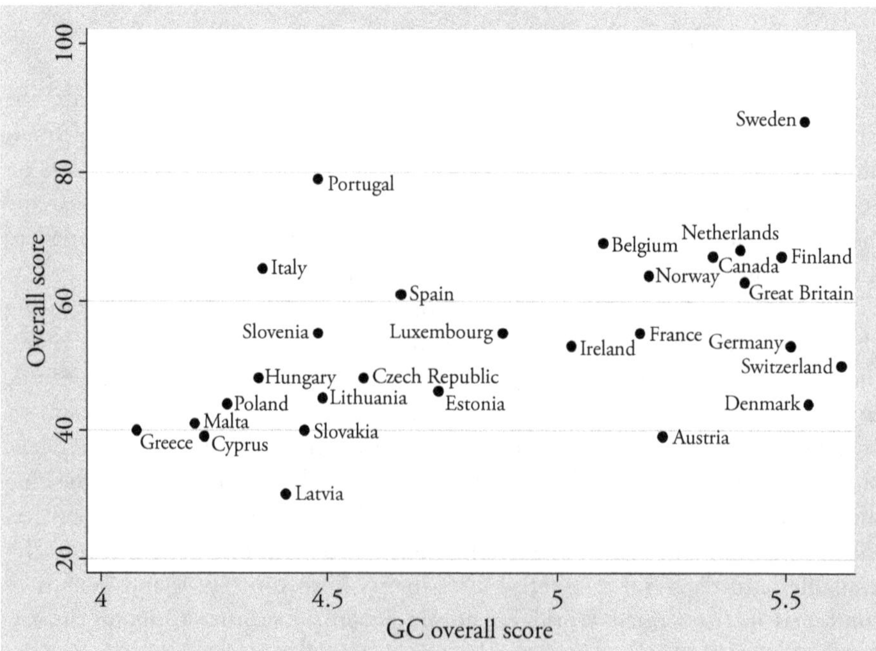

Lisbon Review Index Score – MIPEX Composite Score

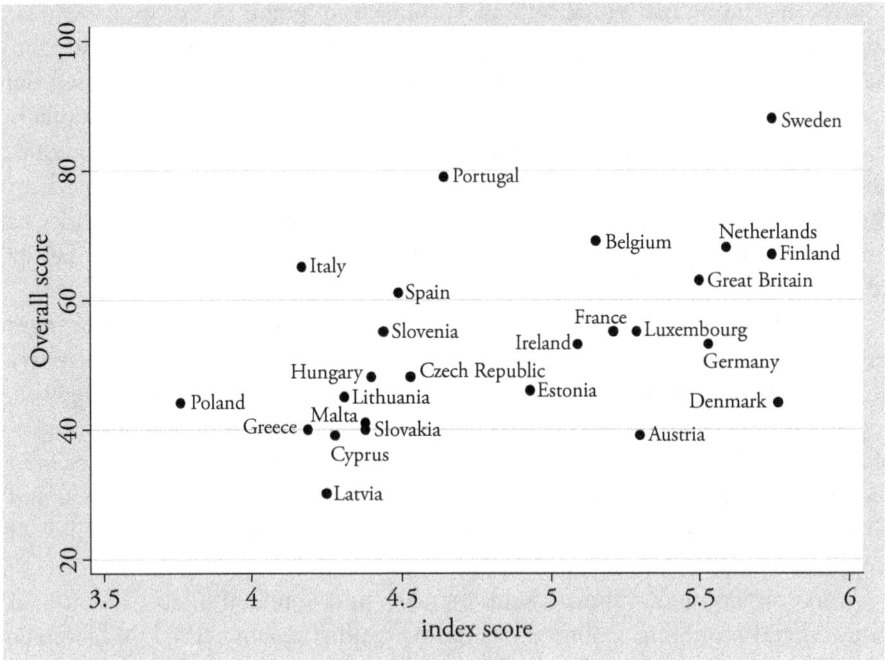

correlation was identified between the MIPEX score and the GC dimension on Health and Primary Education (r=0.511, p-value=0.005). Countries with quality educational and health systems tend to have somewhat more favourable policy frameworks on immigrant integration. Certain countries' integration policies align with their overall economic competitiveness, while, in the major outliers in Southern Europe and Continental Europe, policies aimed at the integration of non-EU citizens and those aimed at economic competitiveness appear little connected.

5. *The Same Path for Gender and Immigrant Equality?*

The civil and human rights movements have been traditionally based on solidarity between the rights of women and of ethnic minorities and immigrants. Gender and immigrant equality are seen as components of the long process of enfranchisement and social change (Benhabib 2004, Soysal 1994). This process primarily take place within the bounds of the nation state and through legal and administrative instruments for inclusion: for instance voting rights, anti-discrimination law, and labour market status. Similar claims have been made and accepted in public debates in the 1970s and 1980s with generally greater success on gender equality than on immigrant inclusion.

This complementary relationship has been challenged in recent populist discourses that frame traditionalist (read Muslim) immigrants in Europe as a threat to Western values and progress on gender equality (Roggeband and Vliegenthart 2007). Case studies in Scandinavia and the Netherlands have analysed the recent divergences on immigrant integration policies within these traditionally pioneer countries on gender equality and multiculturalism (Langvasbråten 2008, Akkerman and Hagelund 2007, Roggeband and Verloo 2007). These us/them dichotomies often hang on the rights of immigrant women vs. the authority of immigrant men/sponsors in the context of labour market participation, family reunion policies, and the tolerance of various cultural practices.

The fact that these very recent framing shifts have only led to policy changes in a handful countries leads to our expectation of a positive and still relatively strong positive correlation between current achievement on women's empowerment and the state of play in developing policies promoting immigrant integration. A hypothesis was also formed that high-achievers on gender equality would facilitate family reunion, since the conditions, security of residence status, and rights accorded to spouses and sponsors can strongly influence the equality of opportunity within immigrant families, particularly between spouses.

Scores on women's empowerment are taken as a potential marker of national political and economic action on promoting gender equality. The UN Development Programme uses the Gender Empowerment Measure (GEM) and Gender-related Development Index (GDI) among the five key indicators in its annual Human Development Index (HDI) for 177 countries. The GEM evaluates to what extent women are able to take up political and economic opportunities and take part in decision-making. The measure takes into account the proportion of women in parliamentary representation, proportion of legislators, senior officials, managers, professional and technical employees, and earnings ratios. The GDI measures to what extent inequalities persist between men and women in terms of health, knowledge, and standard of living. Although the GEM is most pertinent given MIPEX's focus on access to opportunities, this analysis relies on both for a comprehensive picture of empowerment.

The MIPEX composite score is strongly and positively correlated to the GDI (r=0.603, p-value=0.001) and the GEM (r=0.638, p-value=0.003). One should note that the European countries and Canada which are surveyed in MIPEX all receive high GDI-values compared to the rest of the world. The countries with greater equality in development and opportunity for women tend to have more favourable integration policy frameworks for non-EU migrants. The outlier policy frameworks that buck this trend are Austria and Denmark, comparatively less favourable integration policies compared to their achievements on gender equality, and Italy, Portugal, and Sweden, comparatively more favourable. Surprisingly, the linking of family reunion policies and gender equality is very weak (GDI r=0.143, GEM r=0.27). The principles behind a country's policies on family reunion are little related to its achievements on gender equality and empowerment.

The correlation of gender equality with legal equality for migrants is upheld in general, while the link with family reunion policies appears more problematic. Kofman (2004) suggests in her critical review of the family-related migration literature that many family reunion policies adopted in the 1970s were viewed as a secondary, "unwelcome" side-effect of the end of recruitment programmes for temporary (largely male) migrant workers. In this context, female spouses were associated more with other "dependents," such as elderly parents and minor children, than with work, autonomy, and empowerment. The policy paradigm behind family reunion was framed as a balance between the (male) sponsor's right to family life and the state's immigration and welfare interests. This balance was supposedly negotiated by placing conditions upon sponsors (ensuring that he was a breadwinner) and limiting the rights, access, and residence security of the family dependents (ensuring that they were not using family reunion as an economic immigration channel). Furthermore, recent populist impulses would restrict the male sponsor's right to a foreign (that is to say traditionalist) wife. The best way to promote gender equality in this logic would be to increase the obstacles for immigrant women to immigrate through family reunion procedures. The traditional logic behind many family reunion policies thus had little to do with gender equality or socio-economic advancement, while new populist logics try to play off gender and immigrant legal equality.

Table 9: Integration and gender equality

HDI Gender-related Development Index – MIPEX Composite Score

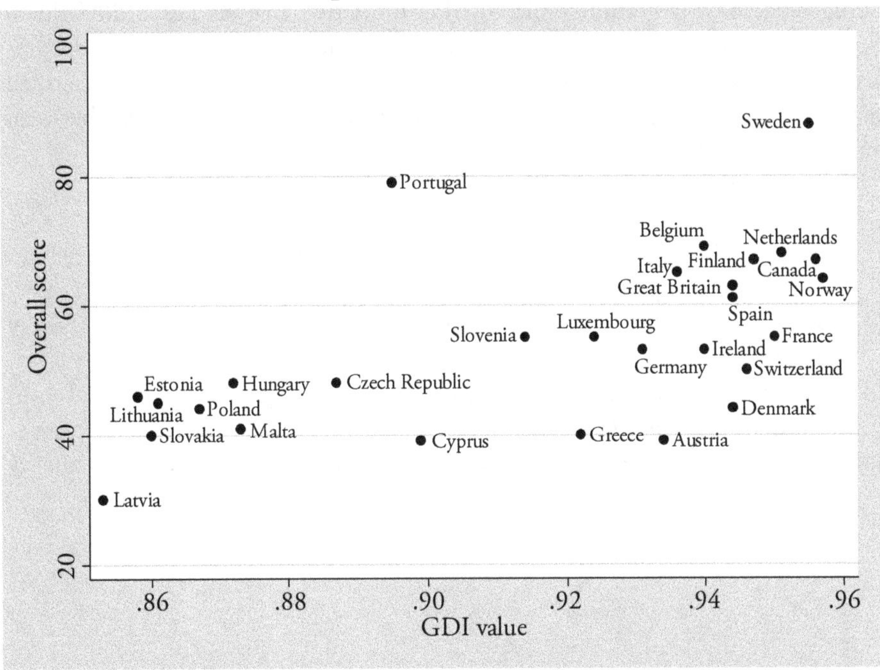

HDI Gender Empowerment Measure – MIPEX Composite Score

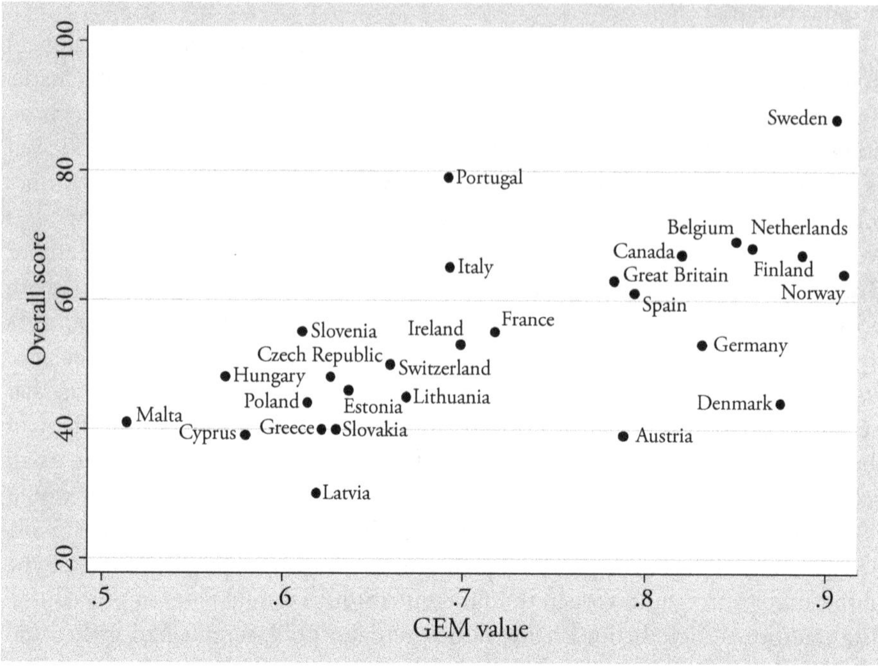

D. *Conclusions and Recommendations for Further Research*

The MIPEX database provides an overview of which countries are or are not doing what on integration policies. This inductive analysis has drilled down beyond these preliminary comparisons to further the discussion on which dynamics, logics, and intentions help explain what countries are doing. It has clarified many statistically significant relationships suggested in the literature between and within integration laws and policies in Europe:

Within integration policies:

(1) Legal eligibility for labour market access and adoption of labour market integration programmes
(2) Definitions of the family and the conditions for acquisition of family reunion;
(3) Tolerance of dual nationality and eligibility for access to nationality (naturalisation and *ius soli*)
(4) Legal enforcement mechanisms on anti-discrimination and national equality policies

Between integration policies:

(1) Conditions for the acquisition of family reunion, long-term residence, or access to nationality
(2) Family reunion and long-term residence law: most dimensions
(3) Long-term residence and nationality law: slight inverse in eligibility
(4) Anti-discrimination laws and access to nationality

Comparisons of MIPEX to similar Indexing exercises placed integration as a part of the broader policy context. Our findings suggest significant statistical correlations between a government's performance on integration policy as scored by MIPEX and its performance on good governance, welfare state generosity, gender equality, economic competitiveness. Particularly high correlations arose between control of corruption and political participation policies as well as welfare state generosity and the securing of residence and political rights. While the strength of the overall correlation differed measurement by measurement, certain countries tended to recur as outlier legal frameworks, significantly bringing down or up these relationships. Integration policy success and coherence in Central Eastern Europe is significantly related to the progress of democratic and economic transition. For how well they score on good governance, welfare generosity, gender equality, and competitiveness towards their own citizens, the countries of Central Europe – Austria, Denmark, Germany, and Switzerland – often come out as remarkably unfavourable on integration policies for non-EU nationals. The countries of the Western Mediterranean – Italy, Portugal, and Spain – are performing remarkably well on integration policies in comparison to their general ratings on good governance, gender equality, and competitiveness. Alone at the top, Sweden emerges as remarkably well-performing on various sets of indicators.

These correlations call for greater comparative research to further bridge the different areas of integration policy and national contexts in Europe. Area specialists are best suited to conduct further quantitative analysis to explore casual relationship within these strands, taking into account the necessary controls and externalities. National specialists can undertake investigations of the political actors at play, discourses, and policy evolutions in various Member States in order to bring out the various logics, intentions, and choices that confront national governments in integration policymaking, the transposition of EC directives, and the implementation of international conventions. This national analysis would be particularly interesting in the case of the recurring outlier frameworks. What explains these divergences between scores on targeted and mainstream policies, for instance in the case of Denmark or the Western Mediterranean countries, and what are their effects on individual integration processes? With future MIPEX editions, these correlations can track immigration policy trends and the possible increasing Europeanisation of immigration policy and norms. This regularly updated quantitative database can give researchers and stakeholders the bigger picture on the changing dynamics behind European immigrant integration policy.

Annex

Second calculation of composite score, standard deviations and standard deviations/means (calculated from the different strand scores for each country).

	Mean	St.dev	St.dev/Mean
Belgium	69	7.24	0.10
Portugal	79	8.52	0.11
Sweden	88	10.32	0.12
Ireland	53	7.62	0.14
Netherlands	68	10.80	0.16
Great Britain	63	10.21	0.16
Germany	53	8.76	0.17
Finland	67	11.61	0.17
France	55	11.97	0.22
Norway	64	14.74	0.23
Czech Republic	48	11.72	0.24
Luxembourg	55	13.68	0.25
Canada	67	17.39	0.26
Italy	65	16.90	0.26
Austria	39	10.21	0.26
Switzerland	50	13.15	0.26
Spain	61	16.30	0.27
Denmark	44	12.78	0.29
Slovakia	40	13.13	0.33
Cyprus	39	12.83	0.33
Hungary	48	17.95	0.37
Slovenia	55	21.13	0.38
Lithuania	45	17.43	0.39
Greece	40	16.26	0.41
Malta	41	18.07	0.44
Poland	44	19.46	0.44
Estonia	46	20.40	0.44
Latvia	30	13.36	0.45

Third calculation without the Political Participation strand

	Mean (without PP)	St.dev	St.dev/mean
Luxembourg	49	4.00	0.08
Belgium	71	5.48	0.08
Slovakia	46	6.62	0.15
Germany	50	7.16	0.14
Great Britain	66	7.75	0.12
Ireland	52	7.79	0.15
Canada	73	8.82	0.12
Portugal	79	9.33	0.12
Cyprus	43	9.84	0.23
Lithuania	51	10.03	0.20
Netherlands	65	10.11	0.15
Finland	64	10.83	0.17
Austria	40	10.94	0.28
Sweden	87	11.03	0.13
Latvia	34	11.09	0.33
Norway	60	12.29	0.20
Czech Republic	50	12.36	0.25
Slovenia	63	12.69	0.20
Greece	45	12.77	0.29
Denmark	42	12.82	0.31
France	55	13.03	0.23
Switzerland	49	14.19	0.29
Poland	50	15.58	0.31
Malta	46	16.43	0.36
Spain	63	17.03	0.27
Hungary	52	17.15	0.33
Italy	67	17.92	0.27
Estonia	49	20.88	0.43

Rule of law (dimension Q3) – MIPEX Composite Score

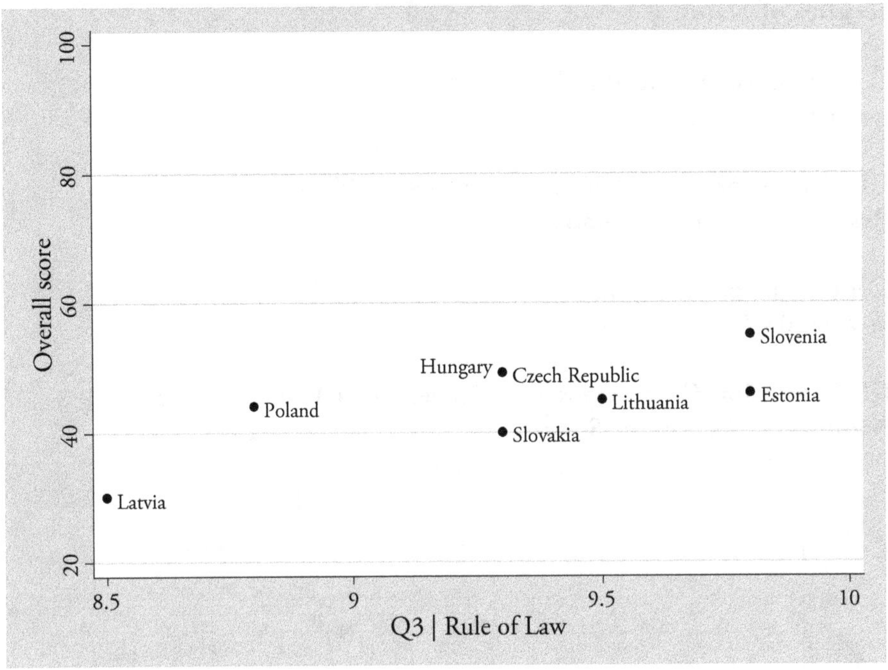

Political and Social Integration (dimension Q5) – MIPEX Composite Score

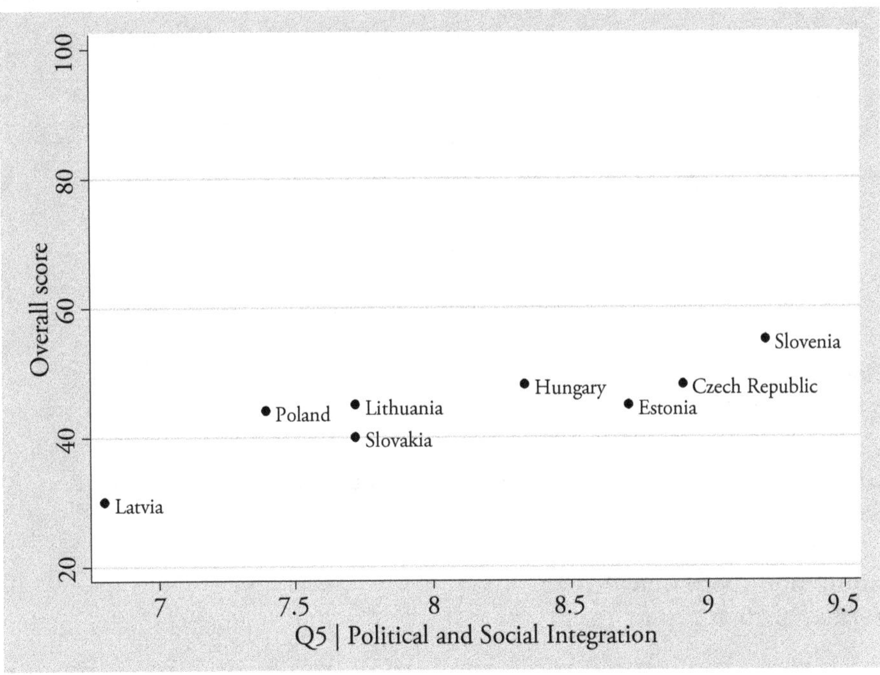

GI: Dimension Government Effectiveness – MIPEX Family Reunion: Security of Status

Correlation coefficient: 0.1144
p-value: 0.5620

GI: Dimension Government Effectiveness – MIPEX Long-term Residence: Security of Status

Correlation coefficient: 0.3437
p-value: 0.0734

GI: Dimension Government Effectiveness – MIPEX Access to Nationality: Security of Status

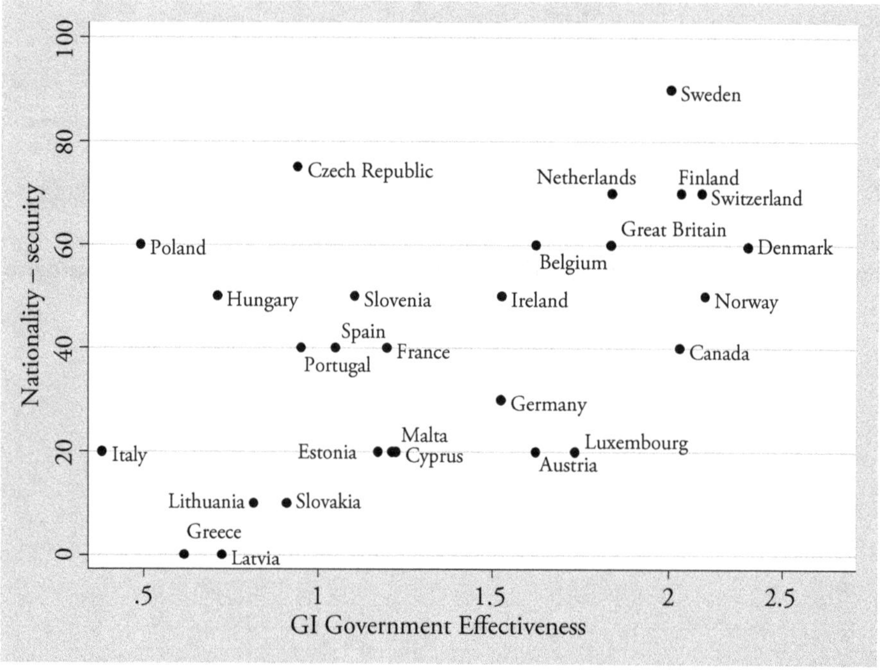

Correlation coefficient: 0.5376
p-value: 0.0032

GI: Dimension Rule of Law – MIPEX Family Reunion: Security of Status

Correlation coefficient: 0.1641
p-value: 0.4040

GC Institutions – MIPEX Composite Score

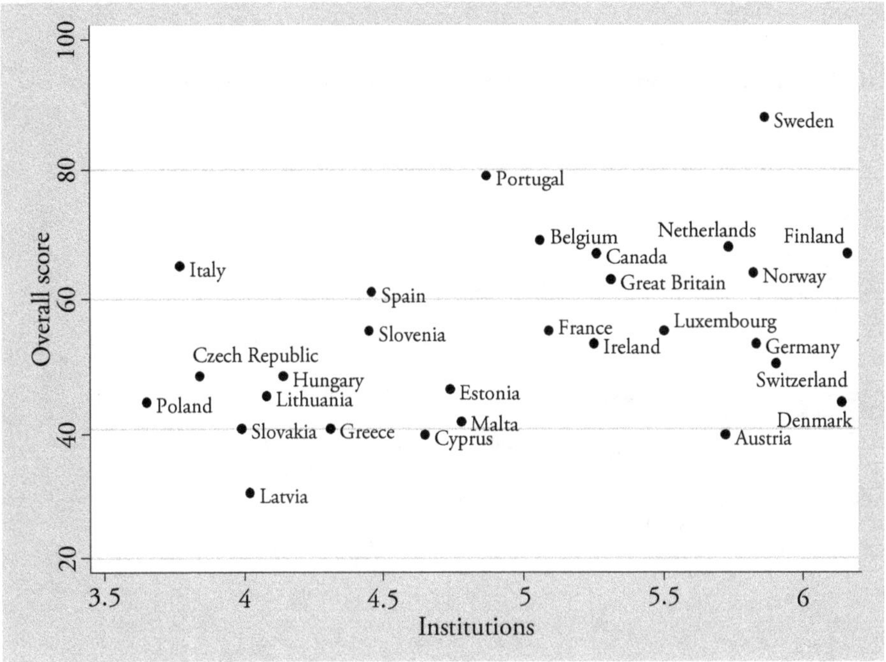

Correlation coefficient: 0.3996
p-value: 0.0352

GC composite score – MIPEX Labour Market Status

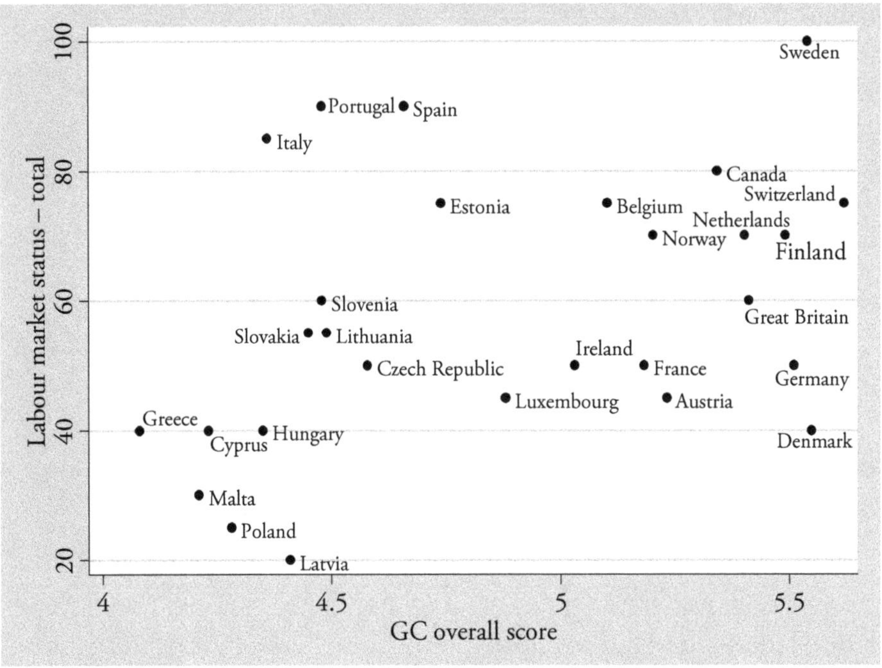

Correlation coefficient: 0.3830
p-value: 0.0443

GC Health and Primary Education – MIPEX composite score

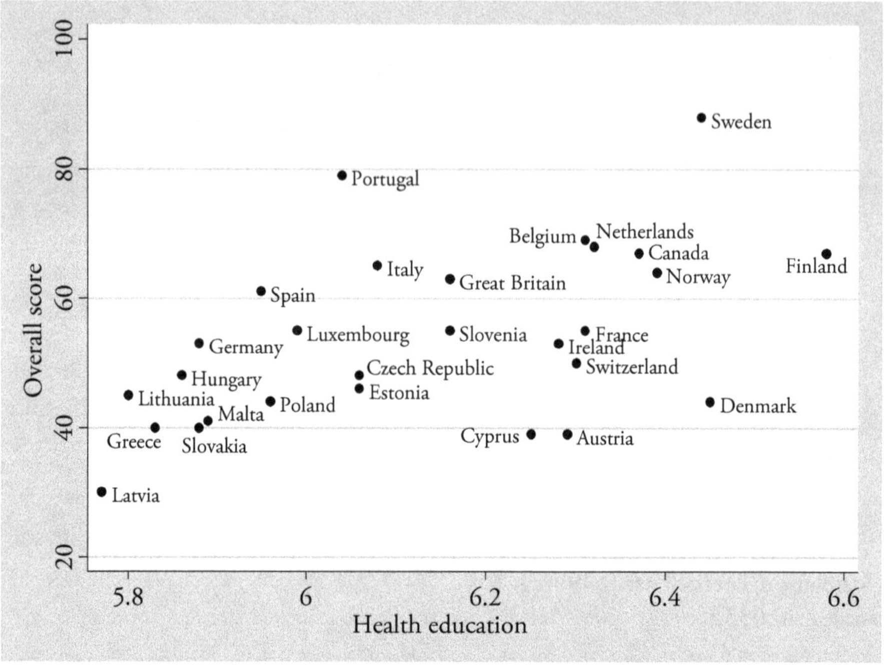

Correlation coefficient: 0.5113
p-value: 0.0054

List of References

AKKERMAN, T. & HAGELUND, A. (2007) 'Women and children first!' Anti-immigration parties and gender in Norway and the Netherlands, *Patterns of Prejudice*, 41, 197–214.

AKULE, D. ED. (2008) *Learning to welcome: the integration of immigrants in Latvia and Poland*, Centre for Public Policy PROVIDUS.

BANTING, K. & KYMLICA, W. (2004) Do Multiculturalism Policies Erode the Welfare State? In VAN PARIJS, ED. *Cultural Diversity versus Economic Solidarity*, Deboeck Université Press.

BAUBÖCK, R. ET AL. (2007) *Citizenship Policies in the New Europe*, Amsterdam University Press.

—— (2006) Migration and Citizenship: Legal Status, Rights and Political Participation, Amsterdam University Press.

—— (2005) *Acquisition and Loss of Nationality: Policies and Trends in 15 European Countries*, Amsterdam University Press.

BELL, M., CHOPIN, I. PALMER, F. (2007) *Developing anti-discrimination law in Europe: the 15 EU Member States compared*, European Commission.

BENHABIB, S. (2007) *The Rights of Others: Aliens, Residents and Citizens*, Cambridge University Press.

BERTELSMANN STIFTUNG, (2008) Bertelsmann Transformation Index 2008: Manual for Country Assessments, http://www.bertelsmann-transformation-index.de/fileadmin/pdf/Anlagen_BTI_2008/BTI2008_Manual.pdf.

BOMMES, M. & KOLB, H. (2006) Migrants' Work, Entrepreneurship and Economic Integration, *The Dynamics of International Migration and Settlement in Europe*, Amsterdam University Press.

BOMMES, M. & GEDDES, A. (2000) *Immigration and Welfare: Challenging the borders of the welfare state*, Routledge/EUI Studies in the Political Economy of Welfare.

BROCHMANN, G. & HAMMAR, T. (1999) *Mechanisms of Immigration Control: A comparative analysis of European regulation policies*, Oxford University Press.

CARRERA, S. (2005) 'Integration' as a Process of Inclusion for Migrants?, *CEPS Working Document.*

CARRERA, S. & APAP, J. (2004) Family Reunification – a case for annulment before the ECJ?, *CEPS Working Document.*

CAUSA, O. & JEAN, S. (2007) Immigrants' integration in OECD countries: does labour market policy matter?, *OECD Working Papers*, 564.

CHOLEWINSKI, R. (2005) Migrants as Minorities: Integration and Inclusion in the Enlarged European Union, *JCMS*, 43, 695–716.

—— (2004) Family Reunification as a Constitutional Right? Justice and Home Affairs in the EU, *CEPS*. 256–267.

DAHLIN, E. & HIRONAKA, A. (2008) Citizenship beyond borders: a cross-national study of dual citizenship, *Sociological Inquiry*, 78, 54–73.

DE SCHUTTER, O. (2006) Three models of equality and European anti-discrimination law, *Northern Ireland Legal Quarterly*, 57, 1–56, http://cridho.cpdr.ucl.ac.be/documents/Working.Papers/DeSchutter_NILQ.pdf.

ENTZINGER, H. (2007) Open borders and the welfare state, *Migration Without Borders: Essays on the Free Movement of People*, Berghahn Books, 119–134.

EUROPEAN COMMISSION (2004) First Annual Report on Migration and Integration, COM(2004) 508 final.

EUROPEAN NETWORK AGAINST RACISM (2007) Realising integration: ENAR policy seminar on migration, integration, social inclusion and anti-discrimination.

EUROPEAN PARLIAMENT (2003) Report on the Communication from the Commission on immigration, integration and employment, A5-0445/2003.

FAIST, T. ET AL. (2004) Dual Citizenship as a Path-Dependent Process, *International Migration Review*, 38, 913–944.

FREITAS, A. (2008) Debating Immigration, Reconsidering the 'Nation': An inquiry into political discourses and public representations in Italy and Spain, *UPF-CIDOB Research Seminar*.

GREEN, E.G.T. (2007) Guarding the gates of Europe: a typological analysis of immigration attitudes across 21 countries, *International Journal of Psychology*, 42, 365–379.

GROENENDIJK, K. (2006) The legal integration of potential citizens: Denizens in the EU in the final years before the imeplementation of the 2003 Directive on long-term resident third country nationals, *Acquisition and Loss of Nationality Volume 1: Comparative Analysis*, Amsterdam University Press, 385–410.

GROENENDIJK, K. ET AL. (1998) *Security of Residence of Long-Term Residents*, Council of Europe.

—— (2001) *The legal status of third country nationals who are long-term residents in a Member State of the European Union*, European Commission.

—— (2007) *The family reunification Directive in EU Member States: the first year of implementation*, Nijmegen, Centre for Migration Law.

GROSS, T. (2005) Integration of immigrants: the perspective of European Community law, *European Journal of Migration and Law*, 7, 145–162.

HAILBRONNER, K. (2006) Nationality in public international law and European law *Acquisition and Loss of Nationality Volume 1: Comparative Analysis*, Amsterdam University Press, 35–104.

HANDOLL (2002) The Migrant as Citizen? Long-Term Resident Migrants in the European Union, *Odysseus Academic Network of Legal Studies*, http://www.december18.net/paper54%20EurLongTermResidents.pdf.

HANSEN, P. (2005) A Superabundance of Contradictions: The European Union's Post-Amsterdam Policies on Migrant 'Integration', Labour Immigration, Asylum, and Illegal Immigration, *Centre for Ethnic and Urban Studies Occasional Papers*.

HANSEN, P. & WEIL, P. (2001) *Towards a European Nationality: Citizenship, Immigration and Nationality Law in the EU*, Palgrave.

HOWARD, M.M. (2009) *Varieties of Citizenship in Europe*, Cambridge University Press.

—— (2005) Variation in Dual Citizenship Policies in the Countries of the EU, *International Migration Review*, 39, 697–720.

IOM (2005) *Towards policy coherence*, IOM Council International Dialogue on Migration.

JOPPKE, C. (2007) Beyond national models: Civic integration policies for immigrants in Western Europe, *West European Politics*, 30, 1–22.

KLICPEROVÁ-BAKER, M. (1999) Post-Communist Syndrome, Open Society Institute Research Support Scheme.

KOFMAN, E. (2004) Family-related migration: a critical review of European Studies, *JEMS*, 30, 243–262.

LANGSVASBRATEN, T. (2008) A Scandinavian model? Gender equality discourses on multiculturalism, *Social Politics*, 15, 32–52.

LAVENEX, S. (2006) Towards the constitutionalization of aliens' rights in the European Union?, *Journal of European Public Policy*, 13, 1284–1301.

LIEBICH, A. (2007), Altneuländer or the Vicissitudes of Citizenship in the New EU States, *in Citizenship Policies in the New Europe*, Amsterdam University Press, 17–38.

MAZZOLARI, F. (2006) Determinants and Effects of Naturalization: The Role of Dual Citizenship Laws, *IZA Working Papers*, http://www.iza.org/conference_files/MEM2006/mazzolari_f2691.pdf.

NIESSEN, J. & HUDDLESTON, T. (2007) *Setting up a system of benchmarking to measure the success of integration policies in Europe*, European Parliament.

OECD (2007) *Jobs for Immigrants (Vol. 1): Labour Market Integration in Australia, Denmark, Germany and Sweden.*

PENNINX, R. ET AL. (2008) Migration and Integration in Europe: the State of Research, Norface, http://www.norface.org/files/migration-COMPAS-report.pdf.

RAXEN (2003) Migrants, minorities and employment: Exclusion, discrimination, and anti-discrimination in 15 Member States of the European Union, *EUMC* http://fra.europa.eu/fra/material/pub/comparativestudy/CS-Employment-en.pdf.

RAY, B. Practices to promote the integration of migrants into labour markets, *HWWA Hamburg.*

REESKENS, T., STOLLE, D., & HOOGHE, M. (2008) Integration Policies and Social Cohesion Indicators in Europe. A Multilevel Test on 19 Countries, *Migration and Immigrant Incorporation Workshop*, Harvard University, 29.

ROGGEBAND, C. & VERLOO, M. (2007) Dutch Women are Liberated, Migrant Women are a Problem, *Social Policy and Administration*, 41, 271–288.

ROGGEBAND, C. & VLIEGENHART, R. (2007) Framing Immigration and Integration: Relationships between Press and Parliament in the Netherlands, *International Communication Gazette*, 69, 295–319.

RUHS, M. & MARTIN P. (2008) Numbers vs. Rights: Trade-offs and Guest Worker Programs, *IMR*, 42, 249–265.

SCHIBEL, Y. (2004) Monitoring and influencing the transposition of EU immigration law: the family reunion and long term residents Directives *European Migration Dialogue*, http://www.migrant.at/EMD-issue-paper%201.pdf

SCRUGGS, L. (2006) The Generosity of Social Insurance, 1971–2002, *Oxford Review of Economic Policy*, 22, 349–364.

SOYSAL, Y. (1994) *Limits of citizenship: Migrant and postnational membership in Europe*, University of Chicago.

SPENCER, S. & COOPER, B. (2006) Social integration of migrants in Europe: a review of the European literature 2000–2006, *OECD*, http://www.compas.ox.ac.uk/publications/papers/Spencer%20Literature%20Review.pdf.

TORFING (2003) Den stille revolution i verfaerdsstaten – fra sorsørgelse og hierarki til aktivering og netvaerksstyring, *Drivkroefter bag arbejdsmarkeds-politikken Denmark*, SFI.

UK CABINET OFFICE (2003) *Ethnic Minorities in the Labour Market*, http://www.cabinetoffice.gov.uk/~/media/assets/www.cabinetoffice.gov.uk/strategy/ethnic_minorities%20pdf.ashx.

UNITED NATIONS (1965) International Convention on the Elimination of All forms of Racial Discrimination, http://www.unhchr.ch/html/menu3/b/d_icerd.htm.

UNITED NATIONS DEVELOPMENT PROGRAMME (2007) Gender Empowerment Measure and Gender-related Development Index http://hdr.undp.org/en/statistics/indices/gdi_gem/.

WALDENRAUCH, H. (2001) *Die Integration von Einwanderen: Ein Index der rechtlichen Diskriminierung*, Campus.

WORLD BANK (2007) *Worldwide Governance Indicators (WGI) project*, http://info.worldbank.org/governance/wgi/index.asp.

WORLD ECONOMIC FORUM (2008) Global Competitiveness Index, http://www.weforum.org/en/initiatives/gcp/Global%20Competitiveness%20Report/index.htm.

WORLD ECONOMIC FORUM (2006) Lisbon Review, http://www.weforum.org/en/initiatives/gcp/Lisbon%20Review/index.htm

Chapter 4

Exploring Regimes of Immigrant Integration: Clustering Countries on the Basis of the MIPEX Data

Marc Hooghe and Tim Reeskens

A. *Introduction*

Although various authors have claimed that integration policies are being harmonised within the European Union, the Migrant Integration Policy Index (MIPEX) data show a considerable amount of variation between states. While some countries devote considerable effort and policy attention to promote integration and equal opportunities, this effort seems to be missing in other European countries. This variation does not necessarily imply that we could refute the existence of a process of "Europeanisation" in this area, but it does seem to suggest that national traditions and policy options still play an important role that cannot be easily disregarded. The ambition of this chapter is limited: we want to investigate whether the MIPEX data reveal clear pattern of differences between countries. Basically this amounts to the question whether it is possible to distinguish groups or families of countries that have comparable patterns of integration policies.

By doing so, we want to shed new light on a long-standing discussion in the field of the study of integration policies. While Joppke (2007) has argued that national cultures have become largely obsolete to explain European integration policies, authors like Jacobs and Rea (2007) have taken an opposite position by arguing that national cultures and national policy traditions still have an important impact on contemporary integration policies. Since the MIPEX figures are cross-sectional and only have a bearing on the situation in the year 2006, this kind of analysis cannot be used to identify trends over time. But if a cluster analysis would demonstrate that national patterns can still be clearly identified, at least this would demonstrate that an alleged process of Europeanisation has not (yet?) smothered all national differences. An analysis on future editions of the MIPEX data set should allow us to establish trends over time in this respect.

The current debates about the nature of European integration policies still is largely determined by the framework that was laid out over a decade ago now by Rogers Brubaker (1992). Although Brubaker himself has since qualified his position, the basic distinction between civic and ethnic integration models remains a structuring element within these debates. While civic models emphasize an adherence to cultural norms and a loyalty to the political institutions, ethnic models imply that full citizenship is only open for those who can claim national ancestry (Brubaker, 1992).

Since Brubakers' original and seminal publication, various new models of integration regimes have been proposed, most of them based on a case study design containing only a limited number of countries. The strength of these research strategies is of course a very rigorous and detailed analysis of the immigrant integration policies. Nevertheless, the main drawback involved in the analysis into integration regimes based on only a small number of cases regards the extent of the generalizations of the findings. Certainly in a European context, it is far from evident to classify the wide range of European countries in the typologies that have usually been limited to France, Germany, Great Britain and the Netherlands (Koopmans et al., 2005).

By gathering 140 indicators covering integration policies for six main domains, namely labour market access, family reunion, long term residence, political participation, access to nationality and anti-discrimination, and this for 28 countries, the Migrant Policy Group (MPG) has made it possible to reach beyond these limitations and has provided researchers with an opportunity for a more quantitative approach to figure out which countries can be seen as a "family" or a coherent cluster. By a "cluster" we refer to a group of countries that has common characteristics that separate them sufficiently from all other countries (or groups of countries). It has to be remembered that in this kind of analysis, clusters are not pre-defined: calculations based on country variables (like the MIPEX figures) will empirically determine which countries "belong" together or not. It also has to be acknowledged that cluster analysis always involves subjective decisions by the researchers. Except in those few cases where a cluster solution is immediately apparent, perennial discussions are possible about how many clusters exactly can be distinguished, and how the cut-off points should be determined. In the analysis reported in this chapter, and given the exploratory character of the analysis, we have opted for a rather data-driven approach toward the analysis, so we have tried to avoid any arbitrary decision about the specific definition of clusters.

The theoretical relevance of the cluster analysis is that identifying a cluster implies that the members of that cluster can be sufficiently distinguished from all other countries (in this case: based exclusively on the 140 measurements in the MIPEX dataset). This implies that if the "hard Europeanisation" thesis would be correct, it would be impossible to distinguish clusters, since basically all European countries should resemble one another. If we succeed in identifying clusters, this by itself would be argument in the discussion about the strength of European identification.

Cluster analysis has another added advantage. It groups countries together based on resemblance and shared characteristics, but at the same time it still allows us to detect variations within the cluster. These variations thus allow for a comparison with countries that closely resemble one another. Given the strong differences between European countries with regard to political institutions or economic development, it often makes little sense to have general comparisons, as the "learning effect" from findings about e.g. the Scandinavian countries is rather limited for a country with much lower levels of economic development. But if we do find differences among the group of rich or less developed countries, this would allow us to define pioneers and trendsetters within these clusters, thus allowing for policy learning effects.

In this chapter, we first briefly review the literature on distinctions in integration regimes, departing from Brubaker's dichotomy. Subsequently, we will empirically explore whether country clusters can be detected based on the MIPEX data. Fourth, we will correlate the country clusters with civic and ethnic nationhood survey conceptions to figure out whether the discovered clusters coincide with preferences among the population of those countries. This effort can also be seen as a first exploration of the usefulness of the MIPEX data in this kind of broad comparative research. Finally, we identify some shortcomings of the current analysis and list topics for future research.

B. *Theorising Models of Integration Regimes*

Jacobs and Rea (2007) have drawn attention to the fact that despite various to harmonise immigration and integration policy in the European Union, strong national differences do seem to remain persistent. A first glance at the MIPEX score cards already makes clear that we can indeed observe huge differences. While Sweden obtains a solid score of 88, this is only 30 for Latvia. These are, however, only country averages. By performing a cluster analysis, we will attempt to look how similar, or dissimilar, countries really are. In the literature on integration regimes, much has been written about dissimilarities regarding countries' policy responses to immigration and the issue of integration. One of the most dominant models in this respect is the distinction, introduced by Brubaker, between civic and ethnic citizenship conceptions. While we will highlight the importance of his work, we will as well pay considerable attention to the analytical challenges posed by it and some recent criticism against the Brubaker model.

1. *Civic and Ethnic Integration Models*

According to Brubaker's model of minority citizenship (1992), national policy can be classified according to two opposite approaches which can be traced back to Germany and France: "for the distinctive and deeply rooted French and German understandings of nationhood have remained surprisingly robust. Nowhere is this more striking than in the policies and politics of citizenship vis-à-vis immigrants."[1] In a civic nation like France the *ius soli* is predominant, as it is open for anyone who is born on French soil. German legislation, on the other hand, traditionally stresses the *ius sanguinis* principle, which makes it easier to acquire citizenship status for those who descend from German stock. Even if these "blood ties" date from centuries ago, like is the case of German populations in Russia, this is still considered as a valid argument for a privileged relation with the German nation and state. According to Brubaker, the German system "is based exclusively on descent, allowing immigrants and their descendants to remain indefinitely outside the community of citizens."[2]

The main foundation for Brubaker's typology can be attributed to Friedrich Meinecke's "Cosmopolitanism and the National State," in which he introduced the notions of civic and ethnic nations. According to his insights, civic nations – the *Staatsnation* – are predominantly a political entity in which people form a nation because "they have willingly come together to form a community of equal citizens irrespective of their racial, religious or linguistic backgrounds."[3] In these states, nationhood is predominantly based on equality among all citizens[4] and the nation as such can be regarded as a form of social contract that in principle is open to all who wish to adhere to it. On the other hand, the ethnic *Kulturnation* "constitutes a distinct people with its own language, way of life, history and homeland."[5] In these nations, society is defined in terms of an ethnic group, which is rather the opposite of the inclusive civic nation. These two types of nation concepts are seen as mutually exclusive: if a society stresses its political character, it cannot simultaneously use references to a shared ethnic identity and an alleged glorious past as its founding myth.

Applying this framework, Kohn (1944) has used the distinction between civic and ethnic nationalism, by defining these concepts as rather fixed and stable characteristics of nation-states. Famously, he portrayed Eastern European societies as primordially ethnic, while the liberal regimes of Western Europe were seen

---

1 Rogers Brubaker, *Citizenship and nationhood in France and Germany*, 3 (1992).

2 Rogers Brubaker, "Civic and ethnic nations in France and Germany" in *Ethnicity*, 114 (1992).

3 David Brown, *The State and Ethnic Politics in Southeast Asia*, 307 (Routledge, 1996).

4 *Id.*

5 *Id.*

as civic. The opposition between the liberal Western and the exclusive Eastern immigrant regimes is still widely present and forms the backbone of Brubaker's distinction between French *ius soli* and German *ius sanguinis* models.

In some of his more recent work, Brubaker (2004) acknowledged two main weaknesses associated with his earlier approach. First, there are analytical ambiguities associated with the civic-ethnic distinction. Within the literature, there is no agreement on the question of which elements refer in an unequivocal manner to civic, and which refer to ethnic concepts of citizenship.[6] It has to be noted here that while Brubaker acknowledges doubt about the operationalisation of the concepts, he does not question the fact that both concepts can be used as ideal types.

The second problem is associated with the normative implications of the distinction. Civic nationalism is portrayed as liberal, universalistic and inclusive while the ethnic form of nationality concepts is regarded as illiberal, particularistic and exclusive. Especially in Eastern Europe and the Balkans, where ethnic divisions do not necessarily coincide with state borders, ethnic and civic conceptualizations of group identity do not necessarily overlap. Brubaker (2004) therefore introduces a further distinction between state-framed and counter-state understandings of nationalism.

Building on and further developing Brubaker's dichotomy, in recent years various studies have tried to elaborate this framework. Castles and Davidson (2000), e.g., argue that countries have three main policy options with respect to managing social diversity. The first option is exclusion, referring to the German guest worker system. In this policy option, countries can import guest workers if there are labour shortages in the economy. Yet, these guest workers will never be accepted as full citizens as they are expected to leave the territory, if there is no longer an economic demand for their services. In contemporary liberal democracies, this model does not longer hold as it not is no longer considered as legitimate, but is has to be noted that this model is still predominant in large areas across the world. The second policy option is assimilation. According to this model, immigrants can be granted full citizenship. The immigrants' distinct culture is seen as in transition and it is expected that they fully adopt the national culture and generally accepted social norms. The third policy option is integration. With respect to this policy option, policy makers are aware that immigrants do not, or cannot abandon their distinct culture immediately and therefore their cultural identity can be considered as an opportunity, for instance on the labour market or in education: "in some way or another a compromise will have to be established between the wish to give ethnic minority groups equal

[6] Rogers Brubaker, *Ethnicity without Groups*, 137 (Harvard University Press, 2004).

access to schooling and to economic opportunities, while allowing them at the same time to hold on to their own distinct cultural identity."[7]

2. *Analytical Challenges Regarding the Study of Integration Regimes*

Following the publication of "Citizenship and Nationhood in France and Germany," various authors have expressed their concern about the empirical validity of broad and encompassing generalizations about the division of ethnic and civic concepts across nations. First, it is striking to note that both concepts are often not strictly defined or delineated. Kymlicka, therefore, notes that "this sort of distinction is almost a cliché in the literature, but it needs to be handled carefully, and can easily be misinterpreted or misapplied."[8] While there is some consensus that adherence to legal principles typically belongs to civic citizenship, while language, descent and religion are more closely tied to ethnic citizenship, the delineation between these various forms is seldom explicitly made.

Second, it is clear that a simple dichotomy is not sufficient to fully understand the varieties of citizenship concepts. Kymlicka[9] for instance claims that "membership" of a nation is not just a question of law or ethnic heritage, but also of culture. This cultural factor is often neglected in the literature on nationalism and identity. Kymlicka uses Quebec and Catalonia as examples of this cultural nationalism: Québécois and Catalans are concerned with the survival of their culture and they do accept immigrants as long as they respect the cultural tradition of these regions. The theoretical insight to be gained here is that citizenship concepts clearly are not just two-dimensional, but incorporate various elements of community, society and politics. Kymlicka proposes that instead of a dichotomy, at least three dimensions of citizenship should be distinguished, namely ethnic, civic and cultural ones.

Third, the question whether these concepts should be considered as mutually exclusive or not, has led to an intensive debate. Miller[10] argues that the various concepts cannot be combined. In his view, societies hold on to either a civic or an ethnic citizenship character (or cultural, if we take Kymlicka's view into account), while it is almost inconceivable to take some middle position. Brubaker on the other hand,[11] strongly opposes this view. He argues that all these various considerations are being used simultaneously. Citizenship concepts within

---

[7] Marc Hooghe, The challenge of diversity: different answers and solutions, in *New citizens, new policies? Developments in diversity policy in Canada and Flanders* 6 (Academia Press 2006).

[8] Will Kymlicka, *Politics in the vernacular: nationalism, multiculturalism, and citizenship*, 243 (2001).

[9] *Id.* at 244.

[10] David Miller, *Citizenship and national identity*, 131 (2000).

[11] Brubaker 139 (2004).

a society are based on a mix of ethnic, civic and cultural considerations, and all these elements are used simultaneously in order to reach decisions on who is considered as a full member of the political community, and who is not.

Fourth, the overlap between civic-ethnic and West-East has been heavily criticised as well. Based on quantitative data, Shulman (2002) argues that ethnic concepts are present just as well in Western European societies, while in Eastern Europe, too, notions of civic identity can be found. Shulman summarises his results by stating that "imperial and communist rule have not pushed Eastern European nationhood in a strongly cultural direction while greatly weakening civicness. And whereas most of the West has a long tradition of democracy and relatively strong and stable political institutions, cultural conceptions of nationhood are alive and well, and support for multiculturalism is relatively weak."[12] Based on survey data from Latvia, Poland and Lithuania, Björklund[13] too claims that Eastern Europe is not a civic desert area: "The results of the Baltic survey do not support the idea of a uniform and specifically East European 'ethnic' concept of nationality." If we consider more specifically the field of immigration and integration policies, Koopmans et al. (2005) assume that these national traditions of civic or ethnic nationhood do remain strong and present as they influence current integration policies. Joppke (2007) has criticised this point of view as he argues that a majority of European countries tends to adopt the same procedures and requirements. To him, it is no coincidence that various European countries almost simultaneously have decided to introduce citizenship tests in order to established who is entitled to have full membership in the host community and who is not. Jacobs and Rea argue against this view by listing various national policy reforms, although they admit that "traditional typologies might have to be re-examined."[14] The new MIPEX data provide us with an opportunity to re-examine whether these traditional typologies indeed still respond to the present reality. The logic of the analysis is that if these typologies do make sense, the countries under investigation should form one specific cluster.

C. *Exploring Country Clusters Using MIPEX*

To investigate whether countries form distinct clusters, it is first of all necessary to discuss our methodology, namely cluster analysis. Subsequently we will

---

[12] Stephen Shulman, Challenging the civic/ethnic and west/east dichotomies in the study of nationalism, 35(5) *Comparative Political Studies* 583 (2002).

[13] Fredrika Björklund, The East European 'ethnic nation' – myth or reality? 45(1) *European Journal of Political Research* 112 (2006).

[14] Dirk Jacobs & Andrea Rea, The end of national models? Integration courses and citizenship trajectories in Europe, 9(2) *International journal on multicultural societies* 264 (2007).

perform this type of analysis on the full MIPEX data set. Later on, we will perform separate analyses on each of the six policy domains, included in the composite MIPEX ranking.

1. *Methodology*

In order to examine whether certain countries have common characteristics with regard to integration policies, we will use cluster analysis. Using this technique, it will be possible to assess the degree of association between various countries on the basis of the variables in the data set. This kind of technique offers more fine-grained information on precise policies, than simply ranking the average scores. For instance, countries A and B may have implemented policies W and X while they have not implemented Y and Z while countries C and D did the opposite. The overall score will rate all four countries equally high while countries A and B are clearly distinct from countries C and D.

Cluster analysis can circumvent this problem by investigating the degree of similarity and dissimilarity between the various cases, i.e. countries, with respect to the variables of interest, the 140 policy indicators that MPG has gathered. A major problem associated with cluster analysis is that this technique is not well equipped to deal with missing data. Therefore we were quite rigorous in eliminating that were not present (or did not meet the quality requirements) for all countries under consideration. In total we are left with 111 policy indicators after this elimination process. The loss of substantial information, however, remains rather modest. E.g., we did not include the variable on whether non-nationals have voting rights on the regional level, because information on that variable was missing in all countries where there are no separate regional elections. Since we do have information, however, on national and local elections (and these are being held in all countries under investigation), the actual loss of information by deleting this variable remains very limited.

Ideally, the result of the cluster analysis should be that the distinction that have been introduced by authors as Brubaker, Koopmans and others, are also empirically supported, so that we should find, e.g., a clear "ethnic" and an equally clear "civic" cluster of countries. With regard to the technical aspects, the clustering method was based on the Ward-estimator, which is, among all available techniques, considered as providing reliable outcomes.

2. *Analysis on the Full MIPEX Data*

Based on the cluster analysis on the pooled data covering 111 indicators, the following results are obtained. The discrimination between the countries points out that two main clusters have emerged. The first cluster contains, with the exception of Slovenia and Hungary, all Eastern European countries, namely Latvia, Czech Republic, Estonia, Slovak Republic, Poland and Lithuania. This cluster is completed with the Mediterranean countries Greece, Cyprus and Malta, and the Western countries Austria and Denmark. All these countries have a rather restrictive integration policy in common. Within this main cluster, we can distinguish two sub-clusters. The first sub-cluster includes all non-Eastern European countries together with Latvia; the second sub-cluster is built up out of Malta and all Eastern European countries, except for Latvia.

The second major cluster contains, next to Hungary, all Western European countries, with the exception of the Mediterranean countries that were clustered in the first group and Austria and Denmark. Interestingly, also this second major cluster is built up around two sub-clusters. The first one contains Finland, Germany, Norway, Spain, Switzerland, France and Netherlands. These countries can be considered to have the most open integration policies. The second sub-cluster includes countries as Belgium, Great Britain, Canada, Portugal, Sweden, Italy, Slovenia, Luxembourg and Ireland. When we take the overall MIPEX scores in mind, it can be argued that Sweden, Belgium and Portugal score remarkably well on these indicators, and therefore could be considered as policy examples; the reverse is true for countries like Austria and Greece that score distinctly bad on these indicators, and therefore have quite some manoeuvring room for policy improvements.

The analysis on the complete migrant integration policies data set already reveals some interesting findings. First, using cluster analysis provides a different kind of information compared with an investigation of the country specific means on the aggregated MIPEX score. While France and the Netherlands obtain different scores on the overall ranking, the cluster analysis nevertheless reveals that they have strong common characteristics with regard to integration policies. A similar kind of reasoning can be applied to other country clusters, like for instance Italy and Slovenia. Their similarity regarding integration policies is clearly stronger than the composed score at first glance would reveal.

Second, the analysis seems to provide further evidence about the existence of a major East-West distinction with regard to migrant integration policies. With just a few exceptions, the main clusters have been formed around the Western European countries, on the one hand, and Central and Eastern Europe on the other hand.

From a policy point of view, the most interesting finding from this cluster analysis is the fact that there are a few exceptions, i.e., countries that do not have the policies that we would expect them to have. Denmark and Austria are obvious examples: we would expect that these countries would fit into the liberal cluster, but they seem to belong quite strongly to the restrictive cluster. It might come as no surprise, therefore, that both countries have had extreme right parties in their governing coalition (the Freedom Party in Austria and the Danish People's Party). Apparently these parties have succeeded in influencing the integration policy of their country in a direction that one would rather associate

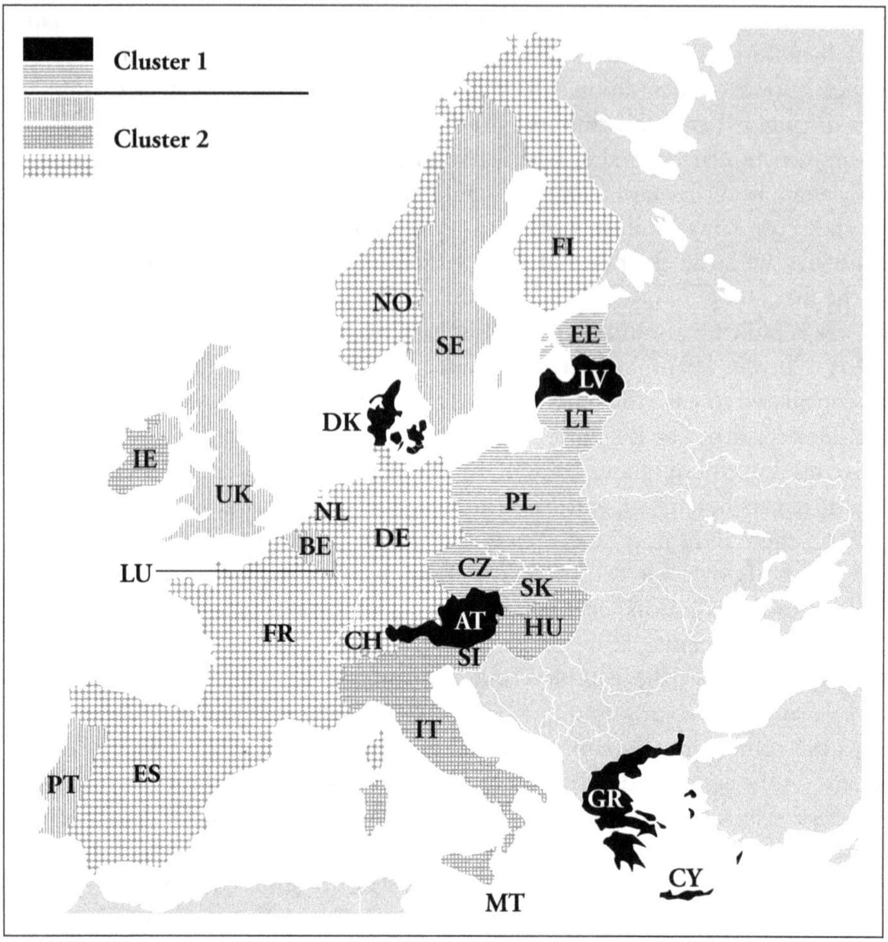

Note: The graph depicts the results of a cluster analysis with ward-estimation method on 111 MIPEX indicators. Country labels: AT = Austria, BE = Belgium, CH = Switzerland, CY = Cyprus, CZ= Czech Republic, DE = Germany, DK = Denmark, EE = Estonia, ES = Spain, FI = Finland, FR = France, GR = Greece, HU = Hungary, IE = Ireland, IT = Italy, LT = Lithuania, LU = Luxembourg, LV = Latvia, MT = Malta, NO = Norway, NL = Netherlands, PL = Poland, PT = Portugal, SE = Sweden, SI = Slovenia, SK = Slovak Republic, U.K. = United Kingdom.

Figure 1: Cluster analysis on the pooled MIPEX data set

with Eastern Europe than with Western Europe. Denmark and Austria are much more restrictive than we could expect basic on their economic development and their geographical situation.

Mirroring this exception is Hungary that does not cluster with its neighbouring countries in Eastern Europe, but clearly belongs to the liberal cluster. The long-standing presence of the minority Roma population may have caused this Central European country to adopt policies that are predominantly found in

Western countries. This, however, is for the time being just a hypothesis, that should be explored further in a case study in that country.

Four, while the cluster analysis confirms an East-West divide, it does not show any indication for a North-South divide, which is often assumed with regard to liberal attitudes and (lack of) ethnocentrism. Scandinavian countries do not seem to perform any better than Portugal, Spain or Italy. Southern Europe is equally divided: while Spain, Portugal and Italy belong to the liberal cluster, Greece and Cyprus belong to the restrictive cluster.

Fifth, relating to our theoretical framework, one of the most interesting topics features the civic-ethnic dichotomy. Applying Brubaker's framework to this model, it seems far from evident that clusters of civic and ethnic countries seem to differentiate on, first of all, the basis of a continuum, and second of all, that France and Germany are ideal types for the two concepts. The analysis has revealed that Germany and France can even be classified into the same minor cluster that is part of the Western European group. Given the various migrant integration policy reforms in Germany, these results may perhaps not come as a surprise. Nevertheless, the finding that Germany and France are so closely related to each other raises some considerable questions about the extent of the still widespread applicability of *ius soli* and *ius sanguinis*. With regard to integration policy France and Germany seem to have more in common than elements that distinguish them. It should be remembered of course that this resemblance is relative, because all Western European countries seem to have much more in common if we compare them to the countries of Central and Eastern Europe.

3. *Disaggregating MIPEX Scores*

The cluster analysis on the complete data set has thus far resulted in some interesting insights on how countries can be grouped regarding their migrant integration policies. Nevertheless, this form of grouping based on aggregate scores, as always, may overlook certain subtleties in the data. Therefore, the next step in the analysis is to disaggregate the data set to its six main domains, namely labour market access, family reunion, long-term residence, political participation, access to nationality and anti-discrimination measures.

With regard to labour market access, a similar pattern can be discovered. Here Hungary joins Denmark, Austria and most countries of Central and Eastern Europe in a restrictive cluster. With regard to labour market access we can observe that (quite exceptionally) France too joins this restrictive cluster. To put it differently: with regard to labour, French policy is much more restrictive than it is with regard to overall integration.

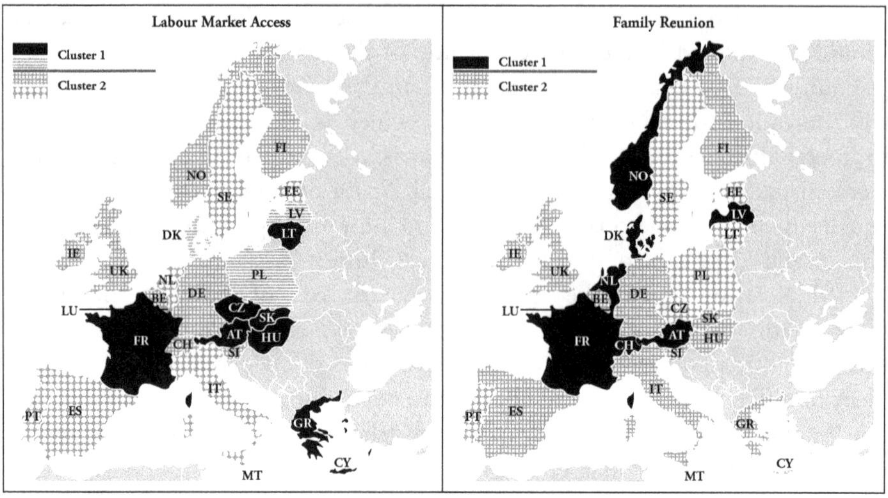

Figure 2: Cluster analysis on labour market access and family reunion

Regarding family reunion, the overall picture is far less clear. Only a limited number of countries form the first cluster, namely Austria, Switzerland, Denmark, France, Latvia, Netherlands, and Norway. All the other countries form the second one, with a first major sub-cluster consisting out of Czech Republic, Estonia, Lithuania, Malta, Poland, Portugal, Slovenia and Sweden. The second smaller cluster is formed by Belgium, Cyprus, Finland, Germany, Spain, Greece, Hungary, Ireland, Italy and Slovak Republic. What is quite interesting to note is the major differences between the Scandinavian countries: while Denmark and Norway cluster together, Sweden and Finland belong to different groups. In general, it has to be acknowledged, however that the cluster on family reunion policies is difficult to interpret.

The country map of long-term residence policies resembles to a considerable extent to the family reunion one. Austria, Cyprus, Germany, Denmark, Estonia, Latvia, Lithuania, Netherlands, Norway and Slovak Republic form the first cluster. Spain, Ireland, Sweden and the U.K. form a first sub-cluster within the second group of countries. Italy, Hungary, Luxembourg and Malta form a second sub-cluster; Switzerland, Czech Republic, Finland, Poland, Portugal and Slovenia form the last one.

With regard to political participation rights, the picture is completely different, since almost all countries belong to a liberal cluster. Apparently, European harmonization has been quite successful with regard to this sub-dimension of integration policy. Only a limited number of countries have a much more restrictive policy with regard to political rights for non-nationals. Latvia and Lithuania also belong to this cluster, and this might be related to their specific

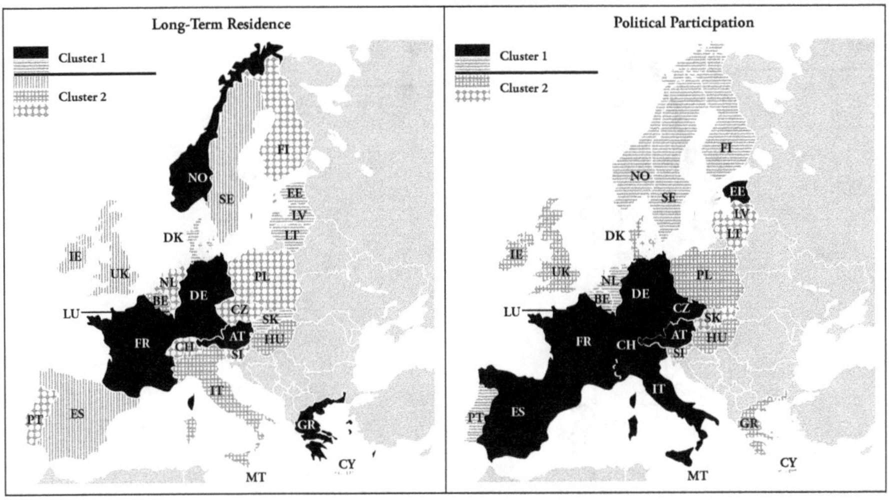

Figure 3: Cluster analysis on long-term residence and political participation

geographical position, neighbouring the strong Russian Federation. It is a bit surprising, however, that Greece, Denmark, the U.K. and Ireland too, belong to this restrictive cluster. As such, we could expect that in these countries there are more abundant possibilities for policy change toward more open political rights for non-nationals.

Access to nationality is the next policy cluster within MIPEX. Liberal policies with regard to acquiring full citizenship can be found in just a limited number of countries, with Belgium, France, Sweden and the U.K. as clear examples. It has to be noted here that there could be a clear trade-off with the previous policy dimension. In countries where it is relatively easy to obtain full citizenship rights, there might be less political pressure to grant voting rights to non-nationals, since it is relatively easy for these non-nationals to obtain citizenship rights in the first place. In general, it has to be noted that most European countries maintain restrictive policies with regard to acquiring full citizenship status.

The sixth and final set of integration policy regards anti-discrimination policies. Once again, most of the Western European countries seem to form one major cluster – Finland, Sweden, United Kingdom France, Portugal, together with Slovenia and Hungary, and Belgium, Italy and Netherlands. The second major cluster consists of all remaining countries, predominantly Eastern European countries, together with Norway, Ireland, Spain, Switzerland, Austria, Malta, Cyprus and Greece. Here again, Denmark, Norway and Ireland score much more restrictive than we could expect.

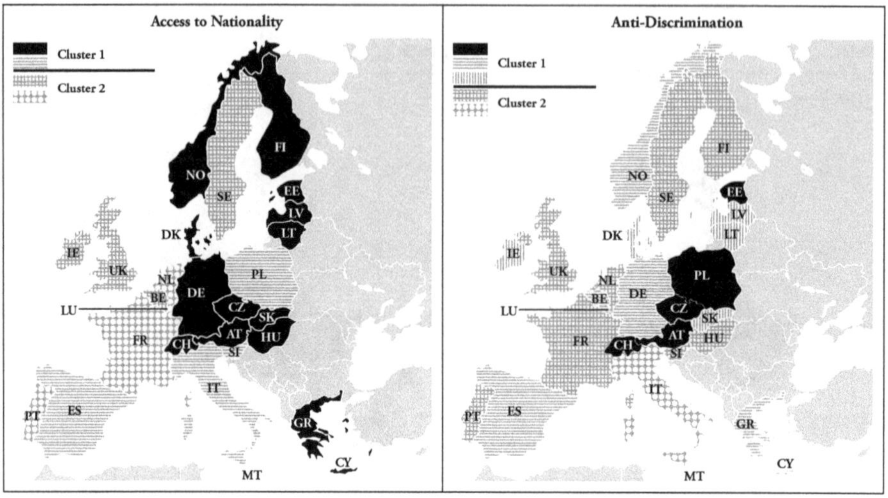

Figure 4: Cluster analysis on access to nationality and anti-discrimination

D. *Relating the Country Clusters to Civic-Ethnic Survey Items*

In this step, we will correlate the cluster divisions with the strength of the civic and ethnic citizenship concept. These figures are derived from the 2003 National Identity wave of the International Social Survey Program (ISSP) 2003. In this wave, respondents in various European countries were asked how much importance they attach to certain citizenship aspects in order to be regarded as a true national of that country. For the purpose of this article, we restrict ourselves to the analysis of two items that can be regarded as typical for the civic-ethnic dichotomy, namely the importance of respecting the national political institutions and laws as an indicator for civic citizenship and having national ancestry as an ethnic citizenship indicator. In final, 19 countries are present in both the ISSP and MIPEX. For these countries, we can ascertain whether there is a correlation between ethnic beliefs (among the population) and the occurrence of restrictive policies, of between civic beliefs among the population and the occurrence of liberal policies.

In Figure 5, we report the country average scores for civic and ethnic citizenship concepts (among the population), for the various clusters that were identified in Figure 1. E.g., we can observe that in the very first (restrictive) sub-cluster, with countries Denmark, Austria and Latvia, the population is more supportive for civic citizenship concepts than for ethnic concepts. The differences between the clusters, however, all clearly very limited as in almost all European countries, support for civic forms of citizenship is clearly more outspoken than for ethnic citizenship. Given the fact that we reveal few differences between the clusters, we can observe that attitudes among the population are not the main determining

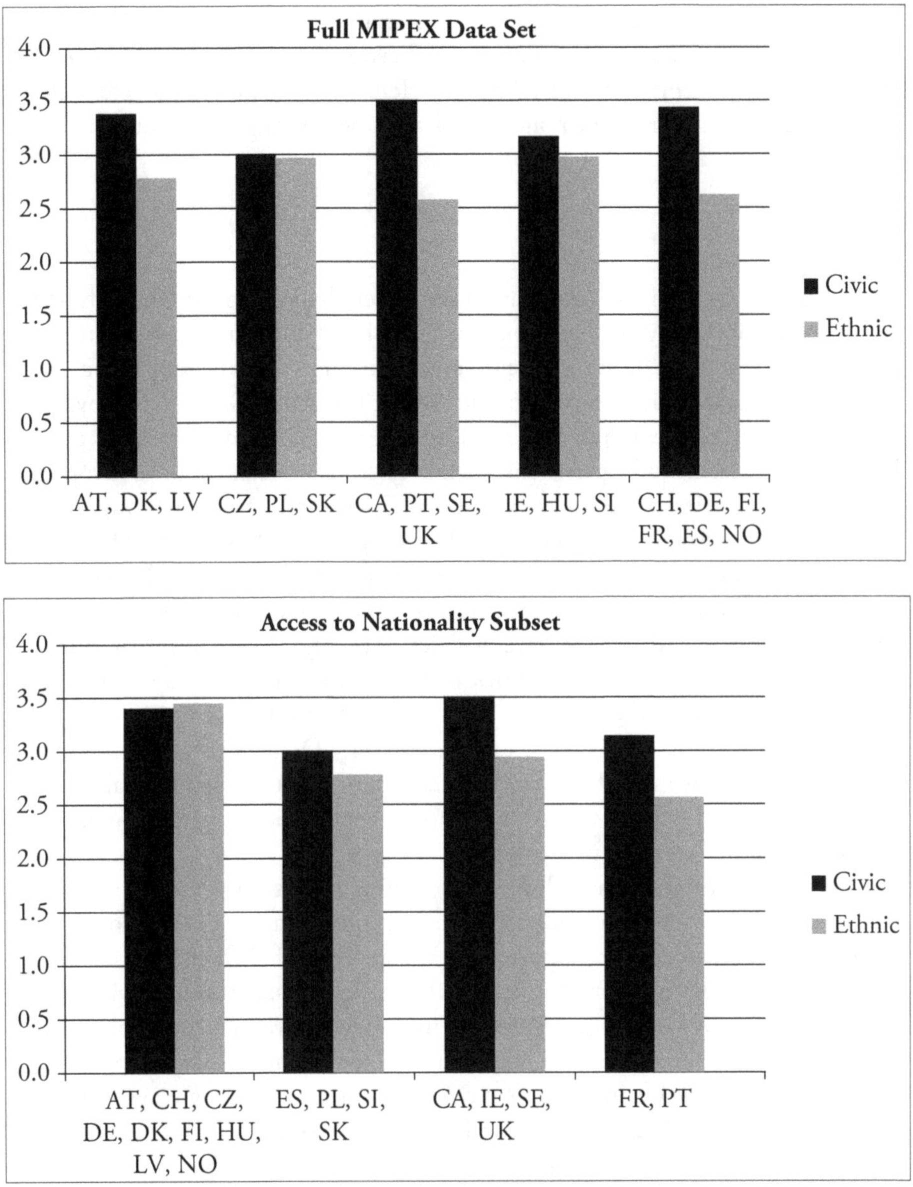

Figure 5: Relation between MIPEX country clusters and civic-ethnic ISSP-items

force for the differences with regard to integration policies. Since public attitudes are basically the same in all clusters, it is clear that the impetus for developing these policies must come from somewhere else.

While these findings might be disappointing, one could still argue that the civic-ethnic dichotomy does not apply to minority policies in general but only to citizenship policies membership. To answer this suggestion, we have correlated the civic and ethnic survey items with the access to nationality clusters as found higher. Even though this picture is slightly different compared with the analysis on the full dataset, the differences between the clusters with regard to civic citizenship seems to be very limited. Here too, we do not observe a clear relation between government policies and attitudes among the population.

E. *Conclusion*

The literature on immigrant integration has generally been concerned with what modes countries apply in managing their stocks of foreigners. In an attempt to investigate which countries resemble one another, we have applied cluster analysis on the extensive set of data the Migration Policy Group has provided. Using this analysis technique, the main finding is that the distinction between East and West seems to be persistent, with Western European countries adopting more liberal policies, while the countries in Central and Eastern Europe seem to prefer quite restrictive policies. Notable exceptions are Austria and Denmark, where integration policies are much more restrictive than we could reasonably assume. Apparently, in these two countries, other policy considerations are at work, resulting in rather restrictive policies with regard to the integration of immigrants. One element that comes to mind is the high score obtained by extreme right parties in these countries, but self-evidently, more empirical research should reveal whether this is indeed the reason why Denmark and Austria score much lower than we could normally expect them to do. It would make sense therefore, to direct efforts to arrive at a more liberal policy toward immigration rights, specifically to these two countries.

A second important remark has to do with countries do *not* form a cluster. First of all, the widespread idea that the Scandinavian countries form one homogeneous block is not supported by the analysis of their integration policies. As we already mentioned, Denmark seems to cluster together with most of the countries in Central and Eastern Europe. Moreover, on the pooled data, Sweden is present in another sub-cluster then Norway and Finland. Investigating the specific domains, in quite few cases the three countries are even present in three different sub-clusters. Second, also the Mediterranean countries are not monolithic. On the one hand, Greece clusters with the Eastern European countries, together with Malta. On the other hand, Portugal seems to cluster quite frequently with Sweden and Western countries like the United Kingdom, with quite liberal policies.

A further interesting result is that the factor solutions can differ quite substantially from one policy arena to another. While France, e.g., has usually a good liberal record, it is highly restrictive with regard to labour market access. And while the United Kingdom, too, most often can be considered as a liberal country, this is not the case with regard to political participation rights. Apparently, there is not just a single country approach toward integration policies. Specific policy arenas and networks, e.g., with regard to electoral reform, social relations or family law might facilitate or hinder policy reforms in these specific arenas. It does not seem to happen all that often that countries score high or low on all policy domains. Specific power configurations in a policy domain, therefore, should be included in this kind of research.

The fact that there are huge differences between the policy domains also sheds new light on the ongoing discussion with regard to the effects of European harmonization. In some areas, like with regard to political participation rights, there is a clear harmonization going on. For other areas, however, we do see sharp national differences that can be related to all kinds of idiosyncratic considerations, like the strength of labour market regulations, types of family law, the strength of extremist parties, etc. The cross-sectional nature of this MIPEX data does not allow us to make any meaningful statements on the trends in integration policies. The strong differences between the policy domains, however, might suggest that the impact of European harmonization is not the same across all policy areas. While in some cases, e.g., where there are no fixed and powerful counterforces, the EU might have a rather easy task in enforcing its rules, this will be much harder in other policy areas. While we certainly cannot claim that we have solved the ongoing debate about the alleged loss of national traditions, our analysis suggests that there might not be a general answer to this question, but that the answer will depend largely on the specific policy domain.

List of References

BJÖRKLUND, F. (2006) The East European 'Ethnic Nation' – Myth or Reality?, *European Journal of Political Research*, 45(1), 93–121.

BROWN, D. (1999) Are There Good and Bad Nationalisms?, *Nations and Nationalism*, 5(2), 281–302.

—— (1996) *The State and Ethnic Politics in Southeast Asia*, London, Routledge.

BRUBAKER, R. (2004) *Ethnicity without Groups*, Harvard University Press.

—— (1996) Civic and Ethnic Nations in France and Germany, *In* Hutchinson, J. & SMITH, A.D. (Eds.), *Ethnicity*, Oxford University Press, 168–173.

—— (1992) *Citizenship and Nationhood in France and Germany*, Harvard University Press.

CASTLES, S. & DAVIDSON, A. (2000) *Citizenship and Migration. Globalization and the Politics of Belonging*, London, Routledge.

JACOBS, D. & REA, A. (2007) The End of National Models? Integration Courses and Citizenship Trajectories in Europe, *International Journal on Multicultural Societies*, 9(2), 264–283.

JOPPKE, C. (2007) Beyond National Models. Civic Integration Policies for Immigrants in Western Europe, *Western European Politics*, 30(1), 1–22.

HOOGHE, M. (2006) The Challenge of Diversity: Different Answers and Solutions, *In* D'HAENENS, L., HOOGHE, M. VANHEULE, D., & GEZDUCI, H. (Eds.), *New Citizens, New Policies? Developments in Diversity Policy in Canada and Flanders*, Ghent, Academia Press, 3–10.

KOHN, H. (1944) *The Idea of Nationalism: A Study in Its Origin and Background*, London, Macmillan.

KOOPMANS, R., STATHAM, P., GIUGNI, M., & PASSY, F. (2005) *Contested Citizenship: Immigration and Cultural Diversity in Europe*, Minneapolis, University of Minnesota Press.

KYMLICKA, W. (2001) *Politics in the Vernacular: Nationalism, Multiculturalism, and Citizenship*, Oxford University Press.

MILLER, D. (2000) *Citizenship and National Identity*, Cambridge, Polity Press.

SHULMAN, S. (2002) Challenging the Civic/Ethnic and West/East Dichotomies in the Study of Nationalism, *Comparative Political Studies*, 35(5), 554–585.

Chapter 5

The Nexus Between Immigrant Integration Policy and Public Opinion in the European Union

Dirk Jacobs and Barbara Herman

It has been claimed by European administrators in a recent article in the *European Journal of Migration and Law* that "without managing public perceptions, it is difficult, or even impossible, to manage migration, especially on a European level."[1] They furthermore state that "perceptions, attitudes and the support of the public shape the content of legislation and influence the impact of policies."[2] Academics like Galya Lahav (2004) have claimed there is indeed an important coherence between public opinion and attitudes of political decision makers with regard to immigration. As a result, one might also expect an impact of public opinion on policy formation in the domain of immigrant integration.

In contrast, authors like Gary Freeman (1995) have claimed that public opinion only is of minor importance for immigration related policies. Freeman claims business and technocratic elites – who often tend to be in favour of immigration in light of a globalising economy – are better organised than the amorphous general public – which tends to be opposed. Elites hence matter much more for policy making. According to this vision, policy is more likely to be made behind gilded doors (Guiraudon, 1997) of meetings at ministerial cabinets and amended in court rooms, away from the public eye. As a result, policy tends to be more "pro" migration than one would expect when looking at public opinion alone.

It is difficult to decide whether authors like Lahav, stressing the importance of public opinion for policy making, or like Freeman, stressing the importance of targeted mobilisation and lobbying for policy making, are closest to the truth

---

1 Ricklef Beutin et al., Reassessing the link between Public Perception and Migration Policy, 9 EJML 390 (2007).

2 *Id.* at 411.

when immigrant integration policy is concerned. We tend to find the hypothesis offered by Freeman to be the most plausible one. Leaving aside the issue that one can debate to what extent public opinion really exists as a coherent phenomenon (Converse, 1964; Zaller, 1992; Saris & Sniderman, 2004), mass opinion needs to be channelled and articulated by political entrepreneurs to be effective in a competition with special interest groups. Obviously, there is by definition some link between public opinion and policy making in democracies. Politicians and political parties cannot systematically act against public opinion and hope to get re-elected. It is nevertheless also true that immigration policies are often linked to economic interests; liberal immigration policies are sometimes seen as a necessary evil by policy makers, regardless of what the ordinary citizen may think about immigrants. Furthermore, there is successful pro-immigrant mobilisation by civil society organisations and academics trying to bring in the human rights perspective and defending immigrant interests. Authors like Yasemin Soysal (1994) have even claimed that a post-national human rights discourse, allegedly on the rise in all liberal democracies, has pushed governments and courts towards expansion of immigrant rights. Last but not least, once policies are in place, citizens can gradually get used to them and eventually perhaps even start to support them.

In this contribution we want to try and shed further light on the nexus between policy making and public opinion with regard to immigrant integration. We will not be able to settle the debate between authors like Lahav and Freeman but want to contribute to the discussions on the topic by pinpointing to the relevance of the Migrant Integration Policy Index (MIPEX) data set. Indeed, we will empirically investigate whether public opinion and policy co-vary across European countries (or not). In doing so, we hence do not limit our attention to a single case study or a small scale comparative analysis, as is done so often, in trying to assess the link between public opinion and policy making, but will focus on 25 EU Member States at once. To this purpose we will make use of the MIPEX combined with the Eurobarometer. Before doing so, we will shortly discuss the interesting analysis undertaken by Meuleman and Reeskens (2008) who, in a similar effort, have already confronted the MIPEX results with data from the European Social Survey (ESS).

A. *Linking MIPEX and the European Social Survey*

Making use of the MIPEX and the ESS, Belgian researchers Meuleman and Reeskens (2008) have examined the relation between the integration regime that a country adopts and measures of perceived ethnic threat and attitudes toward immigrants. They made use of a number of scales present in the first round of the EES (2002–2003), which had a thematic section on immigration.

By means of latent class analysis, Meuleman and Reeskens (2008) constructed a typology of three integration policy types, making use of the MIPEX data set. A first class consists out of countries which have scored high – compared to other countries – on all policy strands of MIPEX. Sweden, the United Kingdom, the Netherlands, Belgium, Norway, Finland, Portugal, Spain and Italy are part of this group. In a second class we find countries which – compared to other countries – consistently score badly on MIPEX. All eastern European countries, Austria, Denmark, Greece and Malta are member of this more restrictive group. A third class of countries shows intermediate results. Typically they only offer limited access to the labour market, to long term residence and to family reunion, but are more inclusive with regard to nationality acquisition and political participation. We find Germany, France, Ireland, Luxemburg and Switzerland as members of this group.

In opposition to claims by authors like Joppke (2007), Meuleman and Reeskens conclude that there is still quite some diversity with regard to immigrant integration policy in Europe (see also Reeskens & Hooghe in this volume). They equally stress that classic theoretical models (Brubaker, 1992; Castles, 1995; Koopmans et alii, 2005) do not seem to accurately catch the current empirical patterns with regard to immigrant integration policy across Europe, as documented by MIPEX.

When relating these three classes of integration policies to public opinion, it turns out that "perceptions that immigration poses serious threats to economic and cultural goods are significantly more widespread in countries with exclusive integration policies" (class two). Denmark is an exception to this pattern, combining exclusionary policies towards immigrants and a relatively low level of perceived ethnic threat (compared to other countries). Meulemans and Reeskens also related the results for the six policy strands of MIPEX separately to the attitude scales. They found that resistance against immigration and the perception of economic threat is less prevalent in countries with inclusive labour market policies. They equally found that countries which offer third country nationals access to political participation tend to have lower levels of perception of economic and cultural threat.

As an overall conclusion Meuleman and Reeskens state that open policies apparently not necessarily have to lead to a white backlash. The empirical evidence thus contradicts the group conflict theory (Blalock, 1967) which predicts "that inclusive integration policies will increase the level of competition between minority and majority groups, and therefore also the perception of ethnic threat among the latter."[3] An alternative interpretation of the findings of Meuleman and Reeskens might be that in those countries where public opinion is favourable to

[3] Bart Meuleman & Tim Reeskens, *The relation between integration policy and majority attitudes towards immigration. An empirical test across European countries*, 23 (2008).

immigration, policy makers are more easily convinced into setting up inclusive policies for immigrants. Once they are introduced they tend to remain in place due to the phenomenon of path dependence (Pierson, 2000).

B. *Linking MIPEX and the Eurobarometer*

As has been stated before, the MIPEX project wants to assess to what extent particular rights are granted to third country nationals (TCNs). We can try and relate the results of countries on MIPEX with general trends in their public opinion towards immigration and migrants, as monitored with standard scales in surveys like ESS. Meuleman and Reeskens did just this in their excellent analysis. They showed there is a moderate link between public attitudes on the one hand and the openness or strictness of integration policies on the other hand.

It would, of course, equally be interesting if we could directly measure the degree of public support for the granting of particular rights to TCNs across EU Member States – and not "just" relate them to general attitudes towards immigration and ethnic minorities. Unfortunately, surveys which explicitly want to measure this (in all EU Member States) hardly exist. We can, however, use at least the following set of questions which were present in Eurobarometer 59.2 (2003) – and in a slight variant formulation in the Eurobarometer 2003.2 Candidate Countries survey – with regard to support for immigrant rights:

(1) Legally established immigrant from outside the European Union should have the same social rights as the (NATIONALITY) citizens
(2) Legally established immigrants from outside the European Union should have the right to bring members of their immediate family in (OUR COUNTRY)
(3) Legally established immigrants from outside the European Union should be sent back to their country of origin if they have been convicted of serious offences
(4) Legally established immigrants from outside the European Union should be sent back to their country of origin if they are unemployed
(5) Legally established immigrants from outside the European Union should all be sent back to their country of origin
(6) Legally established immigrants from outside the European Union should be able to become naturalised easily

Respondents in representative samples from the population of all EU member states could each time chose between two answering categories: "tend to agree" or "tend to disagree." It should be noted that, for the obvious reason that these countries were themselves not yet part of the European Union at the time, in the Candidate Countries the qualification "from outside the European Union" was not present in the question formulation. This might have had an impact on answering distributions, but we are unable to assess the extent of this problem. Comparison of results between "old" EU-member states and "new" EU Member States must, hence, be done with prudence.

As one can see, it was not asked whether one supports the granting of rights to "third country nationals" in European Union member states, which is the interest of MIPEX. The questions were phrased in a more general way, asking about support for the granting of rights to "legally established immigrants from outside the European Union." This is not exactly the same. Third country nationals are indeed legally established immigrants from outside the European Union – so far, so good. A distinctive feature of TCNs is, however, that they do not hold state citizenship of one of the EU Member States. One could argue that the notion of "legally established immigrants from outside the European Union" might refer to a broader category, equally including people with a non-EU immigrant background but who have acquired the nationality of one of the EU Member States. We cannot know whether respondents only had TCNs in mind when responding to the aforementioned items or, in contrast, had the broader category in mind. We can in other words, not guarantee these questions perfectly reflect the opinions with regard to the rights of TCNs. Of course, it comes close, so we might at least consider it to be a good proxy indicator. In any event, it is the only material we have to our disposal across all EU Member States (and the former Candidate Countries).

As Coenders, Lubbers and Scheepers (2003) have shown, the aforementioned questions one, two and six function as one so-called scale, which means they seem to be measuring one underlying attitude. This scale is furthermore "factorially invariant" (which means the questions are probably interpreted the same way all over Europe). The same holds for questions four and five.

Questions one, two, four, five and six are of most interest to the index project and we will focus on their results. Question one shows the support for social rights (table 1), question two shows the support for family reunification (table 2) and question six shows the support for easy naturalisation (table 3). For the results of the latent factor that can be constructed on the basis of these three questions, we refer to the report by Coenders et alii (2003). We will focus here on the results for the questions separately, which facilitates the interpretation of the results.

Question five (table 4) shows to what extent states have not been able to stimulate a positive view about non-EU immigrants among their population (deportation of all non-EU immigrants being a proposal which infringes basic rights of TCNs and which is in breach with several international normative standards). Question four, in turn, shows to what extent the overall population feels unemployed immigrants should be expelled from the country.

Unfortunately data for all these questions are only available in the Standard Eurobarometer of 1997, 2000 and 2003. For some reason, the items have no longer been used in the 2006 Standard Eurobarometer. The most recent data available are thus the results for 2003. It would have been nicer if we had data for 2006, since our MIPEX data concern 2007. It is, however, rather unlikely that big modifications in public opinion will have taken place between 2003 and 2006 since this kind of attitudes towards immigrants tend to remain fairly stable over relatively short time spans.

C. *Public Opinion in Europe on Immigrant Rights*

We will now first present some of the results of the Eurobarometer 2003 before linking them to our MIPEX scores. With regard to the granting of the same social rights to immigrants as those which are enjoyed by the rest of the population (table 1), support seems to be among the highest in a number of newly joined EU member states (Romania, Estonia, Poland, Czech Republic, Slovenia, Slovakia), with support of more than 60 percent of the population. This might, however, be related to the question wording, which refers to legally established immigrants in general (regardless of origin). In some other 'new' EU member States, support is nevertheless quite low (Malta, Hungary). In the 'older' EU Member States, where the question was about legally established immigrants from outside the EU, support is highest for equal social rights in Italy, Sweden, Spain, Portugal, Denmark, the Netherlands, Greece, Ireland and Luxemburg (all over 60 percent support). In most countries a majority of the population supports equal social rights for immigrants, with the exception of Malta (36,6 percent), Hungary (40,7 percent), Belgium (43,3 percent), Germany (45,2 percent), and Lithuania (47,8 percent). There is no correlation between public opinion on the granting of social rights and variables like the number of foreigners in a country or the gross domestic product per inhabitant. There does not seem to be a link with the quality of social protection or the level of social security in a country either.

Table 1: "Legally established immigrants [from outside the European Union] should have the same social rights as the (NATIONALITY) citizens", scores across the current EU-27

Country	Percentage "tend to agree"	S.E.[4]	Country	Percentage "tend to agree"	S.E.
Austria	45,8	1,55	Latvia	53	1,57
Belgium	43,3	1,54	Lithuania	47,8	1,56
Bulgaria	55,6	1,57	Luxembourg	60,6	1,99
Cyprus	55,8	2,26	Malta	36,6	2,15
Czech Rep.	68,3	1,47	Netherland	68,6	1,46
Denmark	68,7	1,46	Poland	68,6	1,46
Estonia	69,1	1,45	Portugal	69,3	1,45
Finland	52	1,56	Romania	73,6	1,38
France	54,8	1,49	Slovakia	60,5	1,51
Germany	45,2	1,10	Slovenia	63,1	1,52
Greece	62,3	1,53	Spain	68,2	1,47
Hungary	40,7	1,54	Sweden	66,6	1,49
Ireland	60,8	1,54	United Kingdom	54,3	1,37
Italy	71,1	1,42			

Let us now look at the public support for family reunion of third country nationals (table 2). A majority in most countries still support this policy, with the notable exceptions of Malta (30,3 percent), Lithuania (39,7 percent), Slovenia (39,9 percent), Belgium (40,8 percent), the United Kingdom (42,7 percent), Latvia (46,3 percent), the Netherlands (47,5 percent), Germany (48,1 percent) and Denmark (49,4 percent). Highest levels of support for family reunification are to be found in Greece and Spain (75,2 percent), Portugal (72,2 percent), Luxemburg (72,1 percent), Italy (71,3 percent), Romania (70,7 percent) and Poland (70,3 percent). There is no correlation between public opinion on family reunion and variables like the number of foreigners in a country, the crude birth rate of the country or the gross domestic product per inhabitant.

[4] Each time the standard error (SE) is provided. Multiplying this standard error by 1,96 provides the confidence limits (to be added to and to be subtracted of the sample percentage). One can assume that, everything else being equal, the real percentage of the population will be situated within the limits of this confidence interval (with a probability of 95 percent). To assess whether a difference between countries is statistically significant, the difference between the proportions has to be divided by the estimated standard error of the difference of these proportions. If the absolute value of the result is larger than 1,96, the difference is statistically significant (at the 0.05 level).

Table 2: "Legally established immigrants [from outside the European Union] should have the right to bring members of their immediate family in (OUR COUNTRY)", scores across the current EU-27

Country	Percentage "tend to agree"	S.E.	Country	Percentage "tend to agree"	S.E.
Austria	50,5	1,56	Latvia	46,3	1,57
Belgium	40,8	1,53	Lithuania	39,7	1,53
Bulgaria	50,5	1,58	Luxemburg	72,1	1,83
Cyprus	52,8	2,23	Malta	30,3	2,05
Czech Rep.	55,6	1,57	Netherland	47,5	1,57
Denmark	49,4	1,58	Poland	70,3	1,44
Estonia	54,5	1,57	Portugal	72,2	1,41
Finland	69,5	1,44	Romania	70,7	1,42
France	54,3	1,49	Slovakia	51	1,55
Germany	48,1	1,10	Slovenia	39,9	1,54
Greece	75,2	1,36	Spain	75,2	1,36
Hungary	55,3	1,56	Sweden	65,7	1,50
Ireland	54,6	1,57	United Kingdom	42,7	1,36
Italy	71,3	1,42			

Easy naturalisation (table 3) is a lot less supported across the populations of the EU member states. Highest support is present in Lithuania (63,5 percent), the Czech Republic (60,9 percent) and Poland (53,6 percent), the only countries to have a majority of the population being in favour of easier naturalisation. The least support seems to be present in Hungary and Malta (29,1 percent), followed by Cyprus (31,4 percent), Estonia (32,2 percent), Denmark (33,3 percent) and Slovakia (34 percent). Once again there is no link with variables like the number of foreigners or the gross domestic product.

Unfortunately deportation of all legally established (non-EU) immigrants (table 4), a clear infringement of basic rights of TCNs, is still supported as an idea by a considerable minority in all EU member states. In no country a majority of the population takes this stance, but peaks are to be noticed in Malta (35 percent), Greece (32,9 percent), Austria (29,6 percent), Germany (28,1 percent), Ireland (27,4 percent), Portugal and Belgium (25,4 percent) and the United Kingdom (25,3 percent) where at least one person in four wants to have all (non-EU) immigrants deported. In every Member State a minimum of nearly 9 percent of the population wants all foreigners out of the country. There is, hence, everywhere still quite some work to do in convincing public opinion that deportation of all legally established immigrants is simply an unacceptable position, which is in breach with human rights.

Table 3: "Legally established immigrants [from outside the European Union] should be able to become naturalised easily", scores across the current EU-27

Country	Percentage "tend to agree"	S.E.	Country	Percentage "tend to agree"	S.E.
Austria	44,8	1,55	Latvia	37,1	1,52
Belgium	38,6	1,51	Lithuania	63,5	1,50
Bulgaria	39,8	1,54	Luxembourg	46,5	2,03
Cyprus	31,4	2,07	Malta	29,1	2,03
Czech Rep.	60,9	1,54	Netherlands	39,7	1,54
Denmark	33,3	1,49	Poland	53,6	1,57
Estonia	32,2	1,47	Portugal	45,2	1,57
Finland	35,4	1,49	Romania	44,6	1,55
France	43,1	1,48	Slovakia	34	1,47
Germany	32,7	1,03	Slovenia	43,5	1,56
Greece	47	1,57	Spain	46,9	1,57
Hungary	29,1	1,42	Sweden	38,3	1,53
Ireland	48,4	1,57	United Kingdom	37,2	1,33
Italy	43,3	1,55			

Table 4: "Legally established immigrants [from outside the European Union] should all be sent back to their country of origin," scores across the current EU-27

Country	Percentage "tend to agree"	S.E.	Country	Percentage "tend to agree"	S.E.
Austria	29,6	1,42	Latvia	20,5	1,27
Belgium	25,4	1,35	Lithuania	17,6	1,19
Bulgaria	9	0,90	Luxembourg	15,9	1,49
Cyprus	21,6	1,84	Malta	35	2,13
Czech Rep.	14,6	1,11	Netherlands	21,9	1,30
Denmark	9,9	0,94	Poland	8,9	0,90
Estonia	12,6	1,04	Portugal	25,4	1,37
Finland	13,8	1,07	Romania	10,1	0,94
France	22,4	1,25	Slovakia	13,5	1,06
Germany	28,1	0,99	Slovenia	22,8	1,32
Greece	32,9	1,48	Spain	22,4	1,31
Hungary	20,6	1,26	Sweden	10,4	0,96
Ireland	27,4	1,40	United Kingdom	25,3	1,19
Italy	19,4	1,24			

Overall, a majority of the populations of EU member states do not want to expel unemployed legal migrants (table not included). Notable exceptions are Malta (63,6 percent) and Italy (50,3 percent). The populations of the Scandinavian countries Denmark (11,8 percent), Sweden (16 percent) and Finland (17,1 percent) are the least harsh on this topic. There is no statistically significant link with the employment rate of the country to be observed here.

Let us now link up these results to the MIPEX data. We will look into the issue to what extent MIPEX scores for long term residence, family reunion and naturalisation are related to the above mentioned public opinions.

D. *Public Opinion and the MIPEX Strand on Long-Term Residence*

There is no statistically significant correlation for the EU-25 between the overall MIPEX policy score on long term residence (and associated social rights) and the support in public opinion for equal social rights for immigrants (Spearman's rho=0.323, sign.=0.115).[5] Although the relationship is not significant from a statistical point of view,[6] the more support their seems to be for equal social rights for immigrants among the population, the higher the index policy score for long term residence is (or vice-versa, if you want). As we have seen earlier in table 1, Malta, Hungary and Belgium seem to have the most trouble in convincing their population that immigrants should have equal social rights. Indeed, when we leave these countries out of the data-set, there is a strong and significant positive correlation between support for equal social rights and the policy score (Spearman's rho=0.592, sign.<0.005). There is clearly no trade-off between the policy score and the support level for equal social rights (or a so-called "white backlash"), since countries like Sweden, Poland, Portugal, and Italy combine high policy scores with high public support. One might furthermore say there is at best a modest link between the public support for equal rights for immigrants and the policy on long term residence.

The second scatterplot seems to suggest there is an inverse relationship between the support among the population for the idea that all immigrants should be expelled on the one hand and the policy score for long term residence. However, from a statistical point of view, there is no significant correlation between the policy score for long term residence and the percentage of the population who would wish that all immigrants be expelled (Spearman's rho=-0.313, sign.=0.128).

[5] Bulgaria and Romania are not included in the analysis since they only joined the EU in 2007 and we were unfortunately unable to include them in the MIPEX preparations.

[6] It should be noted that with only 25 cases, it is difficult to get statistically significant results. This could, in other words, be just a method effect.

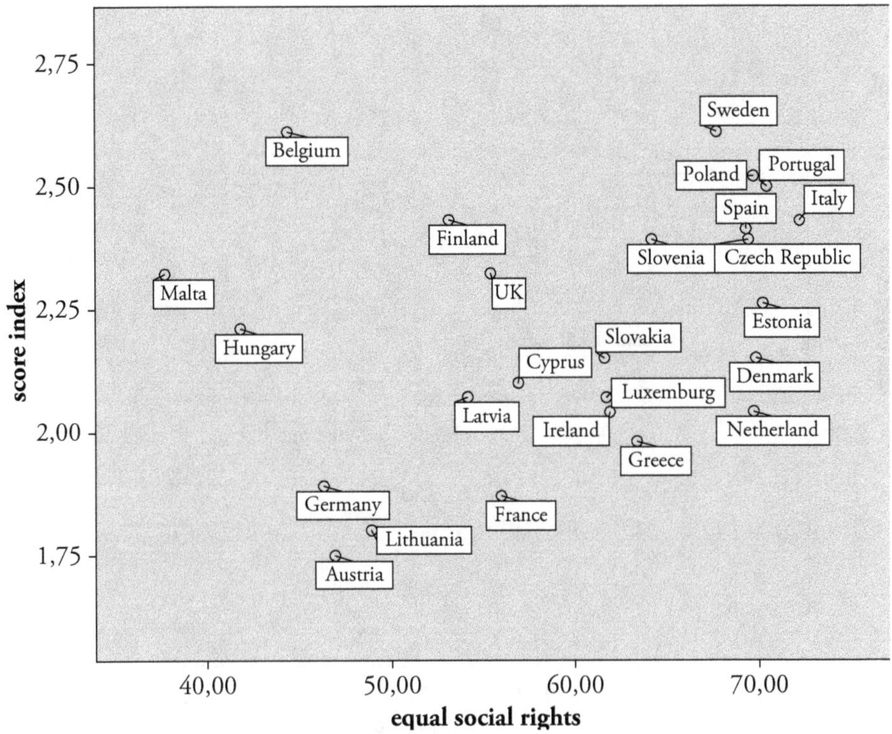

Figure 1: Scatterplot of support for equal social rights (2003) and long term residence policy index score (MIPEX 2007)

The size of the value of Spearman's rank order correlation, nevertheless, suggests a medium sized link, even though the statistical test indicates the association is not significant.[7]

Further analysis also seems to suggest there is an inverse relationship between the support among the population for the idea that unemployed legal immigrants should be expelled on the one hand and the policy score for long term residence on the other hand.[8] However, once again, from a statistical point of view, there is no significant correlation between the policy score for long term residence and the percentage of the population who would wish that all unemployed immigrants be expelled (Spearman's rho=-0.262, sign.=0.205). Furthermore, the effect size (value of Spearman's rho) remains limited and is clearly smaller than the aforementioned result.

One can overall conclude that there is only a very loose link between public opinion and policy on long term residence. The data however clearly show

[7] *Id.*

[8] The scatterplot is not shown here.

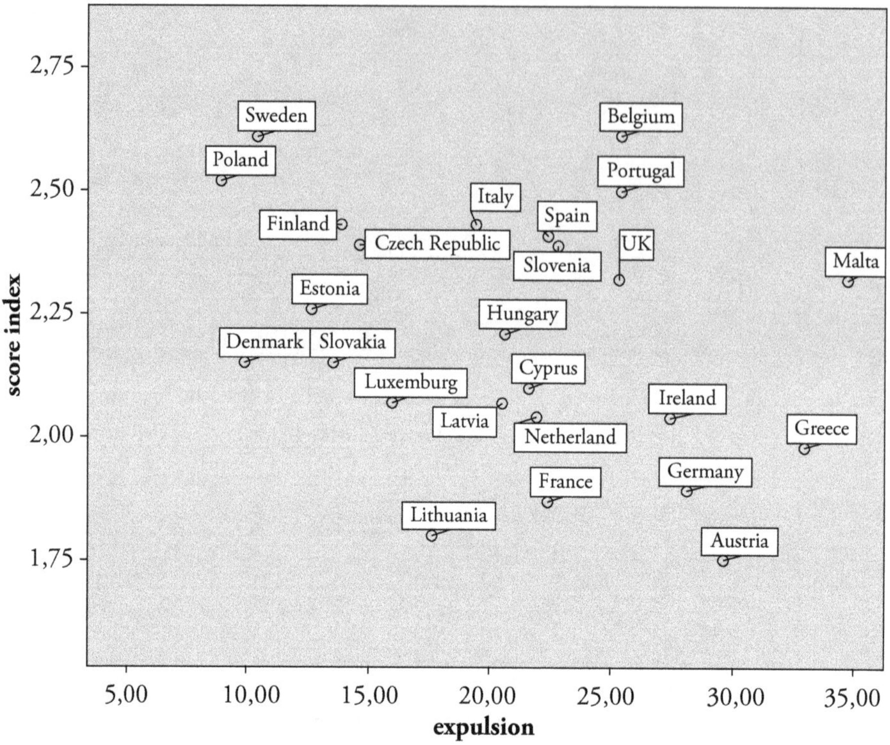

Figure 2: Scatterplot of support for expulsion of all immigrants (2003) and long term residence policy index score (MIPEX 2007)

that countries that have a favourable MIPEX-score are not witnessing a white backlash.

E. *Family Reunion: MIPEX Results and Public Opinion*

Figure 3 shows the scatter plot of the index policy score for family reunion (in 2007) and the percentage of the population supporting family reunion (according to the Eurobarometer in 2003). Although the scatter plot might seem to suggest there is a link, there is no statistically significant correlation (Spearman's rho=0.197, sign.=0.345) for the EU-25 between the overall policy score on family reunification and the support in public opinion for family reunification.

We do nevertheless show the scatter plot because some results stand out. Sweden and Portugal combine a favourable policy score on family reunification and a relatively high level of public support. Luxemburg and Greece have a high level of public support for family reunification but a moderate policy score. Denmark and Austria have a low policy score, although about half of

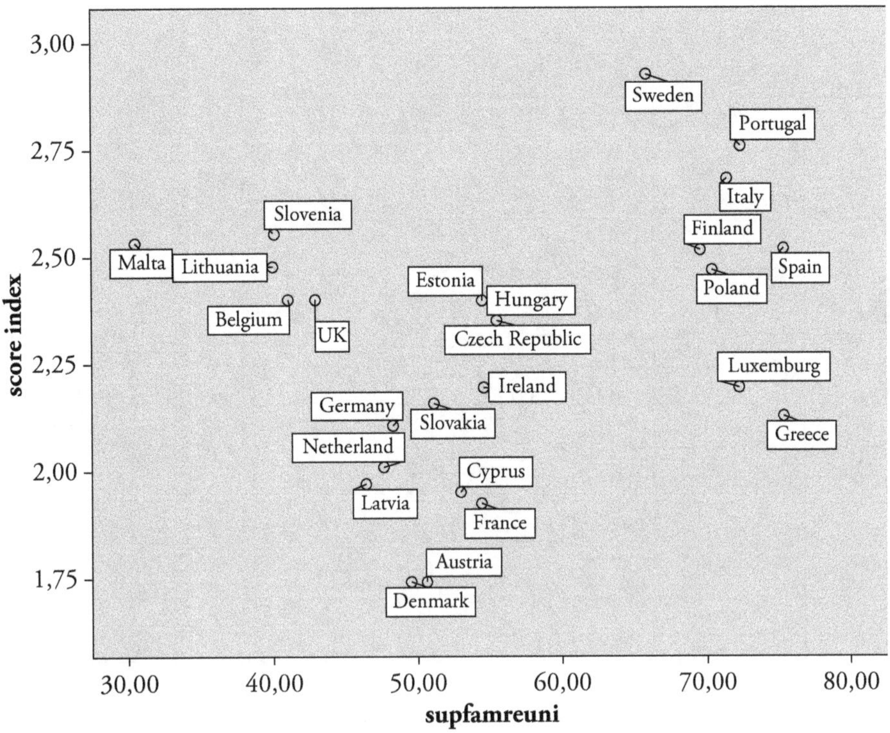

Figure 3: Scatterplot of support for family reunification (2003) and family reunion policy index score (MIPEX 2007)

their population supports the idea of family reunification. In Malta, Lithuania, Belgium and the United Kingdom, support for the idea of family reunification is relatively low, while the policy score is above average.

Overall, the scatter plot shows that there is neither a trade off nor an inverse relationship between the policy score for family reunification and the level of public support for the idea of family reunion. Once more, there seems to be no straightforward link between policy making and public opinion here.

F. *Nationality Acquisition: MIPEX Results and Public Opinion*

Let us now turn to access to nationality. There is no significant correlation (Spearman's rho=0.118, sign.=0.573) for the EU-25 between the overall policy score on nationality acquisition (in 2007) and the support in public opinion for easy naturalisation (in 2003), as can also been seen in scatterplot 4.

Some particular results stand out. In Poland, the Czech Republic and Lithuania there is quite a lot of support for easier nationality acquisition, while their policy score remains moderate. Greece and Spain have relatively low policy scores,

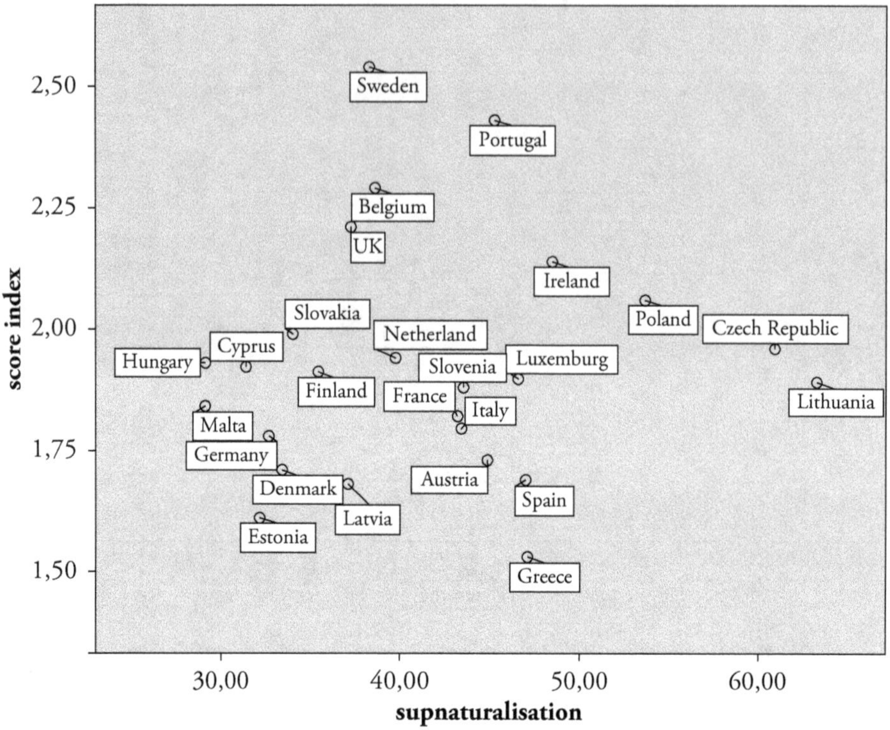

Figure 4: Scatterplot of support for easy naturalisation (2003) and policy index score on nationality acquisition (MIPEX 2007)

while a significant part of the population favours easy naturalisation. Once again, there does seem to be neither a trade off nor inverse relationship between the policy score on nationality acquisition on the one hand and the public support for naturalisation on the other hand. The two seem to be unrelated or only very weakly associated.

G. *Public Opinion on Discrimination*

When linking up the MIPEX results to public opinion, we can make use of more recent data for the strand on anti-discrimination. Indeed, in 2006 a focused survey was undertaken especially on the topic of discrimination (Special Eurobarometer on discrimination). It is worth mentioning that this survey was repeated in 2008. However, as could be expected because of the relatively short interval between the surveys, this new survey showed only very little variation in comparison to the 2006 data. Observed differences could just as well be due to sampling error rather than reflect a genuine evolution over time, so we should

Table 6: General assessment of antidiscrimination policy for the current EU-27 (Special Eurobarometer 2006)

Country	No, not really and No, definitely not	SE	Country	No, not really and No, definitely not	SE
Austria	34,3 percent	1,50	Latvia	61,1 percent	1,53
Belgium	48,5 percent	1,56	Lithuania	52,5 percent	1,58
Bulgaria	38,2 percent	1,52	Luxembourg	44,5 percent	2,21
Cyprus	29,5 percent	2,03	Malta	50,7 percent	2,24
Czech	51,7 percent	1,57	Netherlands	43,2 percent	1,56
Denmark	59,6 percent	1,52	Poland	68,3 percent	1,47
Estonia	46,7 percent	1,57	Portugal	37,8 percent	1,53
Finland	35,3 percent	1,49	Romania	35,3 percent	1,51
France	61,2 percent	1,53	Slovakia	50,3 percent	1,48
Germany	47 percent	1,26	Slovenia	39,2 percent	1,53
Greece	42,5 percent	1,56	Spain	39,9 percent	1,54
Hungary	56,4 percent	1,55	Sweden	68,7 percent	1,46
Ireland	39,3 percent	1,54	United Kingdom	45,5 percent	1,37
Italy	52,9 percent	1,56			

not ponder over them for too long. We hence will only focus on the 2006 results in the remainder of the article.

To assess the public opinion on the antidiscrimination policy per country, we can use the following question: "In general, would you say that enough effort is made in (OUR COUNTRY) to fight all forms of discrimination?" The answering categories were: "Yes, definitely / Yes, to some extent / No, not really / No, definitely not." The results are presented in table six.

As we can see, in Sweden (68,7 percent), Poland (68,3 percent), France (61,2 percent), Latvia (61,1 percent), Denmark (59,6 percent), Hungary (56,4 percent), Italy (52,9 percent) Lithuania (52,5 percent), the Czech Republic (51,7 percent), Malta (50,7 percent) and Slovakia (50,3 percent) a majority of the population thinks that in general more should be done in the struggle against all forms of discrimination. In all countries – with the exception of Cyprus (29 percent), at least 35 percent of the population thinks more could be done in the fight against discrimination. We should note, at the same time, that "don't know" responses are particularly high in Bulgaria (25 percent), Romania (15 percent), Lithuania (14 percent), Estonia (13 percent) and Ireland (11 percent).

Let us now focus on the subjective assessment of the degree of discrimination with regard to ethnic origin per country. The following question is taken from the same Special Eurobarometer: "For each of the following types of discrimination, could you please tell me whether, in your opinion, it is very widespread, fairly

Table 7: Subjective assessment of degree of ethnic discrimination in the current EU-27 (Special Eurobarometer 2006)

Country	very widespread and fairly widespread	SE	Country	very widespread and fairly widespread	SE
Austria	56,3	1,57	Latvia	29,3	1,43
Belgium	78	1,29	Lithuania	23,2	1,33
Bulgaria	42,4	1,54	Luxembourg	45,4	2,21
Cyprus	71,3	2,01	Malta	69,1	2,07
Czech	51	1,57	Netherland	82,9	1,18
Denmark	78,8	1,26	Poland	32,8	1,48
Estonia	36,9	1,52	Portugal	61,1	1,53
Finland	70,2	1,42	Romania	38,9	1,54
France	80	1,26	Slovakia	49	1,48
Germany	47,8	1,26	Slovenia	55,4	1,55
Greece	76,1	1,35	Spain	71,1	1,42
Hungary	66,5	1,48	Sweden	84,6	1,14
Ireland	57,1	1,57	United Kingdom	67,8	1,29
Italy	76,8	1,32			

widespread, fairly rare or very rare in (OUR COUNTRY)? Discrimination on the basis of ethnic origin." We present the results in table seven.

It seems the Swedes (84,6 percent), Dutch (82,9 percent), French (80 percent) and Belgians (78 percent) think discrimination based on ethnic origin is fairly widespread in their country. At the other extreme, a lot less Lithuanians (23,2 percent) and Latvians (29,3 percent) tend to think ethnic discrimination is widespread in their country.

Another question allows us to assess whether the population thinks ethnic discrimination has increased compared to five years earlier: "If you compare the situation with 5 years ago, would you say the following types of discrimination are more common or less common in (OUR COUNTRY?)." The answering categories for "discrimination on the basis of ethnic origin" were: "far more widespread, slightly more widespread, slightly less widespread, far less widespread". The results for this question are given in table eight.

A striking finding is that a very large proportion of the Dutch (76,7 percent) are convinced ethnic discrimination has become more widespread in the five years preceding the survey (which was administered in 2006). As the reader probably knows, during this period the Netherlands experienced quite some political turmoil following the political murders of Pim Fortuyn by a animal rights activist and the murder of Theo Van Gogh by a Muslim fanatic. Other countries where a large majority thinks the problem of ethnic discrimination has become more widespread are Belgium (67,5 percent) and Denmark (67,1

Table 8: Subjective assessment of increased prevalence of ethnic discrimination in the current EU-27 (Special Eurobarometer 2006)

Country	far more widespread and slightly more widespread	SE	Country	far more widespread and slightly more widespread	SE
Austria	47,7	1,58	Latvia	26,2	1,38
Belgium	67,5	1,46	Lithuania	22,9	1,33
Bulgaria	38	1,52	Luxembourg	52,6	2,22
Cyprus	43,2	2,21	Malta	56,6	2,22
Czech	33,6	1,49	Netherlands	76,7	1,32
Denmark	67,1	1,45	Poland	22,3	1,32
Estonia	25,5	1,38	Portugal	49	1,57
Finland	36	1,49	Romania	29,1	1,44
France	60,1	1,54	Slovakia	42,5	1,46
Germany	41,5	1,24	Slovenia	46,4	1,56
Greece	46,7	1,58	Spain	43,3	1,56
Hungary	53,3	1,57	Sweden	49,9	1,58
Ireland	58,7	1,56	United Kingdom	54,5	1,37
Italy	56,7	1,55			

percent). At the other extreme, a far smaller proportion of Poles (22,3 percent), Lithuanians (22,9 percent) and Latvians (26,2 percent) think prevalence of ethnic discrimination has increased.

H. *MIPEX Results for Anti-Discrimination and Public Opinion*

When we now link these results to the MIPEX results, it turns out there is no significant correlation between the general assessment of a country's efforts in tackling discrimination (according to the Special Eurobarometer on discrimination in 2006) and its overall policy score for antidiscrimination for the EU-25 (Spearman's rho=-0.119, sign.=0.570). There is, however, a strong and significant link between the assessment that ethnic discrimination is widespread in a country and its overall policy score for antidiscrimination (Spearman's rho =0.580, sign.<0.005).[9]

[9] This correlation remains in place after controlling for the number of non-nationals in the population.

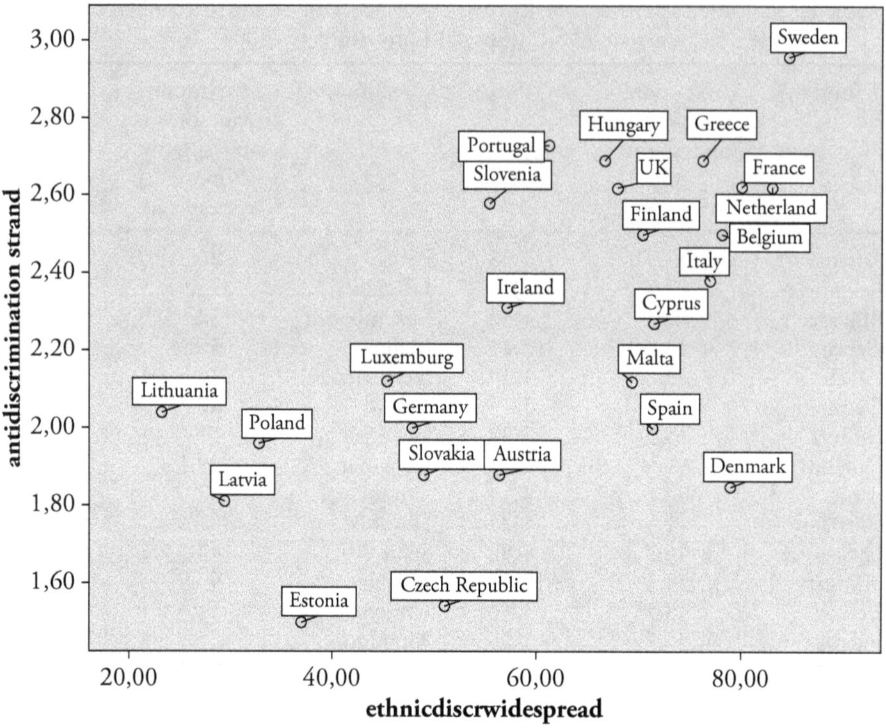

Figure 5: Scatterplot of percentage of population that thinks ethnic discrimination is widespread (2006) and policy index score for antidiscrimination (2006)

In general, those countries which have a large percentage of the population that thinks ethnic discrimination is widespread tend to have a high score on the strand for antidiscrimination policy. Denmark is a notable exception (having a sub-average policy score but a high perception of the prevalence of ethnic discrimination), while also Spain and Malta score relatively low compared to the perceived prevalence of ethnic discrimination.

Interpretation of the tendency in the scatterplot is not necessarily to be done in a straightforward manner. The correlation might be the result of the plausible fact that those countries which are confronted with higher levels of ethnic discrimination have made an effort to boost their antidiscrimination policy to a higher level. It might equally be the case that awareness of ethnic discrimination has been raised in those countries which have developed a more advanced antidiscrimination policy. In fact, both hypotheses might be valid simultaneously.

I. *Labour Market Policy and Public Opinion*

Let us now turn to the perception of (un)equal opportunities on the labour market for immigrants. The following question was taken from the Special Eurobarometer (data on 2006): "Would you say that, with equivalent qualifications or diplomas, the following people would be less likely, as likely or more likely than others to get a job, be accepted for training or be promoted? A foreigner compared to a (NATIONALITY)." The results are given in table nine.

A large majority of the Swedes (82,7 percent), French (78 percent), Belgians (74,2 percent), Dutch (71,9 percent) and Finns (70,7 percent) is convinced it is tougher for a foreigner to get a job, be accepted for training or be promoted. At the other extreme, a smaller proportion of Romanians (24,5 percent), Latvians (27,4 percent) and Lithuanians (27,8 percent) think there is a problem concerning equal opportunities for foreigners on the labour market.

As we can see in figure 6, with the exception of Luxemburg, there is quite an important correlation between the number of respondents who think there is a problem of unequal opportunities on the labour market and the gross domestic product per inhabitant (Spearman's rho=0.676, sign.<0.001). The link remains intact after controlling for the number of foreigners and third country nationals. Apparently, the richer a country is, the more the inhabitants say there are unequal opportunities in the labour market.

Table 9: Perception of unequal opportunities on the labour market in the EU-27

Country	less likely	S.E.	Country	less likely	S.E.
Austria	56,6	1,57	Latvia	27,4	1,40
Belgium	74,2	1,36	Lithuania	27,8	1,41
Bulgaria	30,8	1,44	Luxemburg	38,1	2,16
Cyprus	61,9	2,16	Malta	36,6	2,15
Czech	47	1,57	Netherlands	71,9	1,41
Denmark	62,8	1,50	Poland	37,4	1,53
Estonia	44,8	1,57	Portugal	49	1,57
Finland	70,7	1,42	Romania	24,5	1,36
France	78	1,30	Slovakia	49,8	1,48
Germany	54	1,26	Slovenia	55,3	1,55
Greece	61,2	1,54	Spain	61,5	1,53
Hungary	35,5	1,50	Sweden	82,7	1,19
Ireland	44,1	1,57	United Kingdom	54,2	1,37
Italy	56,8	1,55			

Are they willing to do something about this? A number of questions in the Special Eurobarometer 263 (data on 2006) try to assess the support for positive action in favour of different minority groups. One question asks to what extent positive action on the basis of ethnic origin is being favoured: "Would you be in favour of or opposed to specific measures being adopted to provide equal opportunities for everyone in the field of employment? Specific measures for people depending on their...ethnic origin." The answering categories are: "Totally in favour / Somewhat in favour / Somewhat opposed / totally opposed."

Interestingly and somewhat surprisingly, in all EU member states, with the exception of Denmark (but with a score of 47,9 percent support), a majority is in favour of special measures (positive action) on the labour market, taking ethnic origin into account.

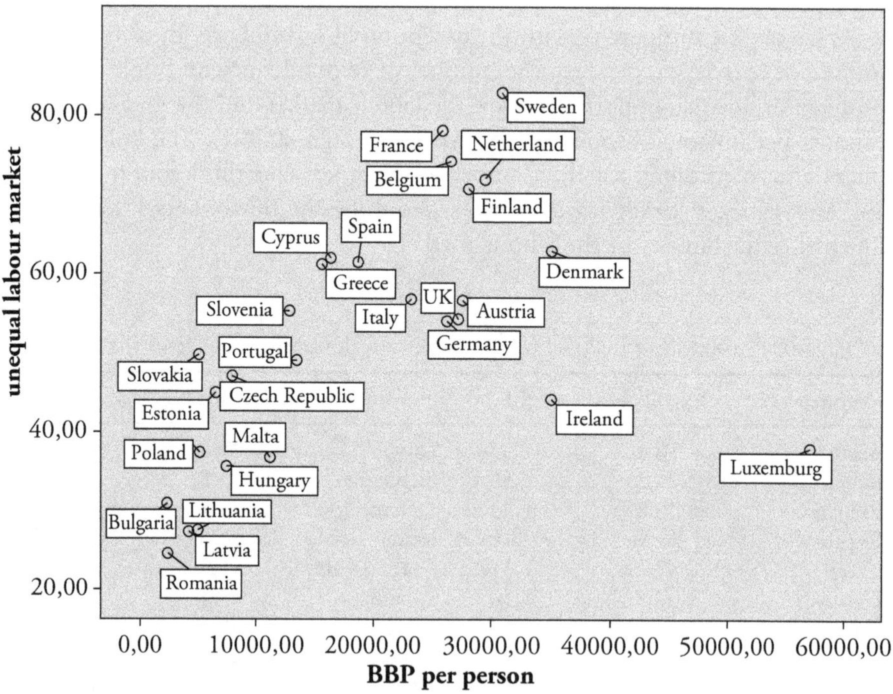

Figure 6: Scatterplot of percentage of population that thinks there are unequal opportunities for foreigners on the labour market (Eurobarometer 2006) and the gross domestic product per inhabitant (Eurostat 2006)

Table 10: Support for positive action based on ethnicity in the current EU-27 (Special Eurobarometer 2006)

Country	Totally in favour and Somewhat in favour	SE	Country	Totally in favour and Somewhat in favour	SE
Austria	56,2	1,57	Latvia	61,9	1,52
Belgium	65,3	1,48	Lithuania	75,2	1,36
Bulgaria	71,5	1,41	Luxemburg	68,5	2,07
Cyprus	73,9	1,96	Malta	63,5	2,15
Czech	69,7	1,45	Netherland	64,3	1,50
Denmark	47,9	1,55	Poland	77,5	1,32
Estonia	77,5	1,32	Portugal	85,9	1,09
Finland	74,3	1,36	Romania	78,5	1,30
France	68,9	1,46	Slovakia	77,5	1,24
Germany	63,7	1,21	Slovenia	78,9	1,27
Greece	81,1	1,24	Spain	81,3	1,23
Hungary	71,2	1,42	Sweden	67,3	1,48
Ireland	72,8	1,41	United Kingdom	72,9	1,23
Italy	64,7	1,50			

Let us now make the link with MIPEX. There is a strong and significant link between the percentage of people (according to Special Eurobarometer 2006) who think there are unequal opportunities for foreigners on the labour market[10] on the one hand and the overall policy score for labour market status on the other hand (Spearman's rho=0.577, sign.<0.005).[11] As can be seen in figure 7, countries in which a large part of the population states there are unequal opportunities for foreigners on the labour market, tend to be countries with a high score in the index with regard to labour market status of TCNs.

Once again, the interpretation of the tendency in the scatter plot is not necessarily to be done in straightforward manner. The correlation might be the result of the plausible fact that those countries which are confronted with a high level of unequal opportunities for foreigners on the labour market have made an effort to improve the labour market position of foreigners. It might equally be the case that awareness of unequal opportunities for foreigners on the labour market has

[10] "Would you say that, with equivalent qualifications or diplomas, the following people would be less likely, as likely or more likely than others to get a job, be accepted for training or be promoted? A foreigner compared to a national" (question from the Special Eurobarometer 2006).

[11] This correlation remains in place after controlling for the number of non-nationals in the population.

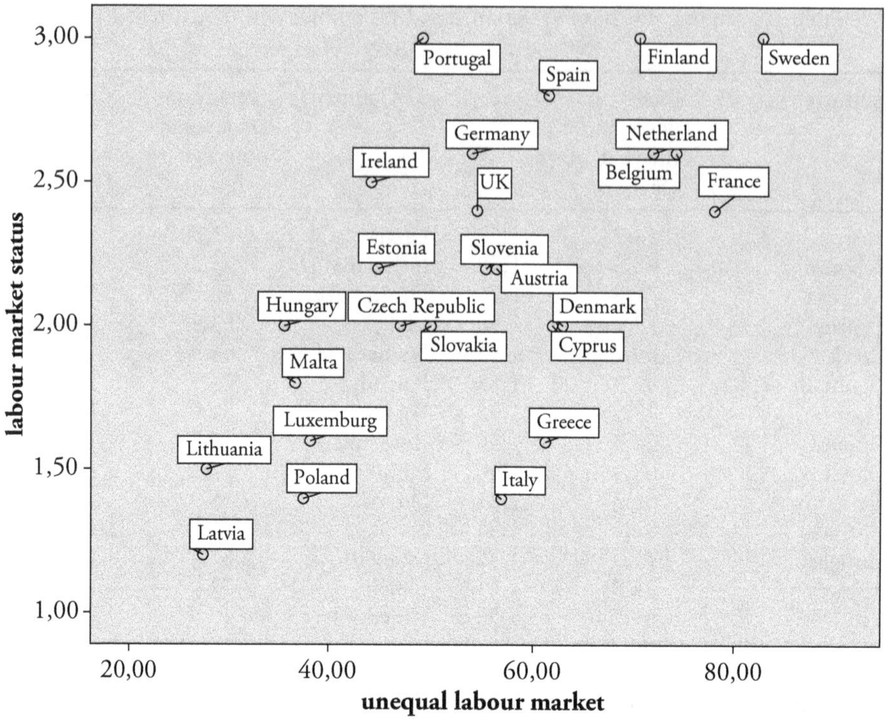

Figure 7: Scatterplot of percentage of population that thinks there are unequal opportunities for foreigners on the labour market (2006) and the policy index score for labour market status (2006)

been raised in those countries which have developed a more advanced labour market integration policy. In fact, both hypotheses might be valid simultaneously. If we repeat the MIPEX exercise in the future, we will perhaps one day find ourselves in the position to formally test both hypotheses by taking into account timing of legislative changes and changes in public awareness.

In figure 8 we have linked the MIPEX score for labour market access to the gross domestic product per inhabitant. They are correlated in a significant way (Spearman's rho=0.500, sign.: $p < 0.05$). We cannot prove that there is a causal link between an open labour market policy for immigrants on the one hand and economic wealth on the other hand, but there is clearly a positive association between the gross domestic product per inhabitant and the labour market policy for immigrants. This might be an artefact related to unobserved underlying patterns, but with the variables we have to our disposal we could not show it is a spurious relation. We suspect that it is not the openness of the labour market for immigrants which creates wealth, but that it is higher economic productivity which calls (or has called) for additional immigrant labour force input.

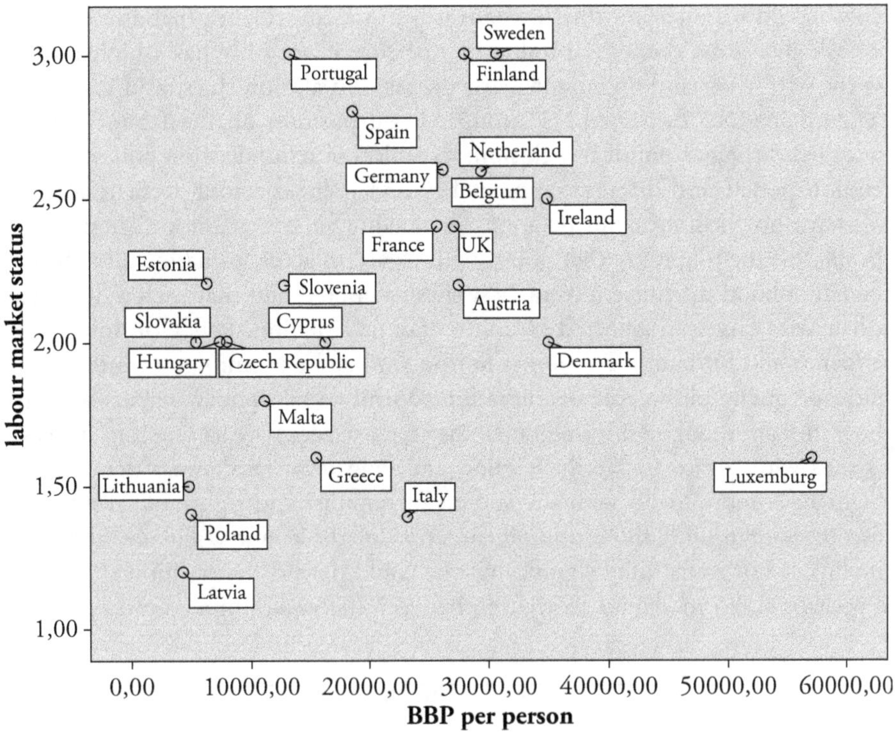

Figure 8: Scatterplot of the policy index score for labour market status (MIPEX 2007) and the gross domestic product per inhabitant (Eurostat 2006)

J. *The Richer the Country, the More Open Its Policies Towards Migrants?*

We have already talked extensively about political participation in another contribution to this book. We will not reopen that topic but just want to show figure 9 in which we associate the MIPEX score for political participation to the gross domestic product per inhabitant. The correlation is very strong (Spearman's rho=0.790, sign.: $p < 0.001$). Just as was the case for the labour market strand, results tend to be better on the MIPEX strand for political participation as the country is richer (measured in gross domestic product per inhabitant). We, of course, do not think that facilitating political participation of immigrants makes countries richer. It is, however, interesting to observe that there is not only a link between being a rich nation and having an open labour market policy, but also with allowing for more political participation of non-nationals. The association is, in contrast, not statistically significant for anti-discrimination policy (Spearman's rho=0.308, sign.: p=0.134), naturalisation (Spearman's rho=0.159, sign.: p=0.447), family reunion (Spearman's rho=-0.174, sign.: p=0.406) or long term residence (Spearman's rho=-0.054, sign.: p=0.799).

How should we interpret this? Perhaps it is just a coincidence that as a country has a higher gross domestic product per person, it not only has a higher score on the MIPEX strand on labour market access but also on the strand for political participation. But maybe a stronger Legal position on the labour market indeed also triggers political inclusion, regardless of naturalisation policy, family reunion policy, anti-discrimination policy and policy on long term residence. We have no theoretical justification for making such a claim and hesitate to speculate. One might say that policy with regard to access to nationality reflects the nationhood discourse a country wishes to uphold and that such a discourse will remain largely unaffected by the economic situation. Policy on long term residence and on family reunion is not only a matter of immigrant integration but can equally play a role in migration control. When policy makers want to show they are though on immigrants, they have in recent years opted to increase barriers with regard to family reunion and long term residence. Such choices might have more to do with the success of populist and right-radical political discourses than with the economic situation of the country. Finally, although the link is not statistically significant, one could defend the position that there is perhaps also a moderate association between the wealth of a country and the

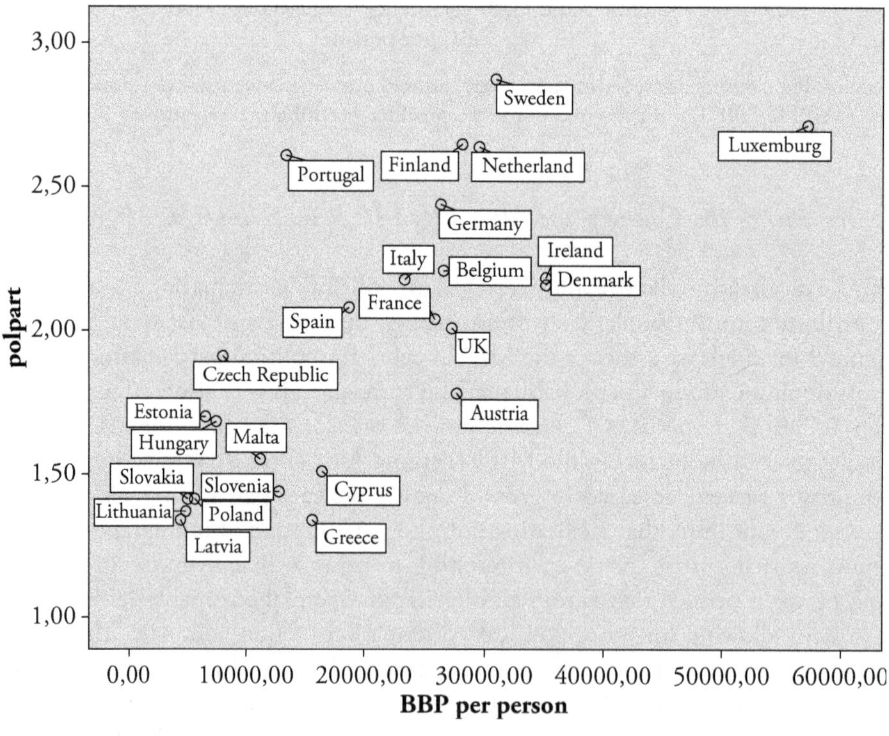

Figure 9: Scatterplot of the policy index score for political participation (MIPEX 2007) and the gross domestic product per inhabitant (Eurostat 2006)

score on the antidiscrimination strand. Would it be the case that more wealth leads to more labour inclusion of immigrants which in turn triggers the trade unions to plead for more and better political inclusion of immigrants? Indeed, in countries like the Netherlands and Belgium the trade unions were among the first actors to mobilise for more political rights for immigrants (Jacobs, 1998). We would have to investigate these hypotheses closer before we could draw such a conclusion.

K. *Conclusion and Debate*

Some authors, like Lahav, have stressed the crucial importance of public opinion for policy making with regard to immigrant integration. Others, like Freeman, have claimed mass opinion is only of secondary importance, since targeted mobilisation and lobbying would be far more important. We agree with Meuleman and Reeskens that there is most probably a dialectical relation between integration regimes and immigration-related attitudes. Firstly, policy measures can be seen as institutionalised values with respect to the rights and duties of newcomers in society. They thus reflect elite-discourse that can influence mass opinion. Secondly, policy measures can lead to more (or less) inclusion of foreigners in mainstream society, impacting on relations between majority and minority groups (and their attitudes). Thirdly, attitudes of the majority population towards immigrants might push policy makers into developing more exclusionary – and in less frequent cases more inclusive – policies. Especially in countries with strong populist anti-immigrant and radical right parties, policy makers will be tempted to opt for stricter policies even though they actually might think this is a bad idea. In contrast, at times of labour shortage, employers will be in favour of immigration and will try and convince both policy makers as the general public of the need for newcomers. Civil society actors, academics and immigrants themselves will furthermore mobilise and lobby for extension of immigrants rights from a human rights perspective. These forms of elite mobilisation are, in our opinion, probably more effective in influencing policy making than vague demands from an amorphous general public, unless the latter are taken on board by populist politicians.

In this contribution we wanted to contribute to the debate on the nexus between policy making and public opinion with regard to immigrant integration. We did not have the ambition to settle the debate. Our main agenda was to highlight the relevance of the MIPEX data set for these kind of debates. Indeed, using MIPEX and large scale European surveys like the European Social Survey and Eurobarometer, one can empirically assess to what extent public opinion and policy co-vary across European countries. We hope that other authors will be inspired and explore further use of the MIPEX data-set in combination with other data sources (and probably with the objective of looking at other research questions). Such exercises will become all the more interesting if the MIPEX exercise were to be repeated in the future, allowing for diachronic analysis on a number of issues related to immigrant integration policy.

List of References

BLALOCK, H. (1967) *Toward a theory of minority-group relations.* New York: John Wiley & Sons.

BEUTIN, R., CANOY, M., HORVATH, A., HUBERT, A., LERAIS, F. & SOCHACKI, M. (2007) 'Reassessing the Link between Public Perception and Migration Policy', *European Journal of Migration and Law,* 9: 389–418.

CASTLES, S. (1995) 'How nation-states respond to immigration and ethnic diversity', *New Community,* 21 (3): 293–308.

COENDERS M., LUBBERS M., SCHEEPERS P. (2003), *Majority populations' attitudes towards migrants and minorities.* Report for the European monitoring Centre on Racism and Xenophobia, Vienne: EUMC.

CONVERSE, PHILIP E. 1964. "The Nature of Belief Systems in Mass Publics." In *Ideology and Discontent,* ed. David E. Apter. New York: Free Press.

FREEMAN, G. (1995) 'Modes of immigration politics in liberal democratic states', *International Migration Review,* 29 (4): 881–902.

GUIRAUDON, V. (1997) "*Policy Change Behind Gilded Doors: Explaining the Evolution of Aliens' Rights in Contemporary Western Europe.*" PhD-thesis Harvard University.

JACOBS, D. (1998) *Nieuwkomers in de politiek. Het parlementaire debat omtrent stemrecht voor vreemdelingen in Nederland en België (1970–1997).* Gent: Academia Press.

JOPPKE, C. (2007) "Beyond national models: civic integration policies for immigrants in Western Europe". *Western European Politics* 30 (1): 1–22.

KOOPMANS, R., STATHAM, P., GIUGNI, M. & PASSY, F. (2005) *Contested Citizenship: Immigration and Cultural Diversity in Europe.* Minneapolis: University of Minnesota Press.

LAHAV, G. (2004) *Immigration and politics in the New Europe. Reinventing borders.* Cambridge: Cambridge University Press.

MEULEMAN, B. & REESKENS, T. (2008) *The relation between integration policy and majority attitudes toward immigration. An empirical test across European countries.* Paper presented at the Dag van de Sociologie, 29 mei 2008, Leuven.

NIESSEN, J., HUDDLESTON, T. & CITRON, L., in cooperation with Geddes, A. & Jacobs, D. (2007) *Migrant Integration Policy Index.* Brussels: British Council and Migration Policy Group.

PIERSON, P. (2000) "Increasing Returns, Path Dependence, and the Study of Politics", *The American Political Science Review,* 94 (2): 251–267.

SARIS, W. & SNIDERMAN, P. (2004) *Studies in Public Opinion: Attitudes, Nonattitudes, Measurement Error, and Change.* Princeton: Princeton University Press.

SOYSAL, Y. (1994) *Limits of Citizenship: Migrants and Postnational Membership in Europe.* Chicago: University of Chicago Press.

THALHAMMER E., ZUCHA V., ENZENHOFER E., SALFINGER B., OGRIS G. (2001), *Attitudes towards minority groups in the European Union. A special analysis of the Eurobarometer 2000 survey on behalf of the European Monitoring Centre on Racism and Xenophobia,* Vienne: EUMC.

ZALLER, JOHN R. (1992) *The Nature and Origins of Mass Opinion.* New York: Cambridge University Press.

Chapter 6

Benchmarking Standards in Anti-Discrimination Law and Policy

Mark Bell

Since the adoption in 2000 of the Racial Equality Directive,[1] there has been considerable focus on EU Member States' legal obligation to ensure that their national legislation complies with the Directive's minimum requirements. The Commission has monitored the implementation process through a Network of Legal Experts in the Non-Discrimination Field,[2] which produces annual reports on national legislation. In conjunction with this periodic monitoring, the Commission has resorted to infringement proceedings against a majority of the Member States with a view to ensuring compliance with all aspects of the Directive.[3] Whilst such processes are designed to bring about harmonisation of minimum legal standards, elsewhere there has been a more subtle trend to promote convergence towards the highest standards in anti-discrimination law and policy.

The main vehicles for the identification of good practices, and their promotion, are a range of EU funding programmes, such as the Community Action Programme on Combating Discrimination (2001–2006)[4] or the "Equal" programme (2000–2008).[5] The Anti-Discrimination Action Programme funded a range of

---

[1] Directive (EC) 2000/43 implementing the principle of equal treatment between persons irrespective of racial or ethnic origin (2000) OJ L180/22.

[2] <http://ec.europa.eu/employment_social/fundamental_rights/policy/aneval/legnet_en.htm>.

[3] Commission, 'Commission acts to close gaps in race equality rules' Press release IP/07/928, June 27, 2007.

[4] Decision (EC) 2000/750 establishing a Community action programme to combat discrimination (2001 to 2006) (2000) OJ L303/23. Its successor is 'Progress': Decision (EC) 1672/2006 establishing a Community programme for employment and social solidarity – Progress (2006) OJ L315/1.

[5] *See* <http://ec.europa.eu/employment_social/equal/index_en.cfm>.

initiatives which sought to "Europeanise" the normal points of reference when formulating anti-discrimination law and policy. Transnational projects developed links between civil society across the Member States, whilst a variety of expert networks promoted a European and comparative outlook, for example, amongst national equality bodies.[6] The cumulative effect of such projects is arguably to alter the perceived boundaries when national policies are framed; the underlying message is that it is desirable to look outside the national arena, to examine policies elsewhere in Europe and to import good practices.[7] In encouraging this type of "free movement of ideas,"[8] it becomes crucial to have a robust mechanism for measuring national performance, a means of identifying the leaders and the laggards. The Migrant Integration Policy Index (MIPEX) provides an innovative contribution to benchmarking through offering a quantitative evaluation of anti-discrimination law and policy in relation to race/ethnicity, religion/belief and nationality.[9] This chapter examines the results from the 2007 MIPEX, both with a view to evaluating the trajectory of national law and policy in this field, but also to reflect on the challenges posed in applying benchmarking to anti-discrimination. In keeping with the structure of MIPEX, four themes are examined: definitions and concepts; the fields of application; enforcement; and equality policies.

A. *Definitions and Concepts*

MIPEX identified four key indicators for measuring anti-discrimination law in relation to definitions and concepts. These are presented below, alongside the average score recorded for the EU-25, EU-15 and EU-10.[10] For each indicator, states were awarded a mark ranging between a minimum of one and a maximum of three.

---

[6] *See* <http://www.equineteurope.org/>.

[7] *See* Gráinne de Búrca, *EU race discrimination law: a hybrid model?* in *Law and new governance in the EU and the U.S.* 97 (Oxford: Hart Publishing, 2006).

[8] This expression can be found within a range of documentation from the Equal programme.

[9] Jan Niessen, Thomas Huddleston and Laura Citron, *Migrant Integration Policy Index* (British Council and Migration Policy Group, 2007). An extended set of the data, which this chapter draws from, is available from the accompanying website: <http://www.integrationindex.eu>.

[10] EU-15 refers to those states who were members prior to 2004, whilst EU-10 refers to those states which joined the Union in that year.

Indicator	EU-25	EU-15	EU-10
The law prohibits direct and indirect discrimination, harassment and instruction to discriminate	2.6	2.6	2.6
The law includes discrimination by association and discrimination based on assumed characteristics	1.7	1.9	1.5
The law applies to natural and legal persons, as well as the public and private sectors	2.7	2.9	2.3
The law prohibits incitement to violence, hatred and discrimination; racially/religiously motivated insults, threats and defamation; instigating, aiding, abetting or attempting to commit such offences	2.6	2.7	2.5

The first indicator directly reflects the Racial Equality Directive, which introduced this four-fold definition of unlawful discrimination. This was subsequently reproduced in the Employment Equality Directive[11] (which covers discrimination on grounds of religion or belief), and incorporated into EU gender equality legislation.[12] As a consequence, this reflects the "hard core" of EU anti-discrimination legislation, where the standards required are particularly unambiguous. Regarding the definition of discrimination, there seems little scope for national experimentation and the Directives exercise a powerful harmonising impact. This seems to be confirmed by the results for this indicator, which reveal a high level of convergence. The maximum score of three points was awarded for any state which prohibited all four forms of discrimination in relation to each of the three grounds under examination: race/ethnicity, religion/belief, nationality. The strong performance under this indicator also reveals spillover effects from the Racial Equality Directive into domestic provisions on nationality discrimination. The Directive expressly states that it "does not cover difference of treatment based on nationality."[13] Although there are other EU legislative instruments which require the prohibition of nationality discrimination,[14] these are phrased in general terms,

[11] Directive (EC) 2000/78 establishing a general framework for equal treatment in employment and occupation (2000) OJ L303/16.

[12] Directive (EC) 2006/54 on the implementation of the principle of equal opportunities and equal treatment of men and women in matters of employment and occupation (recast) (2006) OJ L204/23.

[13] Art 3(2), Directive 2000/43.

[14] In relation to EU citizens, the main equality provision is found in Art 24, Directive (EC) 2004/38 on the right of citizens of the Union and their family members to move and reside freely within the territory of the Member States... (2004) OJ L229/35. Equal treatment rights

with no reference to concepts such as harassment or instructions to discriminate. The MIPEX results demonstrate that fifteen EU Member States have nevertheless chosen to extend the detailed definition of discrimination found in the Racial Equality Directive to their laws on nationality discrimination.

A similar level of convergence can also be found in the results pertaining to the third and fourth indicators. A high score of 2.7 for the EU-25 was recorded in relation to the application of national anti-discrimination law to natural and legal persons, as well as the public and private sectors. Again this reflects a foundational element of the Racial Equality Directive. Article 3(1) states clearly that "this Directive shall apply to all persons, as regards both the public and private sectors, including public bodies...." The unequivocal nature of this obligation has generated a high level of compliance, especially amongst the EU-15 states, where all received the maximum three points under this indicator, with the exception of Denmark.

So far, the impression arises that the EU Directives are the key element in propelling the convergence of national anti-discrimination legislation. The results for the fourth indicator are instructive, because this concerned matters which lie outside the scope of the Directives. Laws relating to incitement to violence and similar activities are generally dealt with at national level within the field of criminal law. At EU level, criminal law issues mainly fall outside the scope of the EC Treaty and have been dealt with separately from the anti-discrimination legislation based on Article 13 EC. Instead, action has been based on Article 29 of the EU Treaty, which sets the objective of "preventing and combating racism and xenophobia." Since 2001, the Member States have been negotiating the adoption of a 'Framework Decision' on racism and xenophobia.[15] The difficulty in reaching agreement on this instrument exposed strong political tensions on the appropriate balance between freedom of expression and combating 'hate' speech, as well as differences of opinion on whether racial and religious offences

for third country nationals are scattered across a range of EC Directives, as well as international agreements with third countries. Perhaps the most significant source of equal treatment rights can be found in Art 11, Directive (EC) 2003/109 concerning the status of third country nationals who are long-term residents (2004) OJ L16/44.

[15] A Framework Decision is akin to a Directive, although EU Treaty, Art 34(2)(b) expressly states that Framework Decisions 'shall not entail direct effect'. This implies that an individual cannot directly enforce rights found within a Framework Decision in proceedings before national courts. Notwithstanding this injunction, the Court of Justice has held that an individual may invoke a Framework Decision in order to ensure that national courts fulfil their duty to interpret national law 'as far as possible in the light of the wording and purpose of the Framework Decision in order to attain the result which it pursues': Criminal proceedings against Pupino, Case C-105/03, para 43 (2005) ECR I-5283.

should be treated in the same manner.[16] Given the absence of a detailed EU legal framework in this area, it might be expected that MIPEX would find more divergence in national law. Surprisingly, the results demonstrate a remarkable level of convergence (2.6), with little difference in performance between the EU-15 and EU-10. This finding indicates that similarities between national anti-discrimination laws cannot simply be ascribed to the impact of the EU Directives. The presence of apparent convergence in an area that is largely unaffected by EU law draws attention to other external sources which may have a role in shaping national practice. One possible explanation for the proximity of results under this indicator is the influence of the International Convention on the Elimination of All Forms of Racial Discrimination (ICERD).[17] This instrument has been ratified by all EU Member States and Article 4(a) requires signatories to prohibit the offences of incitement to violence or discrimination based on race, colour or ethnic origin. In addition, the prohibition of such conduct is also recommended and monitored by the Council of Europe's specialised body, the European Commission on Racism and Intolerance (ECRI).[18]

In contrast to the other indicators adopted under this heading, a markedly lower level of convergence was found in relation to whether national law prohibits discrimination by association or based on assumed characteristics. Here, the EU-25 average result was 1.7, but the individual country results were more polarised. Seven EU states received the maximum rating of three, whilst fourteen received the minimum rating of one. The diversity of national practice seems to reflect the lack of engagement with this issue in European instruments. The Racial Equality Directive does not expressly clarify whether discrimination by association or based on assumed characteristics fall within its scope. In Article 2(1), a broad reference is made to discrimination "on grounds of racial or ethnic origin." This is sufficiently open to support a reading of the Directive which incorporates association and assumed forms of discrimination, but it is not unambiguous. Whilst this lack of clarity may explain the uneven response within national legislation, the legal uncertainty has arguably been dispelled by the recent judgment of the Court of Justice in *Coleman v Attridge Law.*[19] This case arose under the Employment Equality Directive and it concerned a woman who claimed to have experienced discrimination and harassment following the birth of her son, who is disabled. The treatment was allegedly due to her son's disability, as other employees with children were not treated in the same manner.

---

[16] Political agreement on the Framework Decision was reached in April 2007, but it had yet to be formally adopted at the time of writing.

[17] New York, Mar. 7 1966.

[18] Para 18, ECRI, General policy recommendation no 7 on national legislation to combat racism and racial discrimination, CRI (2003) 8.

[19] *Coleman v Attridge Law and Steve Law* Case C-303/06, judgment of July 17, 2008.

This posed the question whether an individual who faced discrimination based on association with a disabled person (in this case, being that person's primary carer) was prohibited by the Directive. The Court of Justice held that the Directive was designed to combat all forms of discrimination based on disability and it was not limited to a particular class of persons.[20] It emphasised that to deny protection to a person in a situation such as that of Ms. Coleman would undermine the effectiveness of the Directive.[21] Although this decision relates to disability discrimination, the legal reasoning would appear equally applicable to the Racial Equality Directive. Notably, the Court mentioned that its interpretation was consistent with the wording of Article 13 EC,[22] which seems a subtle indication that this principle can be applied to all the prohibited grounds of discrimination found therein. An important issue for future editions of MIPEX will be to measure whether this judgment prompts a convergence in national legislation to include discrimination by association.

Overall, the indicators on the definition and concept of discrimination suggest a high level of convergence within the EU Member States. It has been argued that this reflects the relatively precise nature of the Racial Equality and Employment Equality Directives in this area, as well as the requirements of ICERD. Nevertheless, the indicator on discrimination by association or based on assumed characteristics reveals that convergence may be limited when one probes into more detailed interpretation of the concepts, especially in the absence of clear guidance from external legal sources. This finding is significant because it suggests that Member States may discover unanticipated shortcomings in their national legislation as case-law begins to unfold the full extent of the concept of discrimination. A good example is provided by the decision of the Court of Justice in *Firma Feryn*,[23] issued one week before the *Coleman* judgment. In brief, this held that a public statement of an employer that he did not recruit employees of a particular racial or ethnic origin constituted direct discrimination contrary to the Racial Equality Directive. This finding that direct discrimination can arise purely from an employer's statements, without the need for an identified individual victim, reveals another dimension to the concept of discrimination which was not explicit within the text of the Directive.

[20] *Id.* at para 38.

[21] *Id.* at para 51.

[22] *Id.* at para 38.

[23] *Centrum voor gelijkheid van kansen en voor racismebestrijding v Firma Feryn NV*, Case C-54/07, judgment of July 10, 2008.

B. *Fields of Application*

The second area considered by MIPEX is the fields of application of anti-discrimination law. Six indicators were identified in this area, each of which corresponds to a different social good (such as employment or education). The source of these indicators was evidently the material scope of the Racial Equality Directive, which covers an identical list of areas.[24] In each category, the maximum mark of three was awarded if discrimination on grounds of race/ethnicity, religion/belief and nationality was prohibited. If discrimination was only prohibited on two of the three grounds, then a mark of two was assigned, and similarly one mark if only one ground was covered in national law.

Indicator: **Area where national law prohibits discrimination**	**EU-25**	**EU-15**	**EU-10**
Employment and vocational training	2.5	2.6	2.4
Education (primary and secondary)	2.3	2.5	2.0
Supply of goods and services, including health	2.3	2.5	1.9
Supply of goods and services, including housing	2.2	2.5	1.7
Social protection, including social security	2.1	2.5	1.7
Social advantages	2.1	2.3	1.7

A number of observations can be made based on this table. Firstly, it is unsurprising to find that the most extensive protection against discrimination is in the field of employment and vocational training. This correlates with the obligations imposed by EU law. The Racial Equality Directive and the Employment Equality Directive require discrimination in this area to be prohibited on grounds of racial or ethnic origin and religion or belief. Although EU law in relation to nationality discrimination is more fragmented, there are various elements which require non-discrimination in employment, both in respect of EU nationals[25] and third country nationals.[26] Indeed, only Poland from all the EU Member States received a mark below two for this category. A second observation is that the level of convergence declines when one turns to examine other social goods. This might be attributed to the weaker impact of EU law. As the law stands, there are no provisions relating to religious discrimination in areas outside employment, and the scattered instruments on nationality discrimination are

[24] Art 3(1), Directive 2000/43.

[25] Art 39(2) EC.

[26] Art 11, Directive 2003/109.

also less comprehensive.[27] In July 2008, the Commission proposed a Directive which would extend protection against discrimination on, *inter alia*, grounds of religion or belief to cover the full material scope of the Racial Equality Directive (in other words, all the remaining fields covered by the six MIPEX indicators).[28] Finally, there is a marked disparity in the results between the EU-15 and the EU-10. Whereas Austria was the only EU-15 state to receive a score of one for all indicators other than employment and vocational training, there were four such states amongst the EU-10 (Czech Republic, Estonia, Malta, Poland).[29] Indeed, all of these states have been laggards in terms of their compliance with the Racial Equality Directive, with national implementing legislation initially only addressing the employment sphere.[30] Under pressure from the European Commission, this picture is beginning to change and Malta has now extended its legislation on racial discrimination to cover areas outside employment. Notwithstanding such improvements, these indicators provide evidence that embedding anti-discrimination legislation has proven more challenging in the EU-10 than in the EU-15.

The relatively high results recorded in this area might reflect the close alignment between the selected indicators and the provisions of the Racial Equality Directive. In contrast, the other three topics examined in this chapter all include some benchmarking indicators that go beyond the contents of the Directive. Although the indicators selected cover a broad range of areas of anti-discrimination law, one notable omission is policing and criminal justice. Whilst this is not addressed by the Racial Equality Directive, ECRI has recommended that all Council of Europe states prohibit discrimination by law enforcement agencies.[31] The European Network Against Racism has noted that its member organisations continue to identify policing as one of the most common areas where discrimination on grounds of ethnic origin, religion and nationality occurs.[32] Therefore, it may be appropriate for MIPEX to consider adding an indicator relating to this field in the future.

---

[27] For example, the Long-Term Residents Directive (2003/109) makes no express reference to non-discrimination in the field of healthcare.

[28] Commission, 'Proposal for a Council Directive on implementing the principle of equal treatment between persons irrespective of religion or belief, disability, age or sexual orientation' COM (2008) 426.

[29] MIPEX also measured results for several non-EU states (Canada, Norway and Switzerland). Of these, Switzerland received a score of one for all six indicators in this area.

[30] Mark Bell, Isabelle Chopin and Fiona Palmer, *Developing anti-discrimination law in Europe* 43 (Migration Policy Group and Human European Consultancy, 2006).

[31] European Commission against Racism and Intolerance, *General policy recommendation no 11 on combating racism and racial discrimination in policing*, CRI (2007) 39, 29 June 2007, para 5.

[32] Catherine Lynch, *Racism in Europe – ENAR Shadow report 2005* 15 (ENAR, 2006).

C. *Enforcement*

Measuring performance for the first two categories is comparatively straightforward. The focus is exclusively on legislation (its definitions and its scope) and the external benchmarks flow fairly directly from the standards set in the Racial Equality Directive. Enforcement is a more elusive phenomenon. A Member State may possess anti-discrimination legislation with a comprehensive definition of discrimination and a wide-ranging material scope, but if the legislation is very difficult for individuals to utilise, then the overall effectiveness of the law may be low. MIPEX had recourse to a longer list of indicators in order to get a better picture of the various dimensions to enforcement. These are set out in the following table, alongside the results for EU-25, EU-15 and EU-10.

Indicator	**EU-25**	**EU-15**	**EU-10**
State provides financial assistance where victims lack the necessary means	2.6	2.7	2.5
Access for victims to procedures, measured by reference to each ground of discrimination (ethnic origin, religion, nationality)[33]	2.6	2.6	2.6
Protection against victimisation	2.5	2.9	2.0
There is provision for a shift in the burden of proof	2.5	2.7	2.1
Victims have access to judicial and administrative procedures, including alternative dispute resolution procedures (irrespective of the discrimination ground)	2.5	2.7	2.2
Discriminatory motivation is treated as an aggravating circumstance	2.0	2.3	1.7
A range of sanctions is available[34]	2.0	2.3	1.6
The role of legal entities in defending the principle of equality[35]	2.0	2.1	1.9
Average length of procedures[36]	1.4	1.5	1.3

[33] Three points awarded if victims have access to procedures in relation to all three grounds.

[34] States received a mark of one if national law only provided for restitution of rights or damages, and requirements to stop offending. A mark of two was awarded if there were additional sanctions for legal persons. A mark of three was given if national law provided at least five out of a list of eight different types of sanctions. The complete description of the indicators is available from: <http://www.integrationindex.eu/topics/2653.html>.

[35] Three marks were awarded in this category if legal entities could (a) engage in proceedings on behalf on victims; (b) engage in proceedings in support of victims; and (c) bring cases even in the absence of an identified victim.

[36] Three marks were given for procedures lasting, on average, less than six months; two marks for six months to one year; one mark for more than one year.

Some of the indicators are derived from the Racial Equality Directive, such as protection against victimisation or provision for a shift in the burden of proof. Other indicators, such as the range of sanctions or the average length of procedures, are areas where EU legislation does not lay down detailed obligations.[37] There is no obvious correlation in the results between whether or not the indicator is an EU law requisite. Notably, the joint highest result is recorded for whether the state provides financial assistance for victims who lack the necessary means to bring their own complaint, even though there are no stipulations in the Racial Equality Directive on this topic. The mixture of results tends to suggest that the climate for enforcement depends on multiple factors, of which the Directive is merely one. This accords with the reality that in many Member States the avenues for enforcing anti-discrimination legislation are equivalent to those available for any infringement of labour or civil law obligations. Even where the state has created specialised enforcement procedures for anti-discrimination law, these tend to offer an alternative procedure only for first instance hearings; after this, the complainant is typically reliant on the conventional judicial procedures. For example, in the Netherlands, the Equal Treatment Commission provides non-binding adjudication. Should a respondent not comply with the decision of this body, then the individual must resort the normal court system.[38]

The interplay between the enforcement of anti-discrimination law and general features of the domestic judicial system illustrates one of the constraints on the capacity for anti-discrimination law to effect change. It is difficult to disentangle whether the poor scores for the Member States on the average length of judicial (or other) procedures reflects a specific weakness in anti-discrimination litigation, or evidence of more deep-seated problems for any type of litigant. In the future, more insight may be provided by a comparison of the results of MIPEX with the data emerging from the work of the European Commission for the Efficiency of Justice. This body was established by the Council of Europe in 2002 with a mandate to analyse national judicial systems and identify ways of improving their quality, in particular to ensure effective access to justice, as required by Article 6 of the European Convention on Human Rights.[39] To this end, it has compiled an extensive body of data on topics such as the national provision of publicly-financed legal assistance.

[37] Art 15 of the Directive establishes a general standard that sanctions must be 'effective, proportionate and dissuasive'.

[38] Jenny Goldschmidt, *Implementation of equality law: a task for specialists or for human rights experts? Experiences and developments in the supervision of equality law in the Netherlands*, 13 *Maastricht Journal of European and Comparative Law* 323, 327 (2006).

[39] European Commission for the Efficiency of Justice, *European judicial systems*, 9 (Council of Europe, 2006).

As with some of the earlier results, a significant gap emerges in the results between the performance of the EU-15 and the EU-10. In addition to the scores for individual indicators, MIPEX also calculates the aggregate score for each Member State in relation to enforcement, this time on a scale of 100.[40] The average result for the EU-15 was 71, whereas the average for the EU-10 was 49. Six of the seven worst performing countries on enforcement were from the EU-10.[41] The starting point for the EU-10 when implementing the Racial Equality and Employment Equality Directives was evidently different from that of the EU-15. Most of the EU-10 did not have an established framework of specialised legislation on anti-discrimination; where provisions did exist, these tended to be anti-discrimination clauses scattered across different legal codes with little detail on concepts.[42] The comparatively high results on the first category examined above (definitions and concepts) suggest that the EU-10 have made considerable progress in transposing the core elements of the Racial Equality Directive into their national legislation. The poorer results on enforcement indicate, though, that there is some distance to be travelled before these new legal instruments become effective in practice.

As mentioned at the beginning of this section, measuring enforcement is more challenging than the previous categories. In considering the final results, there are some outcomes which might question whether the existing MIPEX indicators have fully captured the reality on enforcement. The top six performing states on enforcement were as follows (aggregate mark in brackets): Netherlands (100); Hungary and Portugal (89); Belgium, Italy and Sweden (83). The presence of Portugal and Italy within the top six is somewhat surprising. The data gathered for the European Network of Legal Experts in the Non-Discrimination Field indicates that these are both states where litigation under anti-discrimination legislation remains at a very low level.[43] Contrasting data also emerges from the EU Fundamental Rights Agency (FRA). It compiled data on the number of sanctions and/or financial awards applied in cases of racial or ethnic discrimination during 2006–2007, as well as the level of these awards.[44] Portugal was one of twelve states where no sanctions/awards had been applied in this period.

The divergence in results relating to enforcement highlights a key indicator which remains absent from MIPEX: levels of litigation. On the one hand, the

---

[40] *See* <http://www.integrationindex.eu/mapscharts/>.

[41] Latvia, Lithuania, Czech Republic, Estonia, Cyprus and Slovakia. Denmark was the worst performing state from EU-15.

[42] *See* Commission, 'Equality, diversity and enlargement' (Luxembourg: Office for Official Publications of the European Communities, 2003).

[43] The 2007 national reports on Italy and Portugal are available from: <http://ec.europa.eu/employment_social/fundamental_rights/policy/aneval/legnet_en.htm#coun>.

[44] Fundamental Rights Agency, *Annual Report 2008*, 17 (Elanders Hungary, 2008).

absolute quantity of litigation does not necessarily disclose the effectiveness of the legislation. If anti-discrimination law were at its most effective, then the need for litigation would evaporate. Similarly, states might choose to place a high emphasis upon mediation; where this is effective, disputes may be resolved without recourse to litigation.[45] On the other hand, various studies indicate that racial discrimination remains commonplace in many European countries.[46] An absence of litigation rings alarm bells as to whether the legislation is suitably equipped for enforcement by individuals. Although an indicator on the level of litigation would seem, prima facie, to be desirable, it faces formidable obstacles in practice. In relation to racist offences, the FRA has reported that only eleven Member States have data collection systems which could be described as "good."[47] Another challenge to constructing such an indicator is the lack of comparability between the different procedures open to individual litigants across the Member States. In some states, such as the United Kingdom or Ireland, a binding process of adjudication is the primary avenue for bringing complaints, even if many complaints lodged may be settled before a final decision.[48] In such systems, it is relatively easy to compile statistics on the number of cases lodged each year and to track their outcomes. In other states, there is a more diffuse system of binding and non-binding avenues for discrimination cases, which may operate in sequence or even concurrently.[49] In Greece, for example, there are three administrative bodies with authority to receive discrimination complaints: the Ombudsman, the Labour Inspectorate and the Equal Treatment Committee. In addition, cases may be brought before the courts.[50]

The differences in the range and type of processes applicable in the Member States render it difficult to devise a common method for comparing the level

---

[45] *Id.* 106.

[46] For example, a major empirical study by the International Labour Organisation (which included Belgium, Germany, Italy, the Netherlands and Spain) found that ethnic minority job applicants faced discrimination in 'more than every third application procedure.' *See* Timo Makkonen, *European handbook for equality data*, 77 (Luxembourg: Office for Official Publications of the European Communities, 2006).

[47] Fundamental Rights Agency, *Trends and developments 1997–2005 – combating ethnic and racial discrimination and promoting equality in the European Union*, 37 (Elanders Hungary, 2007).

[48] In the United Kingdom., employment discrimination cases are lodged with an Employment Tribunal, although mediation is available prior to the tribunal hearing. In Ireland, most types of discrimination case will be brought to the Equality Tribunal, which has a dedicated mediation service.

[49] In the Netherlands, an individual is not precluded from pursuing their complaint simultaneously before the Equal Treatment Commission and the courts: Goldschmidt (n 38 above).

[50] *See* Yannis Ktistakis, *Report on measures to combat discrimination: Directives 2000/43 and 2000/78: Greece*, (2007), available at: <http://ec.europa.eu/employment_social/fundamental_rights/pdf/legnet/elrep07_en.pdf>.

of anti-discrimination litigation. This is evident when the data on sanctions presented by the FRA is subject to closer scrutiny. According to their methodology, the Netherlands performs poorly; only one sanction was imposed for racial or ethnic discrimination during 2006–2007.[51] As the FRA acknowledges, this does not capture the decisions of the Dutch Equal Treatment Commission because these are not legally-binding. Yet they enjoy a relatively high level of compliance.[52]

D. *Equality Policies*

The final category considered by MIPEX aims to provide an assessment of national equality policies. As with enforcement, this is a more difficult concept to measure and a range of indicators were adopted.

Indicator	**EU-25**	**EU-15**	**EU-10**
Powers of specialised agency to assist victims[53]	2.4	2.5	2.2
Specialised agency has a mandate to combat discrimination based on race/ethnicity, religion/belief, nationality	2.3	2.2	2.5
Restrictions on freedom of association, assembly and speech are permitted when these impede equal treatment	2.0	2.2	1.8
Powers of specialised agency to instigate proceedings and investigations	1.8	1.9	1.7
Law provides that the state disseminates information and ensures social and civil dialogue in relation to discrimination	1.8	2.0	1.5
Legal standing of specialised agency[54]	1.6	1.5	1.7
Mainstreaming equality policies	1.4	1.3	1.5

Considering the above results, it is notable that no particular disparity emerges between the performance of EU-15 and EU-10 states. Instead, the most striking feature is the lower level of results when compared to the other categories.

[51] Fundamental Rights Agency, 19 (2008).

[52] The respondent voluntarily complies with the Commission's decision in around two-thirds of cases; *Id.* 20.

[53] Three marks were awarded for bodies that could both provide advice to individuals and undertake independent investigation of the facts of case.

[54] Three marks were awarded where the specialised agency had the power to engage in judicial and administrative proceedings on behalf of the complainant.

This suggests that the enhancements to anti-discrimination legislation in recent years have not been embedded within a wider framework of equality policies. For example, the indicator on dialogue between the state on the one hand, and the social partners and civil society on the other, confirms the finding of the European Network of Legal Experts in the Non-Discrimination Field that this element of the Racial Equality and Employment Equality Directives has received "the least formal implementation by the Member States and probably the most varied response."[55] The weak results under these indicators testify to the shortcomings in the change provoked by the Directives. Formal revision of the legal framework is the first step and, albeit imperfectly, one which most states have taken. Breathing life into the new legal provisions and making sure that the underlying policy goals are actually achieved is considerably more challenging.

Of the four themes examined under anti-discrimination by MIPEX, "equality policies" seems the area where the indicators selected are most open to debate. Although the heading indicates a shift in focus away from legislation, in fact most of the indicators are concerned with legal provisions, such as the powers and functions of specialised agencies. Three marks would be awarded where a specialised agency has the power to instigate proceedings in its own name, lead its own investigation and enforce its findings, but this does not reveal whether, in practice, the agency actually exercises these powers. For example, the Cypriot equality body can issue sanctions, but has taken a policy decision to limit itself to recommendations and mediation.[56] A key variable in the capacity of specialised agencies is their resources, both human and financial. Yet finding a yardstick for measuring the resources provided remains difficult. Many of the agencies have mandates for a wider range of discrimination grounds than those examined by MIPEX, whilst some have broader remits relating to human rights[57] or infringements of rights by the public administration.[58] This diversity in institutional arrangements hinders any attempt to measure the resources devoted by the state to supporting victims of racial, religious or nationality discrimination.

Questions could also be posed about the construction of some of the indicators in this area. The indicator relating to the possibility for restrictions on freedom of speech, assembly and association where these impede equal treatment is perhaps slightly out of place under the heading "equality policies." Indeed, it might be more appropriately twinned with the indicator on whether national law prohibits incitement to violence, hatred and discrimination (which was under the

---

55 Mark Bell, Isabelle Chopin, & Fiona Palmer, *Developing anti-discrimination law in Europe*, 72 (Office for Official Publications of the European Communities, 2007).

56 FRA 18 (2008).

57 For example, the British Equality and Human Rights Commission.

58 For example, the Polish Commissioner for Civil Rights Protection.

"definitions and concepts" heading). Perhaps the most interesting indicator in this group is that relating to "mainstreaming equality policies." Three marks were awarded here if national law provides: (a) a mechanism to ensure compliance of current and future legislation within anti-discrimination law; (b) an obligation on public bodies to promote equality; (c) an obligation on public bodies to ensure that contractors respect non-discrimination; and (d) for the introduction of positive action measures. This indicator bundles together a variety of options from the equality policy menu, ranging from mainstreaming to procurement to positive action. Like the earlier indicators, the shortcoming is the focus on what legislation provides rather than on what happens in practice. Most Member States *permit* positive action to be taken, in accordance with the approach in the Racial Equality Directive.[59] This tells us relatively little, though, about whether public and private actors take advantage of this opportunity. This can throw up surprising results; under the mainstreaming equality indicator, Lithuania receives a maximum score of three, whilst the United Kingdom receives the minimum mark of one. This seems peculiar; the United Kingdom has the most elaborate legal framework in the EU for the promotion of race equality within the public sector.[60] Such quirks in the marks do not invalidate the overall results produced by MIPEX. They do, however, serve as a reminder of the limits of quantitative analysis in capturing more subjective phenomena which are less easy to measure. Although there is sufficient evidence to support the contention that the United Kingdom has more experience with positive action than Lithuania, it would be extremely taxing to find an objective mechanism for ranking the *extent* to which positive action or mainstreaming has been used in practice within the Member States. The value of the MIPEX indicators lies in their focus on objective criteria, which allows for comparative classification and measurement.

E. *Conclusions*

In addition to the detailed indicators discussed above, MIPEX also provides an aggregate analysis of national performance on anti-discrimination according to a 100-point scale.[61] This confirms some of the findings which emerged in this chapter. Whilst the average score in the EU-25 was 58, there was a marked gap between the EU-15 average (66) and that of the EU-10 (48). This indicates that there is room for improvement across the Union, but progress is especially required in central and eastern Europe. The discussion in this chapter has revealed

[59] Art 5, Directive 2000/43.

[60] *See* K. Monaghan, *Equality Law*, 625 (Oxford University Press, 2007).

[61] Niessen, Huddleston & Citron 18 (2007).

a pattern where the basic definitions and scope of national legislation are often in tune with the European benchmark, but domestic practice remains variable in the domains of enforcement and equality policies. This picture poses a challenge for the European Union; its capacity to shape national law and policy is arguably stronger in relation to the formal text of legislation, where inconsistencies can be pursued via infringement proceedings before the Court of Justice. Procedures for enforcement, and the remedies attached thereto, have traditionally been a matter where broader national autonomy has been enjoyed, in order to respect the diversity of legal systems within the Union. In the field of gender equality, the Court of Justice counter-balanced national discretion with an emphasis on ensuring the *effectiveness* of equal treatment legislation.[62] In essence, Member States could freely select enforcement methods and remedies in keeping with national traditions, but only insofar as these were consistent with the principle of effectiveness. The MIPEX results suggest that a similar degree of intervention may be required to ensure better enforcement of national legislation on ethnic and religious discrimination. In its first interpretation of the Racial Equality Directive, the Court has signalled that it will adhere to a similar effectiveness test:

> Directive 2000/43 thus imposes on Member States the obligation to introduce into their national legal systems measures which are sufficiently effective to achieve the aim of that Directive and to ensure that they may effectively relied upon before the national courts in order that judicial protection will be real and effective.[63]

Promoting best practice in relation to equality policies is a thornier task. The benchmarks established within EU legislation are less helpful; for example, the Racial Equality Directive merely permits positive action, but creates no obligations to proceed down this avenue. There is no indication that the Commission intends to promote more stringent legal obligations in fields such as positive action or mainstreaming. Notably, the 2008 proposal for a Directive on discrimination outside employment retains the status quo on positive action found in the Racial Equality Directive, and it contains no mention of mainstreaming.[64] Instead, the Commission advances benchmarking as a key lever for stimulating enhancement of national equality policies.[65] To this end, it has established a "non-discrimination governmental expert group" through which it intends to exchange information on good practices and "develop benchmarks."[66] This trajectory underscores

---

[62] Paul Craig & Gráinne de Búrca, *EU law: text, cases and materials*, 313 (Oxford University Press, 2008).

[63] *Firma Feryn NV* Case C-54/07, Para 37, judgment of July 10, 2008.

[64] European Commission (2008) 426.

[65] Commission, 'Non-discrimination and equal opportunities: a renewed commitment' COM (2008) 420, 9.

[66] *Id.*

the relevance of MIPEX as a tool for reflection on the state of national and European practice. The Commission's ambition to deploy benchmarking also emphasises the importance of continuing a critical evaluation of what constitutes "best" practice on anti-discrimination. The vagueness of EU benchmarks in relation to equality policies illustrates the need for a broad horizon, taking into account reference points outside the EU legislative *acquis*. In the field of racial, religious and nationality discrimination, it would be logical to draw upon the work of ECRI, which has been engaged in European standard-setting for over a decade. This is best witnessed in its general policy recommendations.[67] These provide a more comprehensive analysis of the measures that states need to take; as mentioned earlier, ECRI's most recent recommendation addresses the topic of policing, an area where the EU has struggled to find any consensus.

Reaching agreement on what constitutes the European benchmark is always likely to provoke a degree of controversy. Some of the value choices made within the existing MIPEX indicators are certainly open to debate.[68] Nevertheless, the importance attached by the Commission to benchmarking as a method for anti-discrimination policy evolution confirms the need for detailed scrutiny of how "best practice" within Europe can be identified.

---

[67] There are eleven in total: <http://www.coe.int/t/e/human_rights/ecri/1-ecri/3-general_themes/1-policy_recommendations/>.

[68] One example would be the indicator on whether restrictions on freedom of assembly, association and expression are permitted where these impede equal treatment. The appropriate point at which such freedoms should be curtailed remains highly contentious within Europe and, in part, explains the EU's difficulty in adopting the Framework Decision on racism and xenophobia.

Chapter 7

Acquiring Nationality: Is it a Goal, a Tool, or an Assessment of Integration?

Judit Tóth

Nationality law and practice may reflect on the integration policy of the 25 Member States measured in the Migrant Integration Policy Index (MIPEX) by making a typology or a scale system. It would be based on how each state considers naturalisation and other procedures for the acquisition of nationality; is it the final aim of the long process of migrant's integration? Is this acquired status a necessary legal instrument for promoting integration through social and economic equality and accession to the political community? Or is it used as a benchmarking system to evaluate an individual's level of integration and abilities? This typology could determine the stability as well as the acquisition of this status. Nevertheless, the key terms of nationality, citizenship and integration of migrants[1] are used by decision-makers and stakeholders without common agreement or a univocally clear terminology. For operative purposes, this chapter will define nationality as a legal tie of individuals to the state of a titular nation that may contribute to becoming active, responsible and integrated citizens of the given community.

[1] Citizenship is applicable on the grounds of political theory, law and sociology to national citizenship (containing reserved prerogatives and responsibilities for nationals such in the public sector), denizenship, civic citizenship enjoying e.g. certain political rights at local level, active citizenship (participating in civil sector, community and political life), European/union citizenship (with own complementary rights to the national citizenship residing in another member state), global, corporate or transnational citizenship (it reflects on global responsibility for ethical, environmental and economic issues of mankind, it steps across the state and company borders). All of meaning of citizenship has influence on community and individual identity but at different scales. *See* INTI Technical Seminar Paper, *The acquisition of nationality, citizenship and national identity*, (European Commission, 2007).

Nationality law is a part of citizenship policy containing numerous non-normative components, such as information campaigns on procedures, regular counselling on naturalisation, free training and tests, language courses etc. And yet citizenship policy is hardly isolated from integration and migration policy. Therefore analysis shall be based not only on normative or legislative analysis but also complemented with the experiences of law practitioners and NGOs, statistical data, and the literature on nationality. The most comparative existing research projects, NATAC[2] and the MIPEX, cover different geographical scopes and are based on diverse methods. Taking into account these various sources, policy or legal-driven analysis and diverse indicators it has become possible to designate the current trends in nationality law.

A. *International Legal Principles*

Searching for normative tools for nationality policy evaluation, we have to answer whether the most relevant principles and requirements of the international agreements and customary law are inserted into national legislation or not. Although those have significantly influenced legislation and legal practice in developed countries, neither NATAC nor MIPEX investigates the presence of all relevant instruments in the Member States. For instance, both indicate the ratifying states of European Convention on Nationality (1997) but more important substantial and procedural guarantees are not evaluated or *contra legem* regulations are not criticised.

What are the most influential internationally accepted (though not always respected) principles relevant to the integration nexus? The effective, genuine link between the national and his/her state is defined in the infamous Nottebohm case at the International Court. A normative tool could identify how many countries have, *inter alia*:

(1) grounds for *ex lege* acquisition based on territorial elements (birth on the territory of the state or double *ius soli* if both the parent and the descendent were born in the territory)
(2) residence within the territory (on the ground of *ius domicilii*)
(3) or option rights based on these elements

Despite the great variety in these provisions, their aim is always to promote the integration of persons permanently living on a state's territory. It would be desir-

[2] *The Acquisition and Loss of Nationality in Fifteen EU Member States*. Project Co-ordinator: Rainer Bauböck. It finally extended the analysis on new member states.

able to include the territorial link in national legislation on nationality grounds for acquisition allowing the choice between some alternatives (option, declaration).[3] The MIPEX eligibility dimension contains indicators on this principle but states of acquisition (and loss) without genuine link are not identified.

Since the prevention or reduction of statelessness as principle was inserted into the European Convention on Nationality, its acceptance can be determined through the ratification of this Convention instead of the separate UN Convention on the Reduction of Statelessness (1961).[4] Furthermore, the legal stability of stateless persons' status is regulated in the UN Convention on stateless persons (1954), requiring facilitated acquisition of nationality in merit and in proceedings in the case of habitual residence.[5] A MIPEX eligibility indicator refers to provisions for the second generation, including stateless persons born on the territory of state who can obtain nationality *ex lege* or by option, whether or not the parent is a lawfully habitually resident for a certain number of years. These rules facilitate acquisition for the second generation. However, the absence of facilitated acquisition (on the grounds either the European Convention on Nationality or the UN Convention are not that clearly indicated in MIPEX. It could also map other means of losing nationality than withdrawal that would lead to statelessness.

The *acquis* contains the UN Convention on Status of Refugees (1951) which has its own legal consequence on facilitated acquisition of nationality such as the reduction of financial burden of the procedure in receiving states.[6]

The UN Convention on Child's Rights (1989) ensures a baby's right to a nationality at birth preventing his/her statelessness (Art. 7). It can be granted on the basis *ius sanguinis, ius soli* or other grounds for the acquisition of nationality, especially for the second and third generation born in the host country. Through the most unfavourable practice towards refugees and children, the scores in the

---

[3] Gerard-Rene De Groot, *Conditions for Acquisitions of Nationality by Operation of Law or by Lodging a Declaration of Option*, in *Migration, Integration and Citizenship*, 187–223 (2005).

[4] Its ten operative articles contain rules on how to provide nationality for stateless born child on the ground of *ius soli, ius sanguinis a matre*, and it grants nationality for the second generation. Moreover, it defines provisions on responsibility of state in changing sovereignty on the territory and population, as well as on loss of nationality prohibiting deprivation of nationality on racial, ethnic, religious or political grounds (Art. 1–10). Just for these substantial commitments on nationality law it has been ratified in small circle of states.

[5] Article 32: The Contracting States shall as far as possible facilitate the assimilation and naturalization of stateless persons. They shall in particular make every effort to expedite naturalization proceedings and to reduce as far as possible the charges and costs of such proceedings.

[6] Article 34: The Contracting States shall as far as possible facilitate the assimilation and naturalisation of refugees. They shall in particular make every effort to expedite naturalisation proceedings and to reduce as far as possible the charges and costs of such proceedings.

MIPEX eligibility dimension indicate which Member States neglect to facilitate these two groups on the ground of human right commitments.

The UN Convention (1957) grants an independent standing in nationality law for married women, regardless of the husband's nationality and changing marital status, as well as a facilitated acquisition of nationality.[7] More generally, the equality of parents and the couple is required (*ius sanguinis a patre* and *a matre*, particularly in the case of the nationality of children birth in wedlock). This principle is only partly captured in MIPEX.

The European Convention on Nationality's rules on the acquisition and loss of nationality formulate provisions in the case of state succession setting up rules on non-citizens' status (Art. 20) including social and economic rights as a prelude of long-term residents' standing as well as another document on statelessness.[8] All of these provisions may draw the attention to *de facto/de jure* stateless persons (e.g. in Baltic and Balkan regions) whose status and integration is not related to international migration. This whole segment is not captured in MIPEX.

What is more, the European Convention is the first attempt at the international arena to establish a number of rules on procedures in the area of nationality. The Convention contains a long list of persons whose naturalisation must be facilitated. According to the Explanatory Report, facilitation implies a reduction in the length of the required residence period, less stringent language requirements, easier procedures and lower procedural fees. All of these major procedural guarantees can be detected through MIPEX evaluation of eligibility criteria and conditions.

The general principle of equality and non-discrimination is a fundamental element of international human rights. It has been recognised as such in Article 7 of the Universal Declaration of Human Rights, Article 26 of the International Covenant on Civil and Political Rights and in similar provisions in other international human rights instruments. In this respect, the relevant provision in the

---

[7] Article 1: Each Contracting State agrees that neither the celebration nor the dissolution of a marriage between one of its nationals and an alien, nor the change of nationality by the husband during marriage, shall automatically affect the nationality of the wife. Article 2: Each Contracting State agrees that neither the voluntary acquisition of the nationality of another State nor the renunciation of its nationality by one of its nationals shall prevent the retention of its nationality by the wife of such national. Article 3 (1) Each Contracting State agrees that the alien wife of one of its nationals may, at her request, acquire the nationality of her husband through specially privileged naturalization procedures; the grant of such nationality may be subject to such limitations as may be imposed in the interests of national security or public policy. (2) Each Contracting State agrees that the present Convention shall not be construed as affecting any legislation or judicial practice by which the alien wife of one of its nationals may, at her request, acquire her husband's nationality as a matter of right.

[8] Council of Europe, *Convention on the avoidance of statelessness in relation to state succession*, ETS No. 200 (2006).

European Convention on Human Rights (ECHR) is Article 14. The European Commission against Racism and Intolerance (ECRI), the Steering Committee for Equality between Women and Men (CDEG) and the Steering Committee for Human Rights (CDDH), have considered the possibility to reinforce ECHR guarantees in these two areas. Thus the 12th Protocol to the ECHR prohibits discrimination in all public relations, which forms the nexus between the authority and the individual.[9] This ban has been taken to be comprehensive in two senses. The notion of discrimination has been interpreted consistently by the European Court of Human Rights in its case-law concerning Article 14 of the Convention. This case-law has made clear that not every distinction or difference of treatment amounts to discrimination. As the Court has stated, for example, in the judgment in the case of Abdulaziz, Cabales and Balkandali v. the United Kingdom; "a difference of treatment is discriminatory if it 'has no objective and reasonable justification', that is, if it does not pursue a 'legitimate aim' or if there is not a 'reasonable relationship of proportionality between the means employed and the aim sought to be realised.'"[10] According to the Explanatory Report, the scope of protection covers only persons who are discriminated against:

(1) in the enjoyment of any right specifically granted to an individual under national law;
(2) in the enjoyment of a right which may be inferred from a clear obligation of a public authority under national law, that is, where a public authority is under an obligation of national law to behave in a particular manner;
(3) by a public authority in the exercise of discretionary power (for example, granting certain benefit);
(4) and by any other act or omission by a public authority.

In brief, the scope also has to radiate on nationality law. Indeed, the number of ratifications by party states has remained low due to this precise complexity. Non-discrimination is indirectly and in part scored in MIPEX through the dimension on (mandatory or discretionally evaluated) conditions of acquisition. In the future it would be important to clearly differentiate between procedures for facilitated acquisition on the grounds of international human right commitments and those for purely political reasons (ethnical ties, colonial or

[9] Article 1 (1): The enjoyment of any right set forth by law shall be secured without discrimination on any ground such as sex, race, colour, language, religion, political or other opinion, national or social origin, association with a national minority, property, birth or other status. (2) No one shall be discriminated against by any public authority on any ground such as those mentioned in paragraph 1.

[10] Abdulaziz, Cabales and Balkandali v. the United Kingdom, Series A, No. 94, paragraph 72, May 28, 1985.

historical past, cultural proximity preferences). Taking into account the neutral definition of nationality in European Convention on Nationality,[11] its ban on discrimination[12] and the obligations of a constitutional state and the rule of law even in nationality issue procedures – the 12th Protocol of ECHR can be used as a key indicator of whether or not Member States are ready to guarantee a non-discriminatory approach in all activities of authority and to ensure remedy in case of its violation. This Protocol provides for complainant systems, including national courts and the ECtHR.

The following benchmarking table is based on only the "dry" facts on ratification of the abovementioned human rights documents. These indicators produce five distinct groups of states concerning citizenship policies promoting international human rights.

(1) Only one state (the Netherlands) presents itself as a best practice by ratifying all international conventions determining the substance of acquisition and loss of nationality;
(2) The second group (Denmark, Finland, Germany, Hungary, Luxembourg, Romania, Slovakia, and Sweden) would qualify as having a favourable approach to nationality requirements, with ratification the European Convention on Nationality and/or the 12th Protocol to ECHR prohibiting all discrimination in public sphere. But as always, all simplification of a grouping is incorrect. For instance, Hungary has made reservations to the European Convention on Nationality excluding the major procedural guarantees (legal remedy against refusal and reasoning of decision in rejected naturalisation and withdrawal of nationality) while the free procedure does not involve any fees. This is also an amalgam of ethnic preferences (kin-minority as major group of applicants is coming from the poorer adjacent countries)[13] and an orthodox interpretation of state sovereignty where one cannot argue with the authority's discretion power;[14]

[11] "Nationality" means the legal bond between a person and a State and does not indicate the person's ethnic origin (Art. 2a).

[12] Article 5 – Non-discrimination (1): The rules of a State Party on nationality shall not contain distinctions or include any practice which amount to discrimination on the grounds of sex, religion, race, colour or national or ethnic origin. (2) Each State Party shall be guided by the principle of non-discrimination between its nationals, whether they are nationals by birth or have acquired its nationality subsequently.

[13] *See* the same rationale in Code of Greek Citizenship (3284/10-11-2004 OJ 217 A) which provides that a fee is not paid if applicant is Greek origin.

[14] Judit Tóth, *Principles and Practice of Nationality Law in Hungary, Regio* Vol. 8, 21–39 (2005).

(3) The halfway group of states (Austria, Bulgaria, Cyprus, Czech Republic, Ireland, Latvia, Slovenia, Spain, United Kingdom) have ratified only four documents and some have accepted neither the European Convention on Nationality, nor the 12th Protocol;

(4) The near-worst group of countries (Belgium, France, Greece, Italy, Lithuania, Malta, Poland, and Portugal) ratified three important documents that nevertheless contain only partial commitments concerning nationality law, granting them wider legislative freedom;

(5) Finally, one state (Estonia) accepts only the bare minimum of international human rights commitments in this field.

Table 1: Ratification of most relevant human rights documents on nationality law by Member States

Country	Stateless 1954[15]	Refugees 1951	Married women 1957[16]	Child's rights 1989	Nationality Conv. 1997[17]	Protocol to ECHR[18]
(1) Netherlands	X	X	X	X	X	X
(2) Denmark	X	X	X	X	X	
Germany	X	X	X	X	X	
Finland	X	X	X	X		X
Hungary	X	X	X	X	X	
Luxemburg	X	X	X	X		X
Slovakia	X	X	X	X	X	
Romania		X	X	X	X	X
Sweden	X	X	X	X	X	
Austria		X	X	X	X	
(3) Bulgaria		X	X	X	X	
Cyprus		X	X	X		X
Czech Rep.		X	X	X	X	
Ireland	X	X	X	X		
Latvia	X	X	X	X		
Slovenia	X	X	X	X		
Spain	X	X		X		X

[15] Convention relating to the Status of Stateless Persons adopted on September 28, 1954 by a Conference of Plenipotentiaries convened by Economic and social Council resolution 526 A(XVII) of April 26, 1954, entry into force June 6, 1960, in accordance with article 39 (UNDOC status June 10, 2008).

[16] Convention on the Nationality of Married Women, Opened for signature and ratification by General Assembly resolution 1040 (XI) of January 29, 1957 entry into force August 11, 1958, in accordance with article 6 (UNDOC status June 10, 2008).

[17] Council of Europe, Treaty Office, status June 11, 2008.

[18] Protocol No. 12 to the Convention for the Protection of Human Rights and Fundamental Freedoms, Council of Europe Treaty Office, status June 11, 2008.

Table 1 (*cont.*)

Country	Stateless 1954	Refugees 1951	Married women 1957	Child's rights 1989	Nationality Conv. 1997	Protocol to ECHR
UK	X	X	X	X		
Belgium	X	X		X		
France	X	X		X		
Greece	X	X		X		
Italy	X	X		X		
Lithuania	X	X		X		
(4) Malta		X	X	X		
Poland		X	X	X		
Portugal		X		X	X	
(5) Estonia		X		X		

We have to underline that this one-sided approach only draws attention to differences in national legislation on citizenship policy if the Member States takes seriously the rights and duties in acquisition, loss and procedural guarantees imposed by these international instruments. Divergent levels of seriousness among the Member States would need to impact on re-grouping the states. Summing up, legal indicators on the ratification of the most relevant international treaties is needed together with an evaluation of whether or not the principles emanating from treaties and international customary law are respected in each state's national legislation and practice.

B. *Other Normative Determinants: European Community Law*

Does EC law facilitate or hinder the promotion of integration through the acquisition of nationality? When acquisition and loss of nationality is nominated as an indicator of citizenship policy and integration one unavoidable question is whether Union citizenship hinders or inspires the harmonisation of integration policy for migrants, applicants and Diaspora. The Treaty of Maastricht (Art. 17–22),[19] the Treaty of Amsterdam, the European Constitution and the Treaty of Lisbon ensure citizenship of the Union for all nationals of Member States – with some exceptions[20] – as a complementary and functional nationality

[19] *See* Art. 12–13, 23, 39, 61, 137, 141, 194–195, 255 and 286 of the EC Treaty, as well as Para. 9 of the Preamble and Art. 2(1) of EU Treaty.

[20] *See* the member states' declarations on definition of nationals that explain who shall be considered for instance, British, Danish, German, Spanish or Italian nationals.

for Community purposes.[21] Legislation on nationality belongs to the sovereignty of the Member States and the Union has, strictly speaking, no direct competence to regulate legal entitlement of acquisition or loss of nationality. That said, Community law and legal principles effectively impact on Member State sovereignty. The nationality legislation in Member States must respect the general principles of Community law (such as solidarity, equality, non-discrimination) and its rules, in particular on free movement of persons.[22] Furthermore, national legislation cannot be contradiction with human rights and international public law on nationality law.[23] However, national citizenship policy has fabricated a (national) identity, political community and loyalty that Union citizenship may create as a European demos and identity only in the long term. For this reason it may be important to consider an evaluation of these indirect impacts.

Due to this functional link one could predict that the EU would increasingly try to influence citizenship policy including the grounds for acquisition and loss of nationality in the Member States through various effective instruments. This set of tools includes EC legislative competence on and supporting measures for immigration control, reception, integration of migrants, cohesion, equality, and employment policies. On another front, the autonomy of the Member States is gradually weakening through the transposition of directives, national action plans concerning EU funds, and recommended open method of co-ordination in matters of nationality law.[24]

The debate around the legal status of the Charter of Fundamental Rights of the Union[25] will be finished by the Lisbon Treaty – at least for the majority of Member States.[26] The Art. 6 of TEU provides a cross-reference to the Charter rendering it directly legally binding for the European institutions, bodies, offices,

21 Gerard-Rene De Groot, *Towards a European Nationality Law, Migration, Integration and Citizenship*, 13–54 (2005).

22 The European Court of Justice underlines the importance of union citizenship itself as a fundamental status. *See* the Micheletti case C-369/90.

23 *See* the cases of C-179/98, C-64/96, C-65/96.

24 Rainer Bauböck et al., *Acquisition and Loss of Nationality. Policies and Trends in 15 European States.* Summary and Recommendations 28 (2006).

25 OJ C-364/1, December 7, 2000.

26 The position of United Kingdom and Poland constitutes one of the most controversial exceptions asking for a special positioning in respect of the applicability of the Charter to their national stages. According to the Polish unilateral Declaration, the Charter will not affect the right of the member states to enact legislation in the areas of public morality, family law, the protection of human dignity and the respect for human physical and moral integrity. The U.K.'s Protocol says that Charter does not extent the ability of ECJ or any court or tribunal in the United Kingdom to find that the laws, regulations or administrative provisions, practices or action of the United Kingdom are inconsistent with the fundamental rights, freedoms and principles that it reaffirms.

agencies as well as Member States when they implement Union law. Further on, the Art. 6(2) of TEU establishes that the EU shall accede to the European Convention for the Protection of Human Rights and Fundamental Freedoms (1950) without affecting the Union's competences as defined in the Treaties. Both of these provisions shall redouble the onus upon Member States to respect fundamental rights when legislating, implementing and exercising nationality law and policies. One can therefore assess to what extent fundamental rights can be applicable to citizenship policies.

(1) Art. 3 (1) everyone has the right to respect for his/her physical and mental integrity – so integration or citizenship courses, tests must not overstep these limits;
(2) Art. 7 everyone has the right to respect for his/her private and family life, home and communication. Together with Art. 9 on right to found a family and Art 19 on protection in the event of removal, expulsion or extradition, naturalisation and withdrawal, the procedure has to evaluate an individual's conditions and follow the imperative to respect his/her privacy, dignity and security – in accordance with the best interest of the child in Art. 24(2) and the legal, social and economic protection of family in Art. 33(1) and ECHR by Art. 52(2)(3);
(3) Art. 20 and 21 provides the equal treatment of persons before the law and prohibition of discrimination – *inter alia* – on the ground of race, colour, ethnic origin, language, religion or membership of a national minority. In addition, a vague promise for positive discrimination of communities can be interpreted from Art. 22 defining the Union respecting for cultural, religious and linguistic diversity, which fits to the diversity and intercultural nature of the EU as recognised in Art. 151 of the EC Treaty;
(4) Art. 46 provides a right to diplomatic and consular protection of Union citizens outside the territory of the Union. The Lisbon Treaty takes a step back in comparison to the European Constitution giving entitlement to adopt directives establishing co-ordination and co-operation measures, while it is a progress in comparison to the existing rules. However, (enhanced or refused) protection of dual nationals of Member States remains intact in spite of their growing rate;
(5) Art. 47 contains the requirement of a fair procedure for violation of the rights and freedoms guaranteed in Union legal acts, including effective remedy, public hearing, free legal aid and genuine access to justice.

A special monitoring system would be able to indicate whether or not fundamental rights in matters of nationality law are ensured in each Member State as a component of citizenship policy. In the absence of an existing specialised monitoring, this evaluation can be assessed within the MIPEX and strengthened perhaps in co-operation with the new FRA.[27]

Beyond the open method of co-ordination among the Member States, what are the additional (indirect) influential instruments in Community law for a more unified citizenship policy including the conditions of acquisition and loss of nationality in an internally borderless and socially heterogenic Union?

Community law ensures common minimal rights for settled, long-term migrants,[28] determining the scope of efforts on integration and equality rules enforcement. Member states "may require third-country nationals to comply with integration conditions, in accordance with national law" (Art. 5). It inspires the conditionality of integration without giving a clear definition on the requirements or method of evaluation on the attained level of integration. This wide discretionary power for authorities can limit the freedoms and rights of long-term migrants. For instance, knowledge of a national language as an indicator of the willingness to integrate looks like an objective precondition, but academic circles would argue for a more sophisticated evaluation including knowledge of a mediator language or a local or regional language. The only objective component in the EC directive on long-term residence is the maximal five years residence prior to submission of the application for this status (Art. 4). That said, there is a debate on whether or not this period must be uninterrupted in the same EU Member State and what periods of residence can count for this assessment – a debate which comes up again regarding the grounds for losing a long-term residence status.

In numerous states the long-term residence status relates to naturalisation and free movement. However, this status (like denizenship, quasi citizenship providing vote and protection against expulsion) is a great competitor of nationality, leaving less and less untouched territory for nationals' legal positions (e.g. in public sector, social rights)[29] at least in the Member States that are obligated to implement the Directive.[30] This competition or parallelism of national and Community denizenship is particularly obvious if facilitated access for certain

---

[27] European Parliament Resolution, March 15, 2007 *on compliance with the Charter of Fundamental Rights in the Commission's legislative proposal: methodology for systematic and rigorous monitoring.*

[28] European Council Directive 2003/109/EC (November 25, 2003) *concerning the status of third-country nationals who are long-term residents* (OJ L 16/44, 23.1.2004).

[29] Elspeth Guild, *The Legal Elements of European Identity – EU Citizenship and Migration Law*, 242–244 (2004).

[30] The United Kingdom and Ireland opted out from the Directive, and Denmark was automatically excluded from it. All other member states must apply by January 23, 2006.

legal status of third country national is based on ethnic criteria.[31] "Since it will be awkward for Member States to run parallel national and Community systems regarding long-term residence status, there is a good chance that many or all Member States will align themselves to the EC model. This is desirable if the EC system represents an improvement on the national system; but if it does not, the Directive will have resulted in a reduction of standards."[32] This assessment appears in a special project on transposition[33] exclusively from the point-of-view of the mandatory and optional rules of Directive without comparisons to the citizenship policy. However, integration and the European denizen status has been analysed for years.[34]

The family unification rules[35] have inspired integration programmes directed at future applicants for naturalisation or long-term migrants, while transposition of the Directive has led to a diversity of integration requirements (for instance its absence in France until late 2007 and its strong conditions in the Netherlands) and personal scope (e.g. dual nationals are excluded from its implementation in Austria, Belgium, Czech Republic, Estonia, France, Germany, Greece, Hungary, Latvia, Lithuania, Luxembourg, Poland, Portugal, Slovakia, Slovenia and Spain).[36] Similarly the EC directive allows some negative integration signals to be sent to potential applicants for the acquisition of nationality, for example the exclusion from reunification of a child over 12 who has not complied with an "integration requirement" (Art. 4.1). Furthermore, while Directive confers greater protection for the EU citizen and family member[37] against expulsion, it states that procedural safeguards will depend on how long the individual in concern has resided in the territory and what is the level of his/her social, economic and cultural integration, state of family and health conditions[38] – without

[31] Maria Kovács M. and Judit Tóth, *Kin-state responsibility and ethnic citizenship: The Hungarian case*, in *Citizenship Policies in the New Europe*, 135–159 (Amsterdam University Press, 2007).

[32] Steve Peers & Nicola Rogers, *EU Immigration and Asylum Law: Text and Commentary*, 639 (Martinus Nijhoff, 2006).

[33] *Seminar on the Long-term Resident's Directive*, February 10, 2006 – Radboud University, Nijmegen, the Netherlands.

[34] Sergio Carrera, *'Integration' as a Process of Inclusion for Migrants? The Case of Long-Term Residents in the EU*, (2005).

[35] European Council Directive 2003/86/EC (September 22, 2003) *on the right to family reunification* (OJ L 251/12, 3.10.2003).

[36] Kees Gronendijk, *The Family Reunification Directive in EU Member States – The First Year of Implementation* (2007).

[37] Directive 2004/38/EC of the European Parliament and the Council (April 29, 2004) *on the right of citizens of the Union and their family members to move and reside freely within the territory of the member states amending prior Regulations*

[38] Art. 28 defines that before taking an expulsion decision on grounds of public policy or public security, the member state shall take account of consideration such a show long the individual

stating what is the threshold or evaluation method on measuring integration. It also leads to divergent national practices (almost) regardless of non-discrimination rules. The newly introduced right of permanent residence which is almost unconditional and equally available to family members from a third country also offers protection against expulsion stabilising their status and urges integration.[39] Assessments of these national practices are available in comparative research on the implementation of Directive in national legislation. MIPEX is monitoring the access to nationality (married or unmarried) couples and their children, its correlation to family unification policy, the independent legal status of migrant spouses, the principle of family unity in nationality status. How those legal frameworks assist the integration of the first and second generation in practice could be tested systematically.

Implementation of the Race Directive[40] has led to different models without a methodically well-established controlling system. Although this Directive has been the utmost reported by the EUMC,[41] a comprehensive monitoring of the correct application of anti-discrimination legislation at national and union level in the enlarged EU is urged,[42] and special benchmarking terms on nationality law have not defined yet. Since the scope of Directive does not cover discrimination on the ground of nationality, it would be important to evaluate the equality of migrants who have newly acquired the nationality of their country of residence. Indeed all public activities including nationality law and its practice would be directed by the non-discrimination requirement if each Member State ratified the 12th Protocol to ECHR. For instance, ethnic preference means *de facto* disadvantage for all other applicants, and the European Convention on Nationality prohibits ethnic preference. A Proposal for a Council Directive to implement the principle of equal treatment between persons irrespective of religion or belief, disability, age or sexual orientation would extend the protection from discrimination for millions of people across the Union in areas including social security, education and access to public services. It would also send a clear message that

---

concerned has resided on its territory, his/her age, state of health, family and economic situation, social and cultural integration into the host member state and the extent of his/her links to the country or origin.

[39] Iveta Alexovicová, *The Right of Citizens of the Union and their Family Members to Move and Reside Freely within the Territory of the Member States*, in *Migration, Integration and Citizenship* 73–105 (2005).

[40] Council Directive 2000/43/EC (June 29, 2000) *implementing the principle of equal treatment between persons irrespective of racial or ethnic origin.*

[41] The monitoring system is based on (1) national independent body concerning independent investigations [Art. 13(2)], (2) on national report to the Commission in five years period [Art. 17(1)] and (3) EUMC and social partners' opinion [Art. 17(2)].

[42] Judit Tóth, *On the Structural and Methodological Issues in the Field of Fundamental and Minority Rights after the Eastward Enlargement*, 1–12 (2007).

discrimination in many social areas is not only unjust but unacceptable in the contemporary Union.[43] This proposal raises a unified approach and non-fragmented approach to anti-discrimination law and equality that would also impact on integration and the acquisition of nationality. Statistical data collection, the existence of ethnic statistics,[44] bodies and effective sanctions for discriminative actions are different across the EU, which has led the FRA to support "more targeted research here, to cast light on the various structural and social forces that go to determine whether and how ethnic discrimination cases get reported and handled in the 27 Member States."[45]

In line with the Constitutional Treaty, the Lisbon Treaty will set up a Standing Committee on Internal Security (COSI) within the Council. Its main task is to ensure that practical co-operation on internal security is promoted and strengthened within the Union. This facilitated co-ordination among the competent national authorities will be transparent to a limited extent through the transmission of information to the European and national parliaments on the proceedings the COSI.[46] Moreover, maintenance of law and order, including the safeguarding of internal security, will remain the sole responsibility of Member States. The ordinary legislative procedure will apply to judiciary co-operation in criminal matters and issues related to the establishment of minimum rules in criminal law will be subject to the mechanism of "emergency brake" and "enhanced co-operation."[47] Furthermore, the ECJ will not have jurisdiction to review validity and proportionality of operations carried out by the police and other law-enforcement services in Member States or the exercise of the responsibilities incumbent upon Member States with regard to the maintenance of law and order and safeguarding of internal security. All of it means that sovereign regulation and implementation of exclusion from long-term resident status, nationality or its withdrawal on the grounds of public order and national security will remain as diverse in future as it does today.

However, a nexus between immigration, social, cultural, political integration and citizenship has been recognised, formed by various legal solutions and integration programmes in Member States. These national models are described by

---

[43] 3 July 2008, www.equalrightstrust.org.

[44] EP and Council took a decision No.1578/2007/EC, December 11, 2007 on the Community Statistical Programme 2008 to 2012.

[45] European Union Agency for Fundamental Rights, *Annual Report 2007*, 107 (2007).

[46] It is criticised by the Statewatch, *COSI – Standing Committee on Internal Security rescued from the debris of the EU Constitution, Statewatch News Online*, No.34, (September 28, 2005).

[47] Sergio Carrera and Florian Geyer, The Reform Treaty & Justice and Home Affairs – Implications for the Common Area of Freedom, Security & Justice, *CEPS Policy Brief*, No. 141, August 2007.

Table 2: Setting of integration models

At national level	(a) At country-wide regulation and programmes on integration (Netherlands, United Kingdom, Austria, Germany, Denmark, Latvia, France)	(b) At regional/ autonomous competence (Belgium, Spain)	(c) Regulation and programmes are under preparation (Poland, Hungary, Portugal, Italy)	(d) Regulation and programmes do not exist at national or regional level
Components of programmes and regulation	1. mandatory or voluntary to participate on programmes; 2. sanctioned or not (failure, absence from the programmes); 3. integration level is tested/evaluated before reception or not; 4. integration agreement/contract/individual plan is made with migrant or not; 5. personal scope (e.g. family member, all TCN, some groups of TCN); 6. cultural, linguistic or/and social substance of programmes, and 7. transposed minimal rules of Directives or not (fully).			

academics as the multicultural model based on respect for[48] and protection of cultural diversity; the assimilationist model or republican, universalistic model based on formal equality and complete assimilation into the dominant, traditional values and supposed common identity; the separation or exclusionist model based on restrictive, rigid immigration policy aimed at artificially maintaining the temporary character of an immigrant's settlement. Today a new typology is needed. Accordingly there are two (competing) levels of policy: the Union has only soft law and indirect instruments[49] while national legislators and governments have established at least four versions of the integration model, each with varying programme components, personal scopes of regulation, consequences, and commitments vary at the national and sub-national level.

As regards the linkage between integration and citizenship, it is important that some Member States are increasingly conditioning the naturalisation process leading to the acquisition of the nationality, for instance through the requirement to successfully pass an integration test or to possess a long-term resident status based on participation in integration programmes. For this reason deeper analyses have to take into account integration and exclusionary requirements and practice

[48] Sergio Carrera, *A Comparison of Integration Programmes in the EU – Trends and Weakness, Challenge Papers,* No. 1 (March 2006).

[49] Common Basic Principles for Immigrant Integration Policy (Justice and Home Affairs Council's meeting, November 19, 2004) refers on 11 principles in order to assist member states in formulating integration policies (a non-biding guide), further on the Directive on long-term migrants (2003/109/EC), Directive on family unification (2003/86/EC) and Directive on free movement of EU citizen and family member (2004/38/EC) shall be taken into account.

in the context of family reunification, long-term migrants' authorisation and the personal scopes of other Directives concerning migration and free movement. The Commission's *Third Annual Report on Migration and Integration* takes note of the absence of structural initiatives in national strategies that target the host population to reinforce its ability to adjust to diversity. Integration as a two-way process requires further efforts.[50]

C. *Alternatives in Analysis*

From the numerous attempts to analyse and produce comparable knowledge on nationality and integration policy and regulation, only three are mentioned here. "Access to citizenship for immigrants and their descendants is a crucial condition for integration" was observed the comprehensive NATAC project which was based on country reports on trends in nationality legislation on the naturalisation of first, second and third generation, dual nationality, spouses and gender discrimination, ethnic preference, statistics, as well as rules on emigrants, quasi citizens, refugees, union citizens and stateless persons. The report noted the need for a higher level of coordination among Member States and with sending countries. Moreover, the EU must be more active in the field of nationality law in order to – *inter alia* –

(1) Prevent conflict between free movement and nationality law. When national laws provide for a loss of citizenship after some years of residence abroad, Union citizens may lose their status merely because they have taken up their right to live in another Member State. When naturalisation requires a certain period of continuous residence in one Member State, third country nationals who also use their right to move freely within the Union may find their access to nationality blocked. Moreover, a facilitated naturalisation of EU citizens would be supported in another Member State (e.g. such as in Austria, Italy and Hungary).
(2) Ensure the ratification of the European Convention on Nationality by all Member States, which would standardise the maximum residence requirement for naturalisation (ten years) and the prohibition against discrimination based on how persons acquired nationality. However, it would not automatically require a harmonisation of human rights commitments (e.g. Netherlands, Portugal and the United Kingdom do not facilitate the naturalisation of refugees and stateless persons, while Austria and Denmark recently raised the years of residence required for refugees).

[50] Press Release, January 14, 2008.

Beyond the major trends in nationality law trends and recommendations defined in this project, patterns of citizenship and integration policy can be recognised on the basis of the project findings, without giving indicators on successful integration of migrants:[51]

(1) liberalising change (Finland, Luxemburg, Netherlands, Portugal and Sweden),
(2) restrictive continuity (Austria, Denmark, Greece, Italy and Spain),
(3) partial liberalisation with a restrictive backlash (Germany),
(4) citizenship battles in the historically liberal countries (Belgium, France, Ireland and the United Kingdom),
(5) new European frontier (the 12 accession countries).

The justifications for and application of linguistic and integration test has been discussed and examined in another project *Language and Integration Tests for Newcomers and Future Citizens* (2007–2008).[52] Member states' practice can be analysed in comparison to the different models on naturalisation policy (unilaterally/bilaterally liberal, republican or communitarian model).[53] However, the prepared national reports can also provide comparable information on normative solutions, political theory and integration policy that strongly criticises those principles that run counter to equality and human rights commitments or the acceptance of migrants.

Comparable analysis requires statistics on the acquisition and loss of nationality, at least in last decade. In the absence of comparable data from states due to diverse data settings, definitions and availability, we can only see rather vague trends (e.g. naturalisation, re-naturalisation of former nationals, and other forms of acquisition are not disaggregated in each state and the percentage of the foreign-born population/non-nationals as part of the total resident population is not defined in the calendar year in Eurostat statistics). Accordingly in 2000, approximately 645.000 persons acquired nationality in the 27 EU Member States. 43 percent of all citizenships are granted to other Europeans, 24 percent to Asians and 23 percent to Africans. Compared with 1990, in almost every country the ratio of the number of acquisitions of citizenship to the non-national population has increased with exception of Finland and Luxemburg.[54] Can we measure a

[51] Marc Morje Howard, *Varieties of Citizenship in the European Union*, (2009).

[52] *Language and Integration Tests for Newcomers and Future Citizens* – a seminar was hold at Centre for Migration Law (Radboud University, February 15, 2008). A book of papers is under preparation.

[53] Gerald Neuman, *Justifying US Naturalisation Policies, Virginia Journal of International Law*, 35 237–278 (1994).

[54] Eurostat, *Acquisition of citizenship, Statistics in focus – Population and Social Conditions* 1–2 (2004/3).

correlation between citizenship policy and acquisition rate on this ground? Can we evaluate citizenship policy on the basis of how many percentage of foreign population in the given year in average acquires nationality? The dispersion of rates is between 0.4 and over ten or at least over 7.5 in 1997–2005, leading to approximately four scales.

(1) The best practice (in Hungary, the Netherlands, Sweden and Slovakia) includes yearly five to ten percent of foreign population living in the state concerned (stock data).
(2) The second favourable practice of acquisition (in France, Denmark, Belgium, Austria, Finland and UK) means significant oscillation within the yearly average of 3.8 and 4.6 percent. For instance, the year of enlargement caused a setback both in figures and ratio of acquisition of nationality in these states. Naturally this may be explained more by the changing stock of the foreign population than by any amendments of legislation or/and stringent policy.
(3) The less favourable practice (in Poland, Czech Republic, Spain and Germany) provides for a yearly rate between 3.3 and 1.8 percent in which the rate of acquisition was also decreasing in the year 2004.
(4) Finally, the worst practice (in Italy, Portugal and Luxemburg) means a yearly average of below one percent – based solely on outcomes, the chance for migrants to acquire nationality in those countries appears quite limited.

Table 3: Acquisition of nationality (number and ratio of foreign population in stock)[55]

Country	1997	1998	1999	2000	2001	2002	2003	2004	2005
Luxemburg	749	631	549	684	496	754	785	841	966
(0.4%)	(0.5%)	(0.4%)	(0.4%)	(0.4%)	(0.3%)	(0.5%)	(0.5%)	(0.5%)	(0.5%)
Portugal	1 364	519	946	721	1 082	1 369	1 747	1 346	939
(0.6%)	(1.0%)	–	(1.0%)	–	(1.0%)	–	(0.4%)	(0.3%)	(0.2%)
Italy	9 789	12 016	11 335	9 563	10 382	10 685	13 406	11 934	–
(0.8%)	(1.0%)	(1.2%)	(1.0%)	(0.7%)	(0.8%)	(0.7%)	(0.9%)	(0.5%)	
Germany	82 913	106 790	142 670	186 688	178 098	154 547	140 731	127 153	117 241
(1.8%)	(1.1%)	(1.4%)	(2.0%)	(2.5%)	(2.4%)	(2.1%)	(1.9%)	(1.9%)	(1.6%)
Spain	10 311	13 177	16 394	11 999	16 743	21 810	26 556	38 335	42 830
(2.0%)	(1.9%)	(2.2%)	(2.3%)	(1.5%)	(1.9%)	(2.0%)	(2.0%)	(2.3%)	(2.2%)

[55] OECD Statistics November 20, 2007. It covers all means of acquiring the nationality including standard naturalisation procedures, as well as situations where nationality is acquired through a declaration or by option (following marriage, adoption or other situations related to residency or descent), recovery or former nationality and other special means of acquisition. The rate is based the percentage of foreign population in stock at the beginning of the year. In the first column the average of yearly ratio can be seen in bold.

Table 3 (*cont.*)

Country	1997	1998	1999	2000	2001	2002	2003	2004	2005
Czech Republic	–	–	8 107	8 335	6 321	4 532	3 410	5 020	2 626
(2.4%)			(3.7%)	(3.6%)	(3.1%)	(2.1%)	(1.5%)	(2.1%)	(0.9%)
Poland	–	871	1 000	975	766	1 186	1 634	1 937	2 866
(3.3%)		–	–	–	–	–	(3.3%)	–	–
UK	37 010	53 525	54 902	82 210	90 295	120 125	125 535	140 705	161 780
(3.8%)	(1.9%)	(2.6%)	(2.5%)	(3.7%)	(3.9%)	(4.6%)	(4.9%)	(5.1%)	(5.7%)
Finland	1 439	4 017	4 730	2 977	2 720	3 049	4 526	6 880	5 683
(4.0%)	1.8%)	(4.7%)	(5.4%)	(3.3%)	(2.8%)	(2.9%)	(4.3%)	(6.5%)	(5.1%)
Austria	15 792	17 786	24 678	24 320	31 731	36 011	44 694	41 645	34 875
(4.1%)	(2.3%)	(2.6%)	(3.6%)	(3.5%)	(4.4%)	(4.8%)	(5.9%)	(5.4%)	(4.4%)
Belgium	31 687	34 034	24 273	62 082	62 982	46 417	33 709	34 754	31 512
(4.5%)	(3.5%)	(3.8%)	(2.7%)	(6.9%)	(7.3%)	(5.5%)	(4.0 %)	(4.0%)	(3.5%)
Denmark	5 482	10 262	12 416	18 811	11 902	17 300	6 583	14 976	10 197
(4.6%)	(2.3%)	(4.1%)	(4.8%)	(7.3%)	(4.6%)	(6.5%)	(2.5%)	(5.5%)	(3.8%)
France	–	–	147 522	150 026	127 548	128 092	144 640	168 826	154 827
(4.6%)			–	(4.6%)	–	–	–	–	–
Hungary	8 658	6 435	6 066	7 538	8 590	3 369	5 261	5 432	9 822
(5.0%)	(6.1%)	(4.3%)	(4.0%)	(4.9%)	(7.8%)	(2.7%)	(4.5%)	(4.2%)	(6.9%)
Netherlands	59 830	59 170	62 090	49 968	46 667	45 321	28 799	26 173	28 488
(6.6%)	(8.8%)	(8.7%)	(9.4%)	(7.7%)	(7.0%)	(6.6%)	(4.1%)	(3.7%)	(4.1%)
Sweden	28 867	46 502	37 777	43 474	36 397	37 792	33 006	26 769	39 573
(7.5%)	(5.5%)	(8.9%)	(7.6%)	(8.9%)	(7.6%)	(7.9%)	(7.0%)	(5.9%)	(8.2%)
Slovakia	–	–	–	–	–	–	3 492	4 016	1 393
(10.6%)							(11.8%)	(13.8%)	(6.3%)

In summary, (non-comparable) data and statistics on nationality law can hardly capture the diversity of national legislation and practice where times of legislative change are making exceptions to traditional abstract models. The country report system and attempts for statistical analysis has been spread to a great extent by researchers, but a complex system of indicators on citizenship policy and integration of migrants' nexus is still needed. MIPEX intends to amalgam normative and legal practical, comprehensive evaluation but without making direct statistical effects or arguments. Perhaps it follows the principle that the maximal sophisticated analysis is the minimal obvious comparison to policy makers.

D. *Trends and Questions From the Question on the Integration/ Nationality Nexus*

In MIPEX, the acquisition and loss of nationality is based on inclusion and exclusive conditions that were divided into more and more indicators over the past two editions; within three years its number reaches 28. The residence period prior to submission, a clean criminal record for serious offences, and the provision of information and voluntary courses and oaths of allegiance are considered as inclusive factors in the MIPEX normative framework. On the other hand, the slightest spots on criminal records, interruptions in residence, procedural omissions, multiple (second) nationality, fraud or severe disloyalty may lead to exclusion from and or loss of nationality. In an enlarging Europe, we are witnessing a period of securitization and lock-down in nationality law, regardless of whether or not threat to public order by terrorism and migrants is genuine.[56]

The formal requirement for naturalisation is the period of residence prior to submission of an application or declaration. The rationale behind a residence period is based on supposed spontaneous integration and genuine, effective linkage concept that comes from living together with so-called recipients in the host country. This old presumption of spontaneity or automatism is inconsistent with supported inclusion that is measured by applying conditions for acquisition (economic, cultural, communication ability or criminal conditions of applicant) as standardised factor. Why do we require a longer and longer residence period if we trust the measurability and standardisation of the level of integration of the given individual? Can we assume spontaneous integration of migrants living in a ghetto or in a homogeneous, newborn democratic society, or in a recently independent state? For party states to the European Convention on Nationality, the maximum of required period of prior residence shall not be more than ten years, although legislators are innovative in prolonging this period by requiring a settlement/long term residence status and uninterrupted residence. For instance, Hungary, a party state, requires not only a period of residence of eight years, but also possession of a settlement permit that is available for non-facilitated persons after three years. In the party states Slovakia and Czech Republic this rule is five+five, which makes the waiting period – together with time of procedures – over the maximal lawful period of ten years. Poland is not a party state to the Convention and applicants must live in the territory for at least five years as a permanent resident, which means waiting at least ten years before becoming eligible for Polish nationality, while the waiting period is ten years in Slovenia.

---

[56] For instance, the Law on the Bulgarian citizenship (1998) requires six conditions for acquisition of citizenship: full age (18), permanent residence status for at least five years, clear criminal record, having income or activity in Bulgaria, fluency in Bulgarian language and being released or to be released from its present citizenship. Applicants of Bulgarian origin are exempted from all but two requirements: minimum age and clear criminal record & their procedure takes about 3 months (the others 12 months) – as this amendment was adopted in 2001. The number of applicants was growing sharply in 2001–2006 while the number of granted citizenship was rather stable and low (rejection rate meant 75% of applications) but their 90–99% was ethnic Bulgarian. (Angelina Tchorbadjiyska, *Bulgarian Experiences with Visa Policy in the Accession Process: A Story of Visa Lists, Citizenship and Limitations on Citizens' Rights*, Regio 10 88–105 (2007).

It is obvious that regulation opts more frequently to change the preconditions of eligibility (e.g. applicant must be a long-term migrant or to live in marriage) rather than changing the period of residence. The other similar technique is introducing short *period of absence* allowed previous to acquisition of nationality. This period was shorter than half year in 2004 and 2006 in Belgium, Luxemburg, Spain, Sweden, Italy and the United Kingdom while it became more favourable in Austria, Germany and Portugal. The new Member States belong to the stringent regulation group.

Table 4: Residence requirement for naturalisation

Year	Residing period 3 years or less "liberal model"	Between 3–5 years	Over five years "stringent model"	Remark
2007 MIPEX II	Belgium	France, Luxemburg, Ireland, Netherlands, Sweden, UK	Austria, Finland, Greece, Spain, Denmark, Germany, Italy, Portugal, All new Member States	Malta: there is no rule on eligibility with some exceptions Greece: ten years within 20 years prior to submission
Changes since 2004 in country profiles			Portugal	

As regards *facilitated naturalisation for the first generation*, due to the international commitments, colonial past, cultural influence or kin-state or integration policy, we can see not only a diversity of reasons but also an absence of HR mandatory facilitation (in particular for stateless persons and refugees). Who are the facilitated persons? They are for instance:

(1) refugees (Ireland, Hungary, Spain);
(2) stateless persons (Slovenia, Hungary, Malta);
(3) French university graduates (France) or alumni members of university (Slovenia);
(4) spouse of national (Spain, Lithuania, Latvia, Hungary, Italy, France, Cyprus, Austria, Greece if there is a joint child from the marriage) or partner (United Kingdom, Netherlands, Finland, Belgium);
(5) citizens of former colonies (Spain);
(6) ethnic migrant as descendant of an (ex) Hungarian national; or
(7) Nordic citizens (Sweden, Denmark) or EEA nationals (Hungary).

The *second and third generation* born and educated in the host country have to meet slightly different requirements than their parents. Provisions on access to nationality for second and third generations follow *ius soli* providing stable legal basis of integration and a feeling to belong to the mainstream society. However, this benefit may operate similar to the abovementioned presumption ("the longer the residence, the more integrated the migrant") in a liberal society but in a more illiberal environment second and third generation could be brought up in a ghetto. The conditionality of acquisition is growing and growing, which may indicate a lower efficiency of integrative social conditions and of an accepting environment in the overwhelming majority of countries. The liberal model is a vanishing exception – in most cases a positive, receptive environment should not be assumed in the case of the second and third generation living and growing up in the host society.

Table 5: Nationality for second generation of migrants

Year	Access to nationality *ex lege* at birth "liberal model"	Upon request at the age of majority	On the base of further requirements "stringent model"	Remark
2007 MIPEX II	–	Belgium, France, Ireland, Lithuania, Spain, Sweden, United Kingdom	All other Member States	France: the second generation can acquire nationality by declaration in full age as long as they have lived in France for 5 of the past 7 years. Belgium: Since 27 December 2006 adaptations to the Code on Nationality, one parents must be the equivalent of a long-term resident. Ireland: the second generation's citizenship depends upon of their parents, who must have lived legally in territory for at least of 3 of the 4 years preceding their birth.
Changes since 2004 in country profiles	Belgium, Ireland			

Table 6: Nationality for third generation of migrants

Year	Access to nationality *ex lege* at birth "liberal model"	Upon request at the age of majority	On the base of further requirements "stringent model"	Remark
2007 MIPEX II	Belgium, France, Ireland, Portugal	Lithuania, Spain, Sweden, United Kingdom	All other Member States	Since the 17 April 2006 new nationality law, any child born to a parent also born in Portugal and resident at the time of birth is automatically Portuguese.
Changes since 2004 in country profiles			Portugal	

Test and examinations on language ability, knowledge on state structures, the constitution, daily life and holidays, history of the province, the text of the national anthem – all of them intend to grade applicants on whether or not they share the values, habits, language ascribed to the mainstream society. This cultural integration test is increasingly comprehensive and frequently accompanied by high costs, unpublished exam questions, and guides that come at a cost. Moreover, this illiberal practice is spread in nationality laws, projecting a monocultural society. The idea of language act has become popular in last decade, excluding certain persons from the public sector and acquisition procedure for certain statuses.[57] Offering to change the names of naturalised persons after acquisition of nationality in France, Luxemburg or in Hungary may represent a cultural, assimilationist pressure by the majoritarian society. Communication and cultural tests may not necessarily be based on supportive, integration services or an appreciation of an individual applicant's conditions. This (missing) correlation is an important indicator in each Member State as common basis of integration policy, in particular in comparison to the language proficiency required for migrant workers or long-term residents to access education and training.[58]

---

[57] Language usage in trade, public education, administration or in justice determine level and size of language ability of applicants, too for instance by Welsh Language Act (1993), Gaelic Language Act (2005), Language Act in Finland (2003), in Estonia (1999), in Slovakia (1995) or in Poland (1999). See other details in the reports of experts to FMOW, 2006.

[58] Art. 11 (3) 2003/109/EC Directive defines lawful exceptions from equal treatment with nationals.

Table 7: Testing language and other abilities

Year	No language test	Simple language test	High level language test "stringent model"	Remark
2007 MIPEX II	Belgium, Cyprus, Ireland, Italy, Poland, Sweden	Austria, Finland, France, Greece, Hungary, Luxembourg, Malta, Norway, Portugal, Slovakia, Slovenia, Spain, Switzerland, United Kingdom	Czech Republic, Denmark, Estonia, Germany, Latvia, Lithuania, Netherlands	The May 2006 Conference of Interior ministers gave the Laender significant room for manoeuvre in assessing an applicant's knowledge of the German language
Change since 2004 in country profiles		Germany		
	No citizenship test	Simple test on history, culture, constitution	High level test on history, culture, constitution	
2007 MIPEX II	Belgium, Czech Republic, Cyprus, Finland, Ireland, Italy, Luxembourg, Malta, Norway, Poland, Portugal, Slovakia, Slovenia, Sweden	France, Greece, Hungary, Spain, United Kingdom	Austria, Denmark, Estonia, Germany, Latvia, Lithuania, Netherlands, Switzerland	
Change since 2004 in country profiles	Germany, UK	Austria, Portugal		

It is obvious how the testing method is spreading among the Member States, regardless of its inconsistency with the overall citizenship policy, a cost/benefit analysis or its supportive or alienating impact on the integration process.

The other conditions for acquisition which may be interpreted as indicators of 'integration' relate to the economic position of applicants, such as income, possession of assets, social/health insurance and employment. This requirement seems more inclined to exclude poor migrants than to address problems linked to their economic position, such as fragile fundamental rights and limited participation of applicants in community life and democracy. Indeed, this economic test would be necessary given the proper length of residence prior to submission of application together with (effective) integration services and supportive family unification. However, the number of states requiring a high standard of resources is extended recently in countries like Austria, while a further aspect of economic stability appears in requirement of health insurance in France, Italy, Slovenia and Austria, indirectly excluding these long-term residents from social transfers. The self-subsistence of migrants is a basic rationale, but when confronted with the principle of equality in social rights, it sends vague messages on social disintegration, the burdens of reception, and attitudes in receiving society in a wide circle of states. It would be important to compare the conditions as to resources and sickness insurance with those required for long-term migrants[59] in order to recognise what is the meaning of "integration conditions"[60] and how those relate to integration policy in each Member State.

Criminal record requirements in the substance and practice of justice form a less dynamic and more monotonous trend in Member States. Exclusion for endangering public order and security stretches from a clean criminal record (in Hungary) to the violation of administrative rules (Austria) up to severe offences committed by the applicant. The only common point is the technique of closure regulation, as criminal law and penal court system is indeed diverse. Based on European Judicial System (2006), which includes the number of courts per 100,000 inhabitants competent for a robbery trial, it appears that in Austria the figure is 0.19 while in Bulgaria it is 1.87 and in Spain it is 3.45. Clearly there is a quite substantial difference in the perceived need for courts with the type of jurisdiction depending on the Member State. More striking is the comparison of numbers of criminal cases dealt with by public persecutors. According to data (2004) number of first instance criminal cases received by the public prosecutor per 100,000 inhabitants was between 669 (in Latvia) and 16,531 (in Denmark). Clearly, Denmark uses its criminal court system to a much

[59] Art. 5 (1) of 2003/109/EC Directive entitles member states to require evidence that applicants have for themselves and for dependent family members stable and regular resources which are sufficient to maintain the family (over the level of minimum national wages and pension) without resources from the social assistance system, and to have sickness insurance in respect of all risks normally covered for his own nationals in the member state concerned.

[60] "Member States may require third-country nationals to comply with integration conditions, in accordance with national law." Art 5 (2) of 2003/109/EC Directive.

Table 8: Testing economic parameters

Year	No specific resources requirement "liberal"	Certain requirements (minimal income over the social threshold)	High level economic test "stringent model"
2007 MIPEX II	Belgium, Czech Republic, Greece, Luxembourg, Malta, Netherlands, Portugal, Slovakia, Spain, Sweden, United Kingdom	Cyprus, Estonia, Ireland, Latvia, Lithuania, Poland, Slovenia	Austria, Denmark, France, Germany, Hungary, Italy
Change since 2004 in country profiles		Austria, Portugal	
	No health care requirement	Simple health insurance requirement	All health risks shall be covered by insurance
2007 MIPEX II	All other Member States	France, Italy, Slovenia	Austria
Change since 2004 in country profiles	Austria		

greater extent than Latvia. It may illustrate that the role of criminal justice in the regulation of disputes in European states is substantially different, as well as the number of persons who find themselves engaged in criminal court cases. For instance, in Denmark there is a 16 percent chance of an individual being involved as a defendant in a criminal case each year, while in Latvia it is 0.6 percent. The relationship of a society to its criminal justice system is informed by the frequency with which the members of society find themselves engaged with that system. Such a substantial difference indicates quite a different engagement. The relationship between convictions and acquittals also shows significant differences. While Latvia may not bring many people before the criminal courts, it has a low acquittal rate.[61] These brief examples can explain why efforts of approximation in the EU are painful for sovereign national legislation and cannot have a deeper impact on the criminal justice system in each state. Although there is not a unified policing and criminal law, the Reform Treaty introduces significant changes with regard to Union competence on criminal procedure,

[61] Elspeth Guild & Florian Geyer, *The Search for EU Criminal Law – Where is it Headed*? in *Security versus Justice? Ashgate* 12–13 (2008).

Art. 69e (2), which facilitates mutual recognition of judgements.[62] Due to this trans-border effect applicants may be excluded from acquisition or nationality would be withdrawn in another Member States despite of fragmented criminal law. Moreover, increasingly demanding criminal record requirements is a leading trend in nationality law.

Table 9: Criminal record of applicants

Year	Rejection of application for serious crimes as specified in law	and for serious or repeated offences/crimes	and for other offences (threat to public order or security) "stringent model"	Remark
2007 MIPEX II Change since 2004 in country profiles	Luxembourg, Portugal, Sweden France	Belgium, Ireland, Lithuania Germany	All other Member States	Austria: e.g. a three-month prison sentence for fiscal irregularities or serious and repeated violation of administrative regulations, as drink-driving Hungary: clean criminal record by Hungarian law and no ongoing criminal procedure

While Luxemburg and Sweden adopt their own liberal approach, Belgium and Portugal appear less stringent. Yet overall, all other states including the new Member States implement a restrictive interpretation of the criminal record requirement. This convergent trend is accompanied with a rather vague precondition of good character (2006/2007). Austria, Netherlands and Finland seriously screened applicants, while Ireland, Spain, Greece, Latvia, Estonia and France require it without providing clearly defined conditions. A "suitable citizen of Malta" shall be the norm, but an applicant is excluded if his/her "civic conduct is not good

[62] Valsamis Mitsilegas, *Trust-building Measures in the European Judicial Area in Criminal Matters: Issues of Competence, Legitimacy and Inter-institutional Balance*, in *Security versus Freedom? A Challenge for Europe's Future, Ashgate* 279–89 (2006).

enough" in Czech Republic, while in Hungary the applicant's naturalisation "shall not interfere on the interests of the Hungarian Republic", and similarly, a potential Cypriot shall have a good character in a fully conditional procedure based on discretion power of the Council of Ministers. All of these outmoded preconditions are beyond not only the rationale of criminal law rationale but also the principles of the rule of law. Perhaps this trend relates to securitization in which migrants and offenders, terrorists and extremists are all synonyms, in other words of MIPEX, "[in Slovakia] the state does not consider the migrant's personal [conditions], but rather the 'public interest' and 'opinion of public bodies concerned' such as the police."

Limits for withdrawal and refusal belong to the issue of stability and the security of one's legal status. Question on refusal refers to acquisition conditions and thus its linking in the MIPEX with withdrawal is not useful. On the other hand, both may demonstrate Member States' interpretation with respect to the threat to public order. In the following table the changed answer-options perhaps make the ranking a bit more understandable. Furthermore, withdrawal of nationality could be categorised in the MIPEX based on whether or not it excludes cases that would lead to statelessness and provides an effective legal remedy.

It is obvious that the reasons for withdrawal are many and this long list is attractive for many states. Although the European Convention on Nationality accepts numerous grounds including severe disloyalty, protection against statelessness shall be ensured among the general prohibitions against sovereign decisions on withdrawal/loss of nationality. It is somehow – explicitly or after certain years of acquisition – provided in Slovenia, Poland, France, Denmark, Sweden, France, Finland, Belgium, Ireland, Netherlands, Portugal, UK, Czech Republic, Spain and Hungary (2006/2007).[63] Yet if transparent procedure and effective legal remedy is applicable – the requirements of rule of law and trust of migrants on legal system should be guaranteed. These conditions are fully provided only in Czech Republic, Belgium, United Kingdom, and Sweden. The list of all relevant factors taken into account before withdrawal is determined on an individual basis (personal behaviour, age, length of residence, personal and family consequences, genuine links to host country and of origin, alternative measures) and right to appeal and representation at independent authority as well as obligation of reasoning is also regulated (2006/2007). The majority of states provide legal remedy but neither the reasons of refusal or withdrawal are

[63] Acquisition of Hungarian nationality can be based on presumption which is reversible (e.g. identity of the parent of unknown, abandoned child who was considered *ex lege* Hungarian national from the moment his/her found in the country, but as far as parent's identity becomes clear, child is ceased *ex lege* to be considered as national regardless his/her age, length of residence and good faith. Is it a withdrawal? Formally not, it is a case of loss but s/he is not protected against statelessness in an individual procedure. Examples on legal peculiarities may not be continued in trap of simplification.

Table 10: Refusal and withdrawal for public order

Year	Refusal of the acquisition or withdrawal of status in case of proven fraud	...and for serious threat to public security	...and for other reasons "stringent model"	Remark
2007 MIPEX II	Hungary, Netherlands, Poland	Denmark, Slovenia, Spain, Sweden	All other Member States	Belgium – withdrawal is possible if s/he fails accomplish the citizen's obligations regardless of how many years s/he has been a Belgian national
Changes since 2004 in country profiles	Sweden	United Kingdom		Czech Republic, Poland – on the ground of refusal belongs to the first group but withdrawal of naturalisation is not possible Finland, Hungary, Spain – withdrawal after 5/10/many years is excluded

required, nor are the various aspects taken into account by the determining authorities. In this respect, the rule of law is an empty formality. For this reason numerous guarantees have to be developed in the majority of Member States despite the existence of partial procedural structures.

Furthermore, the reasons for the refusal or withdrawal of nationality on public order grounds should be consistent with ones for long-term migrants inside a comprehensive integration policy and national laws. For instance, rejection or loss of nationality shall be based on a more severe public security threat or risk than for long-term migrant status authorisation,[64] and its reasoning and remedy guarantees must be in harmony with one another.

---

[64] Art. 17 of 2003/109/EC Directive.

The procedure of acquisition may express a symbolic and pragmatic feature of inclusion or exclusion. These rules cover the length of the application procedure. In 2004 the question asked about the time in practice and all states were found to take more than nine months to finish the procedure in practice. In 2006/2007 the question followed the rationale of sovereign authorisation and found that there is no regulation on maximum length at all in Finland, Greece, Luxemburg, Spain, Belgium, Ireland, Denmark, Germany, United Kingdom, Hungary, Malta, Cyprus and Estonia. It is in contradiction with eligibility conditions of long period of residence in many states because data on applicant are available in big files that may lead to a faster decision. If an applicant meets a long list of requirements, s/he can in a fairly short period acquire Latvian nationality, which is similarly to the period not exceeding six months found in the Czech Republic, Lithuania, Portugal, the Netherlands, and Slovenia.

The cost of procedure includes the fee of application, expenditures related to obtaining certain documents and recently the price of (language, cultural, constitutional) test. In 2004, only France and Luxemburg indicated the best practice without significant charges, while up to 2006 Luxemburg remained alone in the enlarged EU. That said, there are some examples on reducing costs: in 2007 Portugal lifted up fees but applicants who can prove an income equal or less than the national minimum wage fees are waived; the fee of constitutional exam was reduced to twenty euros in Hungary. In the cost/benefit analysis, the position of the acquisition of nationality is gradually deteriorating; it is consuming more time and money while prerogatives reserved for nationals are dissolving due to the rights linked with long-term residence.

But the moral and communitarian value of nationality are strengthening through the recent development of naturalisation ceremonies, oaths, and declarations. From a normative point of view, validity of authorisation may involve an oath of allegiance declaring loyalty of accepted new member to national community and state without much formality or other obligations. While some Member States have developed leaflets, solemn and voluntary regulations for an oath at the City Hall, videos on Dutch citizenship or French values of Republic[65] – the new Member States in nation-building epoch represent the best practice in this field by not making the granting of nationality contingent upon ceremony attendance. The normative relevance of this loyalty declaration has worn away but its formality or ceremonial character means a revival of identity—that is, if it does not involve exclusionary requirements from participating or receiving citizenship. Absence from the mandatory Naturalisation Day ceremony applicant

[65] Devenir Francais – Film pour les ceremonies d'accueil dans la citoyenneté francaise (2007).

can lead to refusal in the Netherlands. Obligatory participation in citizenship ceremonies was also introduced in Denmark and Greece.

The level of tolerance to multiple nationality is related to naturalisation conditions and the nationality rights of children born on the territory to a third country national. While the trend of naturalisation (of first generation of migrants) has moved toward toleration (there are more countries that openly or through the growing circle of exceptions respect for dual ties) – the second generation born in the territory are not widely accepted as dual nationals upon birth. Numerous European born children most often face unfavourable requirements for becoming citizens of their country of birth. Few countries fully allow migrants to hold dual nationality. Furthermore, this phenomenon is stable in numerous countries including new Member States in the period of nation building.

Table 11: Dual nationality

Year	Tolerated dual nationality in law "liberal model"	Required but exceptions are provided (renunciation is not allowed, long process or expensive)	Renounce/lose foreign nationality is required to naturalisation "stringent model"	Remark
2007 MIPEX II	Belgium, Cyprus, Finland, France, Greece, Hungary, Ireland, Malta, Portugal, Slovakia, United Kingdom	Austria, Czech Republic, Denmark, Germany, Latvia, Netherlands, Norway, Poland, Slovenia, Sweden	Estonia, Italy, Lithuania, Luxembourg, Spain	Austria, Slovenia, Czech Republic, Spain – strict exceptions Poland – discretion power

However, this indicator is unclear since it may overlap with whether or not *ius soli* is provided for child born in the country from a third-country national or his/her dual nationality is tolerated. For instance, Germany tolerates acquisition under heavy conditions while Hungary tolerates it *ex lege*. But *ius soli* as a legal basis for acquisition of third country national's child born in Hungary is provided *ex lege* only for stateless, the children of settled migrants and those abandoned children found on the territory. The latter meaning is overlapping with indicator of eligibility of second generation, suggesting possible modification in further MIPEX editions.

Table 12: Dual nationality for child

Year	Duel nationality for child of third-country national born in the country is provided *ex lege* at birth "liberal model"	is provided under conditions (born in wedlock or acquired by *ius soli*)	Dual nationality for child of third-country national born in the country is excluded "stringent model"
2007 MIPEX II	Belgium, France, Ireland, Netherlands, Portugal, United Kingdom	Germany, Italy, Slovakia, Spain, Sweden	Austria, Czech Republic, Cyprus, Denmark, Estonia, Finland, Greece, Hungary, Latvia, Lithuania, Luxembourg, Malta, Poland, Slovenia

In summary, a slow progress can be seen in the EU on the acceptance of dual nationality in naturalisation and the acquisition of nationality by the second generation. But this policy is not able to keep pace with the dynamics and needs of a proactive multiple nationality brought on by increasing net migration and the movement of family members, leading to more mixed couples, children born in dual nationality, and applicants with double ties. The growing numbers of those with a dual identity is a social-cultural fact in Europe, but nationality law requires a longer space of time to absorb this phenomenon.

E. *Conclusions*

Nationality law has been in flux; although the legislation on the acquisition and loss of nationality belongs to traditional sovereignty of nation states, its rules and practice are gradually losing their customary diversity in Europe. Regulation and citizenship policy can be grouping together due to external (normative) pressure and internal stakeholders' games. These slightly convergent and altering groups of liberal, partly liberal or stringent models of states on any given indicator are strongly influenced by the following factors:

(1) Whether European states become party states to human rights obligations concerning the acquisition and loss of nationality; how they transpose these obligations into national(ity) law; and whether they are serious about their commitment. In particular, one should take into account the European Convention on Nationality, the Convention on Refugees, on the Status of Stateless Persons and Child's Rights.

(2) Although the Union has no legislative competence on the acquisition and loss of nationality, Union citizenship, the right to free movement, the minimal rules on third country nationals' status can effectively influence nationality law, and the right to mobility in the Union urges a stronger co-operation among Member States on citizenship policy.
(3) There are more and more persons with dual nationality, and increased international migration is pressuring states to tolerate multiple ties and liberalise nationality laws in favour of the second and third generation as well as the great emigrant communities in sending countries. Europe plays dual roles as sending and receiving countries, thus Diaspora and migrant communities are influential on the implementation (and accession to) political rights and general elections as inherent part of citizenship. In this way nationality legislation and citizenship policy have undergone dramatic changes in the last decade faced with inconsistencies with integration, identity and kin-state policy.
(4) Enlargement of the Union has made these changes and inconsistencies more visible due to the ongoing national, democratic and rule of law building that goes on in parallel. Despite these common features, the new Member States have diverse nationality laws.
(5) A systematic monitoring on legal non-discrimination policy would be improved on acquisition and loss of nationality in which there are numerous preferences on the grounds of ethnicity, origin and language – beyond the human rights mandatory facilitation of refugees, stateless persons and minors – that violates the respect for diversity, equality and civic citizenship. Who are we? Who are they? Are migrants potential terrorists, offenders, a labour force, taxpayers, service providers, a demographic benefit or only colours in the European patchwork? Do we have to wait for a constitutional patriotism[66] – as in United States – after the failure of the European Constitution that may unify us in diversity? In Europe there is an identity crisis and security crisis, and citizenship policies are challenged by both of them.

MIPEX as a comprehensive analysis method on impacts of various nationality legislations may assist us to understand whether citizenship policies are based on equality, non-discrimination, and the respect for social cohesion, in the face of the growing diversity of populations and cultures and the pressure towards securitisation. Just as the diverse policies on the acquisition of nationality and its legal practice can be interpreted in terms of a goal or/and tool for migrants becoming integrated citizens, it can also be seen as a parallel indicator of social

[66] Samuel Huntington, *Who Are We? The Challenges to America's National Identity*, (Simon & Schuster, 2004).

Table 13: Integration policy score (in scale 1–100) of 25 Member States in 2007

Overall rankings across 6 strands	%	Long-term residence	%	Access to nationality	%	Diff. %
Sweden	88	Sweden	76	Sweden	71	– 5
Portugal	79	Belgium	74	Belgium	71	– 3
Belgium	69	Spain	70	Portugal	69	+ 2
Netherlands	68	United Kingdom	67	United Kingdom	62	– 5
Finland	67	Portugal	67	Ireland	62	+ 23
Italy	65	Poland	67	France	54	+ 6
United Kingdom	63	Italy	67	Netherlands	51	– 15
Spain	61	Denmark	67	Czech Republic	50	– 13
Slovenia	55	Netherlands	66	Poland	45	– 22
France	55	Malta	65	Luxemburg	45	– 3
Luxemburg	55	Finland	65	Finland	44	– 21
Germany	53	Slovenia	63	Slovenia	41	– 22
Ireland	53	Czech Republic	63	Spain	41	– 29
Hungary	48	Estonia	61	Slovakia	40	– 11
Czech Republic	48	Greece	60	Lithuania	38	– 9
Estonia	46	Austria	55	Germany	38	– 15
Lithuania	45	Germany	53	Hungary	36	– 14
Poland	44	Slovakia	51	Cyprus	36	– 11
Denmark	44	Latvia	51	Italy	33	– 34
Malta	41	Hungary	50	Denmark	33	– 34
Slovakia	40	Luxemburg	48	Malta	29	– 34
Greece	40	France	48	Estonia	26	– 35
Austria	39	Cyprus	47	Latvia	25	– 26
Cyprus	39	Lithuania	47	Greece	25	– 35
Latvia	30	Ireland	39	Austria	22	– 33
Distance:	58	Distance:	37	Distance:	49	

cohesion and the identity of the receiving community. As Table 13 indicates, the distance from the best to the worst in acquisition of nationality is in between the long-term residence conditions and the aggregated integration analysis based on six strands. However, the difference in score within nationality policy is great. The group of best countries in integration policy on the three aspects is really limited and geographically crosses the North-South axis in the Union. Access to nationality scores similar to Long-term residence – as a possible basis for acquisition conditions and policy – only in France, Portugal, United Kingdom, Belgium, Sweden and Luxemburg. Nationality is much more attractive in

Ireland, while it is significantly worse than the long-term residence score in all other countries. It means that in majority of Member States (21 countries) the conditions for acquiring nationality are autonomous of and more restrictive than those on obtaining long-term resident status, which would contain normative requirements on integration. We can conclude that European denizen status is considered as half-way integration in the majority of states that presume that it is the acquisition of nationality that can contribute to deeper integration. However, this rationale has not been justified, and citizenship policy belongs to reservoir of sovereignty of many states. There are numerous examples how the citizenship policy is involved into political games in order to maximise votes including ones from the pro-migration and public order supporters, Diaspora members and migrant communities.[67] For this reason any inconsistency of long-term residence and acquisition of nationality policy might be limited in future.

The EU has strong regulative instruments to influence convergent citizenship policies in Member States. But there is an equal chance that it will strengthen the liberal democratic model or spread exclusionary solutions that preserve the conditionality of residence. MIPEX indicators can test the dynamics of citizenship policy through repetitions of evaluation of Member State scores within a broader context of EC law, Union programmes, and its contribution to human mobility.

[67] Judit Tóth, *Is it Possible to Regulate Citizenship by Referendum? Minorities Research*, 9 88–121 (2007).

Chapter 8

Policies and "Outcomes" for Third Country Nationals in Europe's Labour Markets

Andrew Geddes and Daniel Wunderlich

A. *Introduction*

The Migrant Integration Policy Index (MIPEX) focuses on indicators of policy integration, but in this chapter we give some consideration to what happens "on the ground" in terms, particularly of the labour market position of the EU's third country national (TCN) population. This focus on the labour market situation could be seen as indicative of a relationship between the policies mapped by MIPEX and "outcomes," such as employment and unemployment levels. We argue that such reasoning would be too simplistic. The relationship between policy and outcomes does actually disguise a complex set of relationships that centre on the making of policy and the multiple factors that intervene in the relationship between immigrant integration policy frameworks across the EU and outcomes that may or may not be a consequence of these policies.

We begin by exploring the relationship between immigrant integration policies and the contextual data that we present in this chapter. We then move on to explore the main strands of thinking within the academic literature on the diffusion and impact of international standards and norms on domestic political systems. We pay particular attention to the concept of "Europeanisation" and explore the various ways in which the EU can "hit home" in domestic politics. We then proceed to provide extensive data on the labour market position of Europe's TCN population. We see that some of the countries that perform well in terms of policy frameworks and adaptation to EU law and standards actually perform less well when we explore the labour market position of TCNs.

As a background to the data that we present, it should be noted that data concerning the labour market situation of TCNs can be difficult to gather because of data gaps and a continued inability/reluctance by some states to collect this data. For example, data on the labour market situation of TCNs in Italy is only available at regional level, which makes it difficult to assess the national picture. The European Commission is aware of the need for more specific and reliable information to support EU policies. An EU Regulation has been proposed to tackle difficulties arising from incoherent methods of data collection in the member states and obliging them to collect comparable data also on the labour market status of TCNs (European Commission, 2005).

Different states can have different methods of collecting data, but more than this, they can have different understandings of what type of data should be collected. So, for example, in France there is an engrained hostility to the collection of data that refers to the ethnic origin of migrants. This contrasts markedly with the situation in countries such as the United Kingdom and Netherlands where such data are collected systematically. There is also significant temporal variation here because nationality laws differ across the EU, so it is possible that TCNs can include new migrants and long-term settled 2nd or 3rd generation while the TCN population does not include "ethnic minorities" whose origins lie in immigration, but that have become citizens. The strength of the MIPEX project is its scope and ambition. The data gaps are not the fault of the project. Rather they can be viewed as a result of a "politics of statistics" on immigrant populations and are therefore issues that need to be considered if we are to develop a fully understanding of the effects of EU action.

B. *Policy and Outcomes*

While we assume that immigrant integration policy makes a difference to the lives of Europe's migrant populations, we are also aware that there are a wide range of other factors linked, for example, to the more general organisational characteristics of labour markets and welfare systems that are not ostensibly linked to immigrant integration and that make a difference too.

This leads us to consider the relationship between policy and outcomes. It may be that immigrant integration policies lead to certain kinds of outcomes – whether positive or negative – for migrant populations. They may, for instance, facilitate labour market access, they may combat discrimination or they may provide new resources for mobilisation by pro-migrant groups. It may also be the case that so-called outcomes also generate certain types of policy. To illustrate this point, the current strong emphasis on socio-economic integration and linguistic adaptation by immigrant newcomers can be understood as a response to a perception that previous "multicultural" policies have "failed" (Brubaker, 2001).

This then raises the issue of whether policies "succeed" or "fail" and how we would assess success or failure (Castles, 2003). On this point about "policy failure" our analysis also needs to be nuanced, because it is too crude to talk about policy success or failure as though these can be identified in such simple, dichotomous terms. It is likely that the pay-off structures of success and failure or the identification of winners and losers is far more complex than simple binary dichotomies. This is because the policy process encompasses various stages of debate, design, decision-making and implementation with feedback loops at all stages. Bearing in mind the complexities of the policy process, it is not unlikely that normative assessments of policy failure disguise the ways in which some political actors may view the generated policy outcome as policy success. An example may clarify this point. If migrants are excluded from legal routes to labour market access or encounter the non-recognition of their qualifications then these factors can contribute to the growth of an unregulated and therefore cheap labour supply of irregular migrant workers and can exert pressure on lower waged employment.

We also need to note that policy implementation does not entail the direct translation of policy in a simple, linear fashion. Research has shown that it is not helpful to picture implementation as a top-down process fully controllable from above (Gunn, 1978, Pressman and Wildavsky, 1984) but that it should be rather understood as a "policy-action relationship" (Barrett and Fudge, 1981). In fact, it may well also be the case that policy-making and implementation follow different logics and may have little to do with each other (Brunsson, 1989). By this is meant that policy-makers need to respond to multiple and possibly contradicting demands that feed into policy decisions. From the perspective of those upon whom implementation depends, putting decisions into practice may only be partially feasible. "Street-level bureaucrats" face additional challenges that stem from the immediate environment with which they must deal and which may not have been part of the calculations made by policy-makers when they made decisions about the scope and direction of policy (Lipsky, 1971). The overall result is that policies may affect outcomes, but outcomes may also affect policies. The structure of pay-offs is likely to be complex because of the nature of this process, the variety of actors involved in it and complex loops and feedback processes within it.

The analytical status of immigrant integration policies developed at EU level such as the anti-discrimination, long-term residents and family reunion directives also needs to be specified. We cannot assume that these measures are independent variables that we then use to explain the dependent variables, i.e. the levels of TCN integration. Indeed, a linear causal relationship would be a particularly heroic assumption in a volatile and complex social environment. This becomes apparent when we analyse policy development at national level and assess the impact of international standards in an area of policy such as immigrant integration where national frameworks have been viewed as paradigmatic (Geddes and Guiraudon, 2004) and where tendencies towards "methodological nationalism" have been identified (Wimmer and Glick Schiller, 2002). Moreover, we need to bear in mind that immigrant integration outcomes need not be the result of immigrant integration policies because, if we look at the labour market situation of immigrant populations in the EU, then it is easy to see that the organisation of work and welfare are key structural factors that shape the immigrant integration framework. By this is meant that a range of policy interventions in the arenas of employment and welfare have an impact on migrants, but are not specifically targeted towards migrants. Conversely, policy interventions that promise a positive effect on migrant integration may have to take place at a level that affects a broader range of people than the original target group bringing about the potential for unintended consequences that could be undesirable for policy makers and implementers. There is also significant cross-national variation. Whether a state has liberal, social democratic or corporatist labour market/welfare state structures will make an important difference to the settings within which immigrant integration policy is made. Immigration is a component of debates about European labour markets and welfare state change, but it is not the driver of these debates. This would suggest that we need to bear in mind diverse forms of labour market and welfare state organisation across the EU (Bommes and Geddes, 2000).

As already noted, the academic literature on immigrant integration often emphasises that national policy frameworks embedded within well-established ways of doing things and with significant sub-national dynamics – at city level, for example – are the key drivers of immigrant integration. The scope, impact and diffusion of supranational and international standards and norms are a relatively new dimension to analysis of immigrant integration.

C. *The Scope for Europeanisation*

The MIPEX project explores the impact of EU legislation and other international norms of migrant inclusion such as those propagated by the Council of Europe on domestic immigrant integration policies. At the base of the MIPEX scale are indicators derived from legally binding EC Directives and Council of Europe Conventions as minimum standards as well as more progressive standards from input of EC Presidency Conclusions, Commission legislative proposals, civil society input within the EU environment and recommendations from the EU's Lisbon strategy for economic reform. The focus is thus on the impact of international standards on domestic policies and practices.

This important theme has been the focus of a strand of work within the academic literature on immigrant integration that emphasises the impact of "global" factors and stresses the growing importance of the "post-national." The emphasis within this work is on the view that states are in some sense "losing control" (Sassen, 1996) of key international processes such as international migration and that the sovereign authority of states may be on the verge of becoming irrelevant or redundant in face of these international developments (Soysal, 1994). These global processes can be understood as a process, a discursive practice or as an imaginary (Sassen, 2007), but in all these forms it fundamentally challenges states as "population containers." (Taylor, 1994) Others criticise this post-national view by arguing that rather than states being externally constrained by international factors, the constraints that bind liberal states with regards to the rights of migrants are, in fact, internal components of the self identity as these states *qua* liberal states, i.e. the international system is an external expression of the identities of liberal states not an external constraint upon them (Freeman, 1998, Joppke, 1998, Guiraudon, 1998).

An additional criticism could be that these 'international' perspectives on loss of control and post-national membership can neglect the specificities of regional integration, i.e. the EU as a unique form of supranational governance at a level less than the global and based on geographical proximity and some sense of shared political identity. The EU is unique amongst international organisations because it possesses the capacity through its own institutional system to turn treaties between states into laws that bind those states (Sandholtz and Stone Sweet, 1997). Even in those environments where no legally binding measures have been created as in the case of labour market policy, the Lisbon strategy with its open method of coordination has generated norms of best practise. Similarly contributions of civil society actors and stakeholder to discussions at EU level can frame the policy setting in which regulations and interventions are being planned. In the field of migration politics, it has been argued that states have developed forms of co-operation and policy integration at EU level as a way of resolving domestic immigration policy dilemmas rather than, in some sense, "surrendering" their sovereign authority (Geddes, 2003, Geddes, 2008). Again, this would imply that regional integration within the EU is not an external imposition upon European states, but has been consciously created by those states to further their interests. What may then happen, however, is that, over time, states do lose some control over the scope and development of the EU because once power has been ceded to new institutions at EU level, it is unlikely to be recovered and unintended consequences may arise. Moreover, the pursuit of interests can be difficult in an EU of 27 states where complex negotiation, bargaining and deliberation occurs across a wide range of issues in a multi-level system (Bache and Flinders, 2004).

The MIPEX project is concerned with what could be called the post-ontological phase of EU development, i.e. the diffusion of ideas and policy practices into member states, but bearing in mind that these EU-level developments stem from agreements amongst member states. The research literature on the impact of European integration tells us that the form taken by EU action and the mode of governance in the respective policy field can make a difference (Knill and Lehmkuhl, 1999, Bulmer and Radaelli, 2004). By this is meant that the EU may have direct effects when member states agree to laws in the form of directives or regulations that have direct effect. The EU may also have "softer" effects when it creates scope for new forms of mobilisation, for instance by providing funding for pro-migrant organisations or initiating processes of benchmarking and standards-setting. Such action can then reframe political opportunities at domestic level by creating scope for new mobilisations at domestic level that draw from EU laws and resources. Another important strand of work within the Europeanisation literature emphasises the importance of national gatekeepers who mediate the relationship between the EU and the domestic polity. This may be in the form of particularly powerful NGOs with resources such as membership, financial backing and/or connections with government. The research literature also tells us that when adaptation to the requirements of European integration occurs then it tends to be with "national colours," (Cowles et al., 2001) i.e. that the effects of European integration are channelled by domestic politics. This means that it is probably not appropriate to see the development of EU action in the area of immigrant integration as the movement towards a common model and single understanding. Rather, we see an overarching legal framework and recommendations that can then work its way into national practices and change them, but with distinct elements of the national debate likely to remain prominent.

D. *The Labour Market Situation of Third Country Nationals*

1. *Employment Rates*

Initially, we present data on employment rates for different population groups within Europe. The employment-to-population ratio indicates a country's ability to provide work to working-age TCNs. Table 1 presents the employment rates for nationals, TCNs and citizens of other EU states. The data then is presented in map form (Map 1) in order to facilitate comparison and to show underlying patterns of the labour market situation of TCNs in their respective host countries in a cross-national context.

Map 1, below, shows differences between the employment rates of nationals and TCNs (absolute gap). When the absolute gap shows a positive value, this means that the percentage of employed TCNs out of all working age non-EU nationals in that country is higher than that of the respective citizens of their host countries. In other words, more non-EU nationals between 15 and 64 participate in economic activities than their national counterparts (blue areas). The opposite holds true if the displayed value is negative (red areas).

Table 1: TCN Employment rates

	total	Nationals	non-EU 25 nationals (TCNs)	other EU 25 nationals	relative gap
Austria	70.0	70.8	59.6	72.7	0.8
Belgium	60.4	61.5	33.1	56.5	0.5
Cyprus	69.5	69.0	78.3	66.1	1.1
Czech Republic	65.3	65.2	74.5	75.4	1.1
Denmark	76.9	77.3	65.0	77.7	0.8
Estonia	68.8	68.7	69.1	x	1.0
Finland	69.9	70.2	48.0	71.7	0.7
France	63.0	63.8	42.9	65.5	0.7
Germany	67.0	68.5	47.9	66.5	0.7
Greece	61.0	60.6	70.8	51.3	1.2
Hungary	57.3	57.3	61.1	56.5	1.1
Ireland*	59.8	58.9	58.6	74.8	1.0
Italy**	58.4	57.9	52.9	53.9	0.9
Latvia	65.5	65.4	74.4	x	1.1
Lithuania	63.7	63.6	77.6	x	1.2
Luxembourg	63.6	60.9	47.3	69.1	0.8
Malta	54.3	54.3	46.9	68.2	0.9
Netherlands	74.2	75.0	46.6	74.0	0.6
Norway	75.3	75.5	56.9	83.0	0.8
Poland	53.9	54.0	47.7	41.3	0.9
Portugal	68.1	68.0	72.6	68.7	1.1
Slovakia	59.3	59.2	x	95.7	x
Slovenia	67.2	67.2	57.1	x	0.9
Spain	64.7	63.9	71.9	64.3	1.1
Sweden	73.1	74.0	46.4	71.4	0.6
Switzerland†	77.2	78.7	64.3	77.9	0.8
U.K.	71.3	71.7	62.3	74.1	0.9
EU 25	52.5	53.3	54.2	58.4	1.0

Data second quarter 2006, European Labour Force Survey, EUROSTAT
relative gap = quotient of value for non-EU 25 nationals over the value for nationals
x = no data available
* based on Central Statistics Office Ireland, Quarterly National Household Survey
** annual data based on National Institute of Statistics (Istat), Annual Report 2006
† based on second quarter 2005

When looking at the data, the most obvious conclusion that can be drawn is that the employment situation of TCNs is worse than that of nationals in the majority of European countries. Only in a few new immigration countries in southern and central Europe is this situation reversed.

When analysing data values for the absolute gap between the employment rates of nationals and TCNs, there are only two countries which show equal rates for nationals and non-EU nationals (Estonia and Ireland). We find the largest

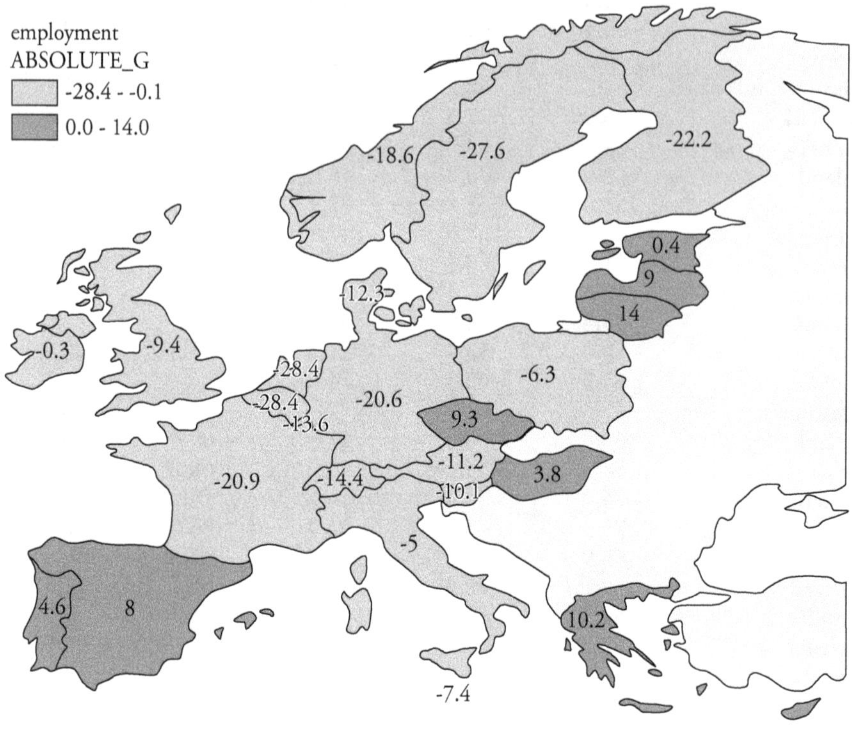

Employment Rates: Absolute Gap between Nationals and Third Country Nationals (%), Quarter 2, 2006 (Switzerland quarter 2, 2005)

Map 1: Absolute gap between employment rates of nationals and third country nationals

gaps of around 20 percentage points in employment rates to be concentrated in Central European and Scandinavian countries where TCNs have lower employment rates than in other European states. A group of countries which perform slightly better in this respect are those with an absolute gap in employment rates of between ten and fifteen percentage points (Austria, Denmark, Poland, Slovenia, Switzerland, and the United Kingdom).

In general terms, older immigration countries of immigration seem to find it more considerably more difficult to provide employment opportunities to their non-EU populations than is the case in newer immigration countries. This does not, of course, say anything about the types of employment, wage levels and labour conditions that non-EU nationals find in their respective host countries nor of the impact of social welfare provisions on the non-working groups amongst the working-age population.

This trend can be described in a more nuanced way when reminding ourselves of the last column of Table 1 (above). In order to make our cross-country comparison independent of each country's economic performance, we calculated the relative gap between employment rates for TCNs and nationals. The ratio describes the likelihood of being in employment as a working-age non-EU national in comparison to someone of the equivalent national population. More than half of all the countries shown in Table 1 are equally successful in bringing their TCN as well as their national populations into employment (14 out of 27 countries with ratios between 0.9 and 1.1). Particularly successful are Lithuania and Greece. Eight countries are less successful (again mostly Central European and Scandinavian countries as well as France). Particularly bad performers in this respect are Belgium, the Netherlands and Sweden. In the Belgian case, only half as many non-EU nationals participate in the labour market when compared to Belgian citizens.

2. *Unemployment Rates*

The unemployment rate indicates the number of those people that are actively seeking employment and unable to find it. Those people that feel discouraged from registering as unemployed do not figure and are only implicitly discernible in the employment rate (see previous section).

Map 2 is derived from Table 2 to show unemployment rates on the base of the absolute gap between unemployment rates of TCNs and national citizens of the host country.

Areas in blue are where differences in unemployment rates between TCNs and the national population are greater than zero. Apart from Greece and the Czech Republic, such incidences seem to occur in all European countries. However, the degree to which this happens differs considerably. While newer immigration

Table 2: Unemployment rates

	total	National	TCNs	other EU 25	relative gap
Austria	4.8	4.2	11.7	6.6	2.8
Belgium	8.4	7.6	32.4	11.1	4.3
Cyprus	4.2	4.1	4.6	4.9	1.1
Czech Republic	7.1	7.1	6.4	4.3	0.9
Denmark	4.0	3.9	12.2	x	3.1
Estonia	6.3	5.5	10.3	x	1.9
Finland	9.0	8.8	29.2	x	3.3
France	8.8	8.3	23.2	8.0	2.8
Germany	10.4	9.5	23.0	11.7	2.4
Greece	8.9	9.0	7.4	x	0.8
Hungary*	7.5	7.5	10.8	0.5	1.4
Ireland**	4.3	4.1	8.1	5.9	2.0
Luxembourg	4.7	3.1	21.1	5.6	6.8
Netherlands	3.9	3.7	12.2	4.5	3.3
Norway	4.0	3.8	13.1	x	3.4
Portugal	7.7	7.6	10.4	x	1.4
Spain	8.6	8.1	12.2	10.5	1.5
Sweden	8.1	7.8	22.9	8.5	2.9
Switzerland†	4.5	3.3	14.1	5.5	4.3
U.K.	5.4	5.1	9.8	6.2	1.9
EU 25	6.4	6.5	18.5	10.2	2.8

Data second quarter 2006, European Labour Force Survey, EUROSTAT
absolute gap = difference of value for non-EU 25 nationals and nationals
relative gap = quotient of value for non-EU 25 nationals over the value for nationals
x = no data available
* based on fourth quarter 2006
** based on Central Statistics Office Ireland, Quarterly National Household Survey
† based on second quarter 2005

countries of Central Eastern Europe, the Mediterranean and Ireland show relatively low differences in unemployment rates between TCNs and nationals, the picture for older countries of immigration varies considerably. In this group, the United Kingdom is a clear outlier where non-EU job seekers experience similarly high levels of employment as in newer countries of immigration. Among the rest of the older immigration countries, two groups are discernible. In Austria, Denmark, the Netherlands, Norway and Switzerland, TCNs have an unemployment rate which is between 7.5 and 10.8 percentage points points higher than that of nationals. In the labour markets of France, Germany, and Sweden and particularly in Belgium, Finland, and Luxembourg, TCNs experience high levels of unemployment.

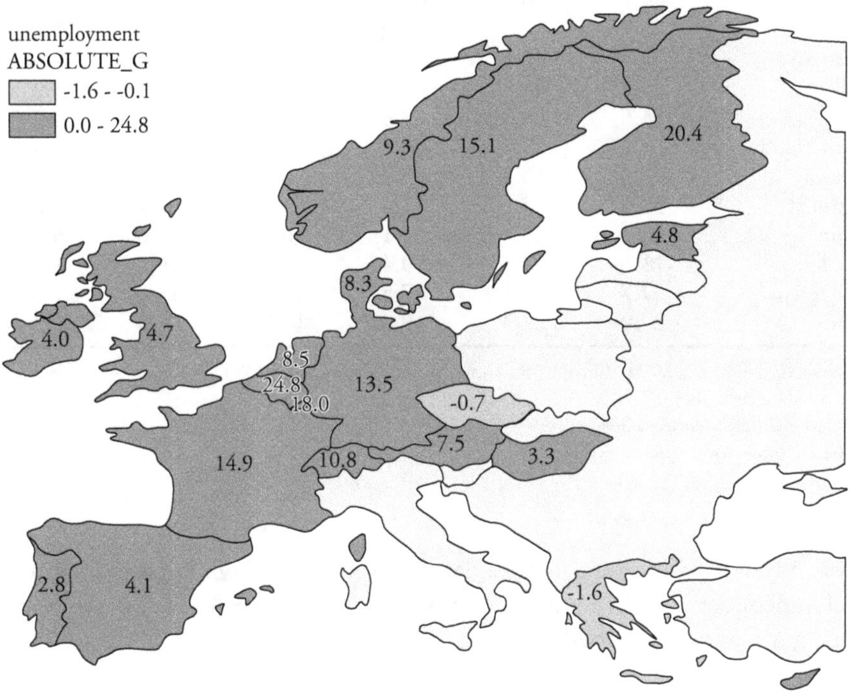

Unemployment Rates: Absolute Gap between Nationals and Third Country Nationals (%), Quarter 2, 2006 (Switzerland quarter 2, 2005, Hungary quarter 4, 2006)

Map 2: Absolute gap between unemployment rates of nationals and third country nationals

Table 3: Long term unemployment

	total	Nationals	TCNs	other EU 25	absolute gap	relative gap
Austria	19.1	16.4	27.9	32.1	11.5	1.7
Belgium	48.1	46.0	59.1	55.1	13.1	1.3
Estonia*	44.7	30.7	68.5	x	37.8	2.2
France	45.7	44.5	49.6	68.4	5.1	1.1
Germany	48.7	46.6	60.2	59.8	13.6	1.3
Greece	49.2	48.8	58.9	x	10.1	1.2
Italy	56.6	58.0	38.8	x	–19.2	0.7
Netherlands	31.1	29.7	44.8	x	15.1	1.5
Norway**	17.3	15.2	35.3	x	20.1	2.3
Portugal	51.6	53.1	11.4	x	–41.7	0.2
Spain	23.1	23.7	21.1	10.8	–2.6	0.9
Sweden	11.6	11.3	19.4	x	8.1	1.7
Switzerland**	37.7	32.1	47.5	41.5	15.4	1.5
U.K.	22.0	22.3	19.8	17.8	–2.5	0.9

Data second quarter 2006, European Labour Force Survey, EUROSTAT
x = no data available
* based on first quarter 2006
** based on second quarter 2005

3. *Long-Term employment*

Table 3 is derived from incomplete data but shows very high levels of long-term TCN unemployment in countries that perform well in the MIPEX ranking such as Belgium and the Netherlands.

4. *Gender Gap*

The gender gap can be understood as women either being less encouraged to participate in the economy of the country or suffering greater difficulties in finding employment than men. The extent of the gender gap is indicated by negative values in the tables below. The gender gap is particularly pronounced (greater than ten percentage points) in Austria, Belgium, Estonia, Finland, France, Germany, Hungary and the Netherlands.

All Scandinavian countries (except Finland) plus Poland, Portugal, and Slovenia, have a lower gender gap in employment rates for TCNs than the other countries (except Cyprus where there are more females than male in employment). Again it seems as though older immigration countries (apart from the Scandinavian countries and Switzerland) are performing worse in terms of the gender gap between TCNs and nationals when compared to newer countries of immigration (minus Hungary).

Table 4: Cross-national comparison of male and female employment rates

	total	Nationals	TCNs	other EU 25	absolute gap
Austria	–14.0	–13.2	–23.5	–17.4	–10.3
Belgium	–13.4	–13.0	–23.3	–14.1	–10.3
Cyprus	–19.8	–22.2	4.7	–19.6	26.9
Czech Republic	–16.8	–16.7	–20.8	–19.4	–4.1
Denmark	–7.4	–7.3	–11.9	–0.6	–4.6
Estonia	–4.9	–2.8	–13.5	x	–10.7
Finland	–3.6	–3.4	–19.0	–9.6	–15.6
France	–10.8	–10.1	–24.6	–17.1	–14.5
Germany	–11.1	–10.0	–21.5	–19.4	–11.5
Greece	–27.1	–26.6	–35.1	–28.3	–8.5
Hungary	–12.8	–12.8	–32.1	3.3	–19.3
Ireland*	–18.2	–17.8	–23.1	–21.0	–5.3
Italy**	–21.2	–21.2	–28.6	26.6	–7.4
Luxembourg	–18.0	–17.4	–25.5	–17.6	–8.1
Netherlands	–13.3	–12.9	–25.6	–12.7	–12.7
Norway	–6.1	–5.7	–11.1	–8.4	–5.4
Poland	–12.4	–12.4	–10.7	x	1.7
Portugal	–11.6	–11.6	–11.9	–10.8	–0.3
Slovenia	–7.5	–7.6	–0.3	x	7.3
Spain	–22.8	–23.4	–18.5	–16.2	4.9
Sweden	–4.9	–4.7	–8.8	–6.2	–4.1
Switzerland*	–13.5	–12.4	–19.0	–16.7	–6.6
U.K.	–11.2	–10.8	–20.1	–12.3	–9.3
EU 25	–14.6	–12.6	–21.1	–16.1	–8.5

Data second quarter 2006, European Labour Force Survey, EUROSTAT
x = no data available
* second quarter 2005
** annual data 2006

The absolute gap indicates whether the gender gap in unemployment rates for TCNs is larger (positive value) or smaller (negative value) than for nationals. An overall gender gap across European countries hardly appears to exist. In most cases, the gender gap in unemployment rates between TCNs and nationals also seems to be rather small. The exceptional cases are Belgium, Finland, and Hungary where female TCNs find it considerably harder to find employment compared to their national counterparts.

5. *Youth, Employment, and Unemployment*

Table 6 shows that youth employment tends to be lower and unemployment higher for TCNs compared to nationals, apart from Greece (EU 25 average, 1.3 times higher youth unemployment for TCNs than nationals). There are particularly high absolute differences between unemployment rates for TCNs and nationals in Belgium, Denmark, Finland and Sweden.

Table 5: Cross-national comparison of male and female unemployment rates (all values as difference between female and male unemployment rates)

	total	Nationals	TCNs	other EU 25	absolute gap
Austria	–0.5	–0.5	–0.2	x	0.3
Belgium	1.2	1.1	10.9	1.4	9.8
Cyprus	1.5	1.9	–1.7	–5.3	–3.6
Czech Republic	3.2	3.1	1.7	x	–1.4
Denmark	0.9	1.0	3.3	x	2.3
Estonia	–1.1	–1.7	2.6	x	4.3
Finland	0.3	0.3	9.0	x	8.7
France	1.3	1.4	4.9	3.2	3.5
Germany	–0.4	–0.1	0.4	0.7	0.5
Greece	7.8	7.7	9.2	x	1.5
Hungary*	0.7	0.6	13.6	x	13.0
Luxembourg	2.7	1.7	3.5	3.9	1.8
Netherlands	0.6	0.8	–3.7	x	–4.5
Portugal	1.9	2.0	0.8	x	–1.2
Spain	5.2	5.2	4.6	3.3	–0.6
Sweden	0.5	0.6	–2.4	0.4	–3.0
Switzerland**	1.2	1.0	4.4	1.7	3.4
U.K.	–0.9	–1.0	1.7	0.0	2.7
EU 25	1.4	1.2	2.1	1.0	0.9

Data second quarter 2006, European Labour Force Survey, EUROSTAT
x = no data available
* fourth quarter 2006
** second quarter 2005

6. *Part-Time Employment*

Table 7 shows that the number of people in part-time employment is relatively similar between nationals, EU nationals and non-EU nationals in most countries. In Denmark, Greece and Italy around one and a half times as many non-EU nationals are in part-time employment compared to nationals. Only in Norway and Switzerland does this hold true in the other direction (see column on relative gap). Of particular interest is that the ELFS posed the question why people decided to take up part time employment. One of the options provided in the survey was the answer "could not find a full-time job." This answer implicitly indicates experience of cases of discrimination by means of comparison of the three population groups. In effect, we can try to uncover patterns potentially contributing to our understanding of the link between policy and labour market outcomes.

In all cases apart from Spain, most nationals have not ended up in part-time occupation when they did not wish to find that type of work. While TCNs find it hardest to find full-time employment, EU-nationals are somewhere in the middle

Table 6: Youth unemployment (15–24 year olds)

15–24	total	Nationals	TCNs	Other EU 25	absolute gap
Austria	8.7	8.2	15.4	x	7.2
Belgium	18.9	17.6	46.6	34.5	29.0
Switzerland*	8.8	6.5	20.8	11.9	14.3
Cyprus**	10.5	8.7	21.5	18.1	12.8
Denmark†	9.4	8.8	34.0	x	25.2
Finland	26.0	25.8	53.1	x	27.3
France	21.6	21.5	27.8	x	6.3
Germany	13.4	12.6	25.4	x	12.8
Greece	24.5	25.8	12.1	x	–13.7
Hungary**	19.6	19.6	34.9	x	15.3
Netherlands††	7.7	7.3	19.8	x	12.5
Spain	18.2	18.6	17.8	x	–0.8
Sweden	26.8	26.3	45.6	x	19.3
United Kingdom	13.7	13.6	19.5	11.6	5.9
EU 25	17.1	16.8	21.1	12.0	4.3

Data second quarter 2006, European Labour Force Survey, EUROSTAT
x = no data available
* second quarter 2005
** fourth quarter 2006
† third quarter 2005
†† first quarter 2006

of these two groups (apart from in Norway and the United Kingdom). If the underlying reason for this distribution is xenophobia, then this would confirm the diagnosis that xenophobia is more directed towards non-EU nationals than other Union citizens (Lahav, 2004). The absolute gap between the experiences of those nationals and TCNs who are in, but did not seek, part-time differs considerably. France has by far the highest incidence of TCNs forced to take up part-time jobs in comparison to nationals (see penultimate column of Table 4 on absolute gap). At the other end of the scale are the Netherlands and Norway where part time work is more established and generally accepted. Here part-time work is mostly a desired experience.

When aiming at a cross-national comparison to reduce the impact of these cultural phenomena, the last column is most revealing. When looking at the relative gap, it is telling that about half or more of all TCNs in part-time employment would have preferred a full-time job when compared to the national population. The cases of Belgium and Switzerland are particularly startling. Although the countries both scored 75% on MIPEX indicators when compliance with European standards on labour access for TCNs was assessed, TCNs in these countries stated more than four times as often that they could not find full-time employment when compared to nationals of those states. The Netherlands

Table 7: Part-time employment and stated reason for no full-time employment

	part-time employment out of total employment						reason for part-time: FTPREAS 5 = could not find a full-time job						
	total	nationals	TCNs	EU 25	absolute gap	relative gap	total	nationals	TCNs	EU 25 nationals	absolute gap	relative gap	MIPEX score on anti-discrimination
Austria	21.5	21.6	20.4	21.6	–1.2	0.9	11.9	10.3	29.6	21.3	19.3	2.9	22
Belgium	22.9	22.9	22.8	23.6	–0.1	1.0	11.7	10.6	44.7	19.8	34.1	4.2	9
Denmark*	22.9	22.6	32.5	28.1	9.9	1.4	15.3	15.7	37.4	33.7	21.7	2.4	24
France	17.2	17.0	20.6	22.0	3.6	1.2	30.1	28.6	71.2	36.9	42.6	2.5	5
Germany*	25.3	25.1	28.8	26.7	3.7	1.1	20.0	18.8	33.9	27.4	15.1	1.8	17
Greece	5.6	5.4	7.4	11.7	2.0	1.4	45.2	43.3	65.8	51.7	22.5	1.5	13
Italy	13.2	12.7	19.5	22.2	6.8	1.5	37.3	35.8	52.0	50.1	16.2	1.5	11
Netherlands	45.8	46.1	41.3	36.6	–4.8	0.9	5.4	5.3	11.1	8.0	5.8	2.1	5
Norway	28.4	28.4	19.4	41.8	–9.0	0.7	13.4	12.8	18.4	33.5	5.6	1.4	16
Portugal*	8.1	8.2	8.1	5.2	–0.1	1.0	31.8	30.7	54.8	38.6	24.1	1.8	2
Spain	12.1	11.5	15.5	21.3	4.0	1.3	34.2	34.9	51.1	33.2	16.2	1.5	17
Sweden	24.3	24.3	29.0	22.3	4.7	1.2	24.9	24.4	40.5	28.1	16.1	1.7	1
Switzerland†	32.2	34.5	23.9	23.8	–10.6	0.7	6.9	5.1	23.8	12.0	18.7	4.7	24
U.K.	24.5	24.8	21.8	17.7	–3.0	0.9	8.8	8.1	19.9	24.3	11.8	2.5	5

Data based on second quarter 2006, European Labour Force Survey, EUROSTAT
* numbers for reasons of part time based on second quarter 2005
† second quarter 2005

and the United Kingdom, which both have long established anti-discrimination standards (both MIPEX score 81, position 5 out of 28) perform only in the mid-range of this assessment. This may indicate the role of cultural factors in provision of full-time employment to TCNs, which are not easily malleable by policy interventions or only in the longer term. Although non-EU nationals find themselves significantly more often in the situation of involuntary part-time employment, this seems to be relatively less often the case in newer than in older immigration countries (with the exception of Germany, Norway, Sweden).

E. *Outcomes Versus Policy*

Following the assessment of the labour market situation of TCNs, we now turn our attention to the issue of the extent to which the dimensions of integration policy analysed in MIPEX connect with TCN labour market performance. In order to develop this section of the analysis we compare MIPEX project results with European Labour Force Survey data for TCNs. The MIPEX measures policies relating to TCN labour market access are the following:

(1) eligibility to work employed or self-employed in most sectors like EU nationals
(2) labour market integration measures such as language courses and professional training, access to vocational training, and recognition of academic and professional qualifications
(3) security of status (work and residence permit)
(4) associated rights (trade union membership, rights to change employer, job, industry and work permit categories)

As has been made clear, MIPEX indicators are based on a normative framework drawn from EC law supplemented by Council of Europe Conventions or European-wide policy recommendations. These standards are then used for a benchmarking exercise to assess policy performance across, in our case, labour market access indicators. The result is a score for each country with respect to these indicators allowing for a ranking per country of its policy compliance with the normative framework (table 3, column 2). We juxtapose this ranking with two types of data:

(1) the employment and unemployment rates of TCNs
(2) the absolute gaps between TCNs and nationals with respect to employment and unemployment rates

These types of data were also ranked per country to provide the base for comparison of policy and outcome shown in Table 3.

Table 8: Cross-national comparison of policy indicators and labour market performance of TCNs

	MIPEX ranking	TCN unemployment rate ranking	absolute gap unemployment rate ranking	TCN employment rate ranking	absolute gap employment rate ranking
Sweden	1	15	17	23	22
Spain	2	9	7	6	*
Portugal	2	7	4	5	*
Italy	4	x	x	x	x
Switzerland	6	13	14	10	17
Estonia	6	6	9	8	*
Belgium	6	19	20	25	24
Norway	9	12	13	16	18
Netherlands	9	9	12	22	24
Finland	9	18	19	17	21
U.K.	12	5	8	11	12
Slovenia	12	x	x	15	13
Slovakia	14	x	x	x	x
Lithuania	14	x	x	2	*
Germany	16	16	15	18	19
Ireland	16	4	6	14	*
France	16	17	16	24	20
Czech Republic	16	2	*	3	*
Austria	20	8	10	13	14
Luxembourg	20	14	18	20	16
Hungary	22	8	5	12	*
Greece	22	3	*	7	*
Denmark	22	9	11	9	15
Cyprus	22	1	3	1	*
Malta	26	x	x	21	11
Poland	27	x	x	19	10
Latvia	28	x	x	4	*
EU 25	12	13	14	17	*

Data based on second quarter 2006, European Labour Force Survey, EUROSTAT
x = no data available
* = no ranking carried out

Table 8 shows that those countries that perform well in the MIPEX with respect to the transposition of European wide standards or recommendations do not necessarily provide the best labour market opportunities for TCNs. To give two examples, Cyprus which was 22nd in the MIPEX ranking has the lowest unemployment and the highest employment rate for TCNs of all European countries. On the other hand, Sweden, the front runner in the transposition of labour market standards for non-EU nationals, is a mid-ranking state when it comes to unemployment rates of TCNs and ranks almost last when it comes to a cross-national comparison of employment rates of the same group. The obvious point here is that Cyprus and Sweden are very different immigration countries and that it is difficult to compare them, but if we look across the data we do tend to see that those countries that do well in terms of policy transposition also have some problems with the labour market integration of TCNs. It may well be that perceptions of dissatisfaction about TCNs' labour market integration informed the policy choices and implementation in the first place, which is then indicated by a high MIPEX score. There is also the possibility that MIPEX mainly assesses a state's ability to transpose EU measures.

In order to provide a more meaningful base of comparison, we calculated the absolute gap between employment and unemployment rates for TCNs and those for nationals. The results of the comparison of absolute gaps with the MIPEX results are similar to those of the un-weighted unemployment and employment rates of TCNs. In some cases the original indication of the MIPEX score is rectified via this new measure, as in the case of Portugal. Overall, however, we do not find a correlation between the scores on the transposition of European wide standards and labour market access for TCNs. It is rather that the results indicate deeper engrained structural factors that labour market integration measures and the like seek to overcome. Although labour market performance indicators have similar tendencies (higher unemployment for nationals and higher unemployment for TCNs), TCNs seem to be disproportionately affected by the overall economic performance of the country with respect to unemployment and employment. This indicates a missing link between the MIPEX results and labour market performance indicators.

F. *Correlation Between Employment and Unemployment Rates With the Level of Economic Integration*

The relation between integration policy and TCN labour market access is less than straightforward, as shown above. Instead of thinking about the relationship in a linear fashion, we have suggested that policy outcomes also influence the way in which integration policies are shaped. This indicates that Europeanisation is a process marked by feed-back loops.

In addition, Europeanisation needs to be understood in the national context in which the transposition of European directives and policy objectives is located. At this point we will assess national factors that influence policy outcomes beyond the influence of integration policies which stem from the supranational level. Attentively, we consider whether the level of integration of an economy impacts on unemployment and employment rates of non-EU nationals and can indicate why the absolute gap between nationals and TCNs differs so widely between member states.

The concept of economic integration that we employ builds on research on "corporatism" and "pluralism" in Western economies. Corporatism refers to an "institutionalised pattern of policy formation... in the shaping of economic policy." (Lehmbruch 1979) The emphasis is on formal interest group intermediation between social groups and the state. Critics argued that the concept of corporatism has been interpreted in too many and incongruent ways (Siaroff 1999) and, despite its theoretical contributions, as such does not count as a convincing explanation of economic performance in Western democracies which demand more fine-grained analysis (Therborn, 1987).

Siaroff 1999 proposes the concept of "economic integration" as an alternative measure to corporatism based on indicators of:

- social partnership
- industry-level coordination
- and policy-making patterns

In contrast to corporatism, this measure is linear and allows a better ranking of countries for cross-national comparison. The latest available data on economic integration is for the mid-1990s which seems satisfactory given that there have been indications of predominantly path-dependent institutional change along the corporatist-pluralist divide in OECD countries over the last thirty years (Armingeon, 2004). Table 9 shows the economic integration scores for seventeen countries in the MIPEX analysis. Unfortunately data were not available for new EU states in Central and Eastern Europe. In Table 9, the higher the score on the right, then the more "integrated" is the economy, i.e. the stronger the social partnerships, the higher the industry-level coordination under particular national policy-making patterns.

Using the economic integration score, we then attempted to various correlations to test our hypothesis that stronger integrated economies may exert a negative effect on the labour market integration of TCNs in comparison to nationals. The results of these correlation exercises are presented in Table 10. Given that our cases are not normally distributed, we present both Pearson's parametric and Spearman's non-parametric correlation coefficients. Due to the small number of cases, our interpretations need to be tentative.

When analysing employment rates, the higher the level of economic integration of a country, the higher the employment rates of nationals but the lower the employment rates of TCNs. In this case, the absolute gap between employment rates of TCNs and nationals has a strong negative correlation with the degree of economic integration. For more pluralist economies, the opposite holds true. This means that more economically integrated countries have a stronger ability to put their national population to work, however, having considerably more difficulties to achieve the same with TCNs in contrast to more pluralist economies.

Table 9: Integrated vs. pluralist economies in the mid-1990s

Austria	4.625
Norway	4.625
Sweden	4.625
Netherlands	4.000
Finland	4.375
Denmark	4.250
Germany	4.125
Switzerland	4.125
Luxembourg	4.125
Belgium	3.750
Italy	3.000
Ireland	2.625
Portugal	2.375
France	2.250
U.K.	2.000
Spain	2.000
Greece	2.000

based on data of Siaroff, 1999: 193f

It seems that integrated economies are more protective of their national workforce against TCNs in the labour market and that this works particularly to the disadvantage of 15–24 year old non-EU nationals. This could indicate a negative influence of strong social partnership arrangements and high industry-level coordination under particular national policy-making patterns in corporatist arrangements on TCN employment and unemployment. Without suggesting causal relationships in this tentative analysis, we have indicated the significance of contextual factors such as the level of economic integration of a country when trying to understand the labour market integration of non-EU nationals in their countries of residence.

G. *Conclusions*

Our analysis has juxtaposed MIPEX data with other data sources that deal with what could be called the contextual or "on the ground" situation. We began by discussing the relationship between policy and outcomes and making it clear that there is little basis to suspect that there is a direct relationship between the kinds of policy frameworks that MIPEX charts and the contextual situations that we find with regards to the labour market integration of TCNs. MIPEX allows in-depth analysis of the transposition of laws and norms from EU level into the national frameworks, but tells us less about the labour market performance of TCNs in the member states. MIPEX does have a strong, policy focus. If we are

Table 10: Correlation of economic integration with level of economic integration, descriptive statistics

		Spearman's correlation coefficient	Pearson's correlation coefficient
employment rates (N=17)	Nationals	0.538*, p = 0.026	0.549*, p = 0.023
	TCNs	–0.311, p = 0.224	–0.440†, p = 0.088
	absolute gap	–0.535*, p = 0.027	–0.693**, p = 0.002
unemployment rates (N=16)	Nationals	–0.263, p = 0.325	–0.326, p = 0.217
	TCNs	0.390, p = 0.135	0.399, p = 0.126
	absolute gap	0.490†, p = 0.054	0.551*, p = 0.027
Youth unemployment rates (N=12)	Nationals	0.343, p = 0.275	0.417, p = 0.177
	TCNs	–0.117, p = 0.718	–0.304, p = 0.336
	absolute gap	0.640*, p = 0.025	0.715**, p = 0.009

† significant at the 0.10 level
* significant at the 0.05 level
** significant at the 0.01 level

to consider the relationships between policies and outcomes, then we need also to account for the wide range of other factors that intervene in the relationship. These could include structural and organisational features of the labour market such as patterns and types of migrant employment, educational systems and attainment levels, vocational training provision, social security assistance and a wide range of other potential factors. We also suggest that 'outcomes' themselves can become inputs and feed into policy reformulation.

Our analysis does show that some of the countries that do particularly well in the MIPEX ranking of policy implementation do less well when we explore the labour market integration of their TCN populations. We were also able to identify clear differences between old and new countries of immigration, particularly in terms of unemployment rates. This may be due to the structure of their economy in terms of the performance of labour intensive sectors and matching the skills levels of migrants with the demand structure of the labour market. The permeability and responsiveness of the education system for migrants and their needs is likely to play a role as well as cultural patterns of discrimination against TCNs as was indicated by our results on part-time employment. Our evidence also suggests a gender gap in female employment rates and a very marked gap when looking at the labour market position of young TCNs. Finally, we also extended our analysis to explore the results of a correlation exercise that suggested the importance of the level of "economic integration" when accounting for the absolute gaps in labour market integration of TCNs in comparison to nationals. Assessment of the level of economic integration does, of course raise much bigger questions about social and economic reform that may involve potentially unpopular remedies and affect a far greater number of people than the migrant target population.

List of References

ARMINGEON, K. (2004) Institutional Change in OECD Democracies, 1970–2000. *Comparative European Politics*, 2, pp. 212–238.

BACHE, I. & FLINDERS, M. (2004) *Multi-Level Governance*, Oxford, Oxford University Press.

BARRETT, S.M. & FUDGE, C. (Eds.) (1981) *Policy and Action. Essays on the Implementation of Public Policy*, London/New York, Methuen.

BOMMES, M. & GEDDES, A. (Eds.) (2000) Immigration and Welfare: Challenging the Borders of the Welfare State, London, Routledge.

BRUBAKER, R. (2001) The return of assimilation? Changing perspectives on immigration and its sequels in France, Germany and the United States. *Ethnic and Racial Studies*, 24, 531–48.

BRUNSSON, N. (1989) The Organization of Hypocrisy. Talk, Decisions and Actions in Organizations, Chichester, John Wiley&Sons.

BULMER, S. & RADAELLI, C. (2004) The Europeanisation of National Policy? *Queen's Papers on Europeanisation, no.1*, http://www.qub.ac.uk/schools/SchoolofPoliticsInternationalStudiesandPhilosophy/FileStore/EuropeanisationFiles/Filetoupload,38405,en.pdf.

CASTLES, S. (2003) Why Migration Policies fail. *Ethnic and Racial Studies*, 27, pp. 205–227.

COWLES, M.G., CAPORASO, J. & RISSE, T. (Eds.) (2001) *Transforming Europe. Europeanization and Domestic Change*, Ithaca/London, Cornell University Press.

EUROPEAN COMMISSION (2005) Commission Regulation (EC) No 430/2005 implementing Council Regulation (EC) No 577/98 on the organisation of a labour force sample survey in the Community concerning the codification to be used for data transmission from 2006 onwards and the use of a sub-sample for the collection of data on structural variables.

FREEMAN, G. (1998) The Decline of Sovereignty? Politics and Immigration Restriction in Liberal States. In JOPPKE, C. (Ed.) *Challenge to the Nation-State. Immigration in Western Europe and the United States.* Oxford, Oxford University Press.

GEDDES, A. (2003) *The Politics of Migration and Immigration in Europe*, London/Thousand Oaks/New Delhi Sage.

—— (2008) *Immigration and European Integration: Beyond Fortress Europe?*, 2nd edition, Manchester, Manchester University Press.

GEDDES, A. & GUIRAUDON, V. (2004) Britain and France and EU anti-discrimination policy: the emergence of an EU policy paradigm. *West European Politics*, 27, 334–53.

GUIRAUDON, V. (1998) International Human Rights Norms and their Interpretation: The Protection of Aliens in Europe. San Domenico di Fiesole, European University Institute.

GUNN, L. (1978) Why is Implementation so Difficult? *Management Services in Government*, 33, 169–176.

JOPPKE, C. (1998) Why liberal states accept unwanted immigration. *World Politics*, 50, 266–93.

KNILL, C. & LEHMKUHL, D. (1999) How Europe Matters. Different Mechanisms of Europeanization *European Integration Online Papers*, 3.

LAHAV, G. (2004) Public Opinion toward Immigration in the European Union. Does it Matter? *Comparative Political Studies*, 37, 1151–1183.

LIPSKY, M. (1971) Street-level Bureaucracy and the Analysis of Urban Reform. *Urban Affairs Quarterly*, 6, 391–409.

PRESSMAN, J.L. & WILDAVSKY, A. (1984) Implementation. How Great Expectations in Washington are Dashed in Oakland; Or, Why It's Amazing that Federal Programs Work at All, Berkeley, University of California Press.

SANDHOLTZ, W. & STONE SWEET, A. (Eds.) (1997) *European Integration and Supranational Governance*, Oxford, Oxford University Press.

SASSEN, S. (1996) Losing Control? Sovereignty in an Age of Globalization, New York, Columbia University Press.

SIAROFF, A. (1999) Corporatism in 24 industrial democracies: meaning and measurement. *European Journal of Political Research*, 36, pp. 175–205.

SOYSAL, Y. (1994) *Limits of citizenship*, Chicago, Chicago University Press.

TAYLOR, P.J. (1994) The State as Container: Territoriality in the Modern World-System. *Progress in Human Geography*, 18, 151–162.

THERBORN, G. (1987) Does Corporatism Really Matter? The Economic Crisis and Issues of Political Theory. *Journal of Public Policy*, 7, 259–284.

WIMMER, A. & GLICK SCHILLER, N. (2002) Methodological nationalism and beyond: nation-state building, migration and the social sciences. *Global Networks*, 2, 301–34.

Chapter 9

Political Participation for Migrants: The MIPEX Results

Dirk Jacobs, Florence Delmotte and Barbara Herman

In this contribution we will discuss the strand on political participation of the Migrant Integration Policy Index (MIPEX). After having discussed the general topic of political participation of foreigners, we will first focus our attention on the choice of indicators in MIPEX. Subsequently we will analyse some of the results of the MIPEX exercise with regard to political participation of third country nationals (TCNs). A number of remarkable results stand out. It turns out political liberties for TCNs are still not assured in all EU Member States. Furthermore, there seems to be no trade off between access to nationality and political rights for non-nationals, although this is often assumed. There does, however, seem to be a link between public opinion on diversity in politics and the openness of a state with regard to political participation of immigrants. Overall, it is safe to say there is still quite some room for improvement as far as policies towards political inclusion of TCNs are concerned.

A. *Political Participation*

One has a tendency to equate political participation foremost with electoral activities, more precisely with the exercise of political rights *stricto sensu*, i.e. the right to vote and the right to stand as a candidate in elections. From a sociological and political science point of view, however, every attempt towards influencing collective decision making (in government institutions) can be considered as a form of political participation (Verba, Schlozman & Brady, 1995). Strikes, manifestations and consultation activities are in this sense often equally forms of political participation. For some groups, they can even function as an alternative to electoral participation and might even coexist, for instance, with high(er) rates of abstention in 'mainstream' political activity (Gaxie, 1993). Moreover, those non-electoral forms of participation, which express a certain level of politicisation, do not necessarily require that electoral political rights have (already) been granted (Manin, 1998). Nevertheless, access to electoral rights undoubtedly constitutes an essential instrument for political integration, given the importance of elections in democratic systems. Political liberties are furthermore an important prerequisite for forms of non electoral participation.

The boundaries between political and non-political activity are not always clear or uncontroversial, if only because some activities which were not explicitly intended to be political might *de facto* have political impact (Verba, Schlozman & Brady, 1995). Furthermore, even political violence, terrorism and corruption could equally be considered to be forms of – albeit illegal – political participation (Martiniello, 1997). Leaving these illegal categories aside, we can thus make an analytical typology of political participation in distinguishing electoral participation and non-electoral political participation.

As we already stated, electoral political participation entails participation in elections (including referenda) and participation in the system of representation linked to democratic state institutions on different political levels (local, regional, national and supra-national). Non-electoral political participation refers to trade union activities, active membership of political parties, participation in civil associations with a political agenda, advisory councils and lobby activities. These forms of non-electoral political participation are often closely linked with political liberties.

In the MIPEX exercise we want to assess to what extent EU Member States allow for and stimulate both electoral participation and non-electoral political participation of TCNs. We constructed a number of indicators to try and measure the degree of openness for political inclusion of foreigners. These will be discussed in paragraph four. Before doing so, we would like to reflect a bit more on the issue of political participation of non-nationals and the broader challenge of political participation of ethnic minorities.

B. *Political Inclusion of Foreigners*

Political inclusion of foreigners should not be taken for granted. Especially with regard to formal electoral political participation (but sometimes equally with regard to non-electoral political participation), nation-states have in the 19th and 20th century – in the process of nation-state formation – had a strong tendency to reserve access to political rights (and to political practices) to state citizens. Modern democratic ideology, however, postulates that every individual should be able to equally influence policy making which regards him/her. One can claim that the link between democratic citizenship and nationalism is historically contingent, and not conceptually necessary (Habermas, 1996;

Fennema, 2001). The history of citizenship has furthermore been characterised by an enlarging, integrative tendency, in which rights – especially political rights – have been first reserved to wealthy men and have then gradually been expanded towards all adult men and finally to all adult nationals, regardless of gender. Since nation-states are not only comprised of nationals but equally have – increasingly in the 20th century – foreign residents among their population, the problem of political exclusion has now shifted to this group. There is hence a tension between modern democratic ideology on the one hand and the logic of nationhood on the other hand.

This tension can be resolved in two ways: foreign residents can be made nationals (through open nationality legislation) or political rights can be granted to all inhabitants regardless of their nationality (Hammar, 1990). Nationality acquisition gives citizens full access to the set of political rights and obligations in the context of a nation-state. States might also wish to grant political rights to non-nationals who cannot or do not wish to take up state citizenship of the host country. This is most often done at the local or regional level. Some supra-national levels have stimulated this development. The European Union is, of course, a case in point. The creation of the notion of European citizenship in the Treaty of Maastricht, granting voting rights at the local level and for European Parliament to all foreign residents holding citizenship of another EU member state under the same conditions as nationals, has further stimulated debate on the granting of local political rights to TCNs.

C. *The Challenge of Representation*

Political participation is one thing – having a political impact is another. Let us discuss the difference with the help of the concept of representation. When talking about political representation, one can make a distinction between two forms: descriptive (or symbolic) representation and substantive representation. There is descriptive representation when the composition of a political body reflects the socio-demographic characteristics of the overall population it is supposed to represent. We talk about substantive representation when interests of subgroups of a population are sufficiently voiced and taken into account in political deliberation. It is often assumed that descriptive representation leads to substantive representation – but there is no guaranteed link between the two.

Political scientists have often analysed to what extent there is descriptive representation in different types of elected bodies. In a perfect world, about half of all members of political bodies should be women. If 20 percent of the population is of immigrant origin, then one in five politicians should be of immigrant background. When ten percent of the population is gay, one in ten politicians should equally be gay, and so on. Descriptive representation could be a goal in any field of society: in elected bodies, on boards of associations, in schools, in the workplace, in the media, *et cetera*.

Whenever a group of people has to choose a limited number of representatives the issue can pop up as to what extent they represent the diversity of the larger group in an equitable way. Ideally, every group of leaders should be a microcosm of the larger group of people affected by decisions made by this smaller group of leaders. This is more easily said than done. When leadership is the result of democratic elections, unaccompanied by measures of affirmative action, there are no guarantees that the diversity of the group will be reflected in the end result, even if all involved normatively agree that descriptive representation is preferable. If candidates all have particular characteristics and/or voters all vote for a typical kind of representative, as is often the case, homogeneity among the leadership will be the result. Voters should make informed choices, taking into account the profile of candidates as one of the elements in decision making.

Furthermore, representation is a matter of power relations. Those in power generally want to stay in power and try to share as little as possible of it. They might like the idea of descriptive representation in theory but dislike it in practice when it means they have to give up their own seat. As a result, descriptive representation sometimes has to be enforced through formal and informal forms of quota. Mere "naming, blaming and shaming" does not automatically work, which is why positive discrimination can be a necessary last resort.

A common objection to this is that formal and informal mechanisms of positive discrimination will hinder quality. One can, however, equally turn that argument around: if availability of qualified personnel is an issue, then more should be done to ensure equal opportunities for all. Failing to do so is wasting valuable human capital. That is one of the reasons why representation of minority groups – in its sociological significance of less powerful groups – is important.

There are nevertheless an important number of normative and practical challenges related to the use of affirmative action in achieving descriptive representation. Even if everyone agrees with the general idea that diversity is important, it still has to be decided what kind of diversity should be taken into account. Then there is the issue of how to organise it in practical terms. Gender balance has become a legitimate goal in most countries, but this is not the case for all other kinds of diversity which might be just as politically relevant. Should one equally take into account ethnic origin, religion, language use, sexual preference and health situation, to name but a few? It is clear there is no easy consensus to be found for these issues. Especially since some people actually do not want to be made visible as being part of a minority group, if only because they do not want to be pinned down to just one aspect of their identity. That is why some of the most ardent critics of quota systems are to be found among minority group members themselves. At least one thing is clear across the board: affirmative action might be an instrument in achieving descriptive representation but it should never be a goal in itself. It is no magical solution. If it exists, its ambition should be to be abolished as quickly as possible once equal opportunities have been achieved.

Suppose descriptive representation is achieved with regard to, say, gender and ethnic origin (with or without formal or informal systems of affirmative action). Will this descriptive representation then be to the benefit of women and ethnic minorities at large? Advocates readily assume it is. This is, however, not necessarily the case. A female politician could take antifeminist political positions, just as a politician of immigrant origin might support points of view which go against the interests of (segments of) the ethnic minority population. It is not difficult to find examples which prove that being a woman or being part of an ethnic minority does not automatically result in proposals which are applauded respectively by the female part of the population or by ethnic minority groups. Numerous female politicians have in the past supported male-oriented policy proposals. Miss Ayaan Hirsi Ali, former member (of immigrant origin) of the Dutch parliament, has defended very critical points of view with regard to multicultural policy and accommodation of Islam in western societies, to give but one very well known recent example. Men can sometimes be better advocates for feminism than women, just as members of an ethnic majority group will sometimes be more considerate of wishes of ethnic minority groups.

That is why political scientists are not just interested in 'counting noses' (descriptive representation) but often also want to investigate what kind of interests are being defended by politicians with particular socio-demographic profiles. The aim is to judge whether minority group interests (substantive representation) are best secured through the presence of members of the same minority group (descriptive representation). One of the challenging methodological problems is, of course, to clearly define and measure group interests (which is not easily done, if only because groups are often difficult to clearly identify and are themselves heterogeneous with regard to profiles and interests). This being said, most studies have shown that descriptive representation indeed enhances substantive representation (Celis, 2006).

So surely the best bet for achieving substantive representation is to start off with descriptive representation. Descriptive representation can even have a value in itself: the symbolic legitimacy of decision making bodies will increase among minority groups if these institutions are more balanced in their composition. Advocates of descriptive representation should however not forget that having token representatives for minority groups can never be the ultimate goal. The final objective should always be to ensure that interests of minority groups are sufficiently voiced and taken account of. What we want is substantive representation. This might be done by anyone; you do not necessarily need minority group members – let alone formal quota – for this.

Ultimately it is the content of the message, the ideology which matters, not the characteristics of the messenger. It is, as we all know, better to listen to what someone tells you than merely judge someone by his or her looks. Merely relying on the symbolic effects of descriptive representation sooner or later backfires. Several political parties in Belgium and the Netherlands have learned this the hard way after blindly recruiting individual minority group members instead of going through the more demanding process of trying to establish links with and through minority associations (Jacobs et alii, 2006).

With this extensive discussion of the notions of descriptive and substantive representation we wanted to show it is no easy and straightforward task to measure political inclusion of minority groups, such as TCNs. As a result, we deliberately opted to limit our focus in MIPEX on the (lack of) openness of public policy in offering opportunities for political inclusion for TCNs, without claiming to be able to assess the success and degree of actual political participation. We suspect that *de jure* opportunity structures will indeed facilitate *de facto* political inclusion, but will not try to demonstrate this here. We want to be very clear about this: we are measuring 'policy input indicators', not 'output indicators' with regard to political inclusion.

D. *The MIPEX Indicators for the Strand on Political Participation*

The degree of political integration and the effectiveness of political participation – in terms of impact on policy – is, as we have discussed, difficult to assess. Adequately comparing substantive representation on a large scale is simply unfeasible without a tremendous research investment. Even verifying to what extent there is descriptive representation is a huge task and furthermore resembles to a methodological minefield. It is not an easy endeavour to correctly classify political actors to particular groups, if only because third party identification and self identification need not overlap. In addition, characteristics of available data vary widely across Europe. MIPEX, hence, cannot possible have the ambition to measure effectiveness of political participation or the degree of actual political inclusion. MIPEX can only assess the extent to which policy is favourable in creating opportunities for political participation and inclusion.

In the political participation strand of MIPEX we want to measure the degree to which EU Member States formally facilitate (or do not hinder) political inclusion of TCNs. We have chosen not to only focus on electoral rights and political liberties, but to equally take a look at advisory and consultative bodies and implementation policies. Taking into account challenges related to data gathering (relative ease of access to information, attempt to limiting problems of interpretation, *et cetera*) we opted for a relatively short list of thirteen indicators (see annexe 1). As we have already stressed, these indicators focus on policy not on outcomes. We did not try to measure the actual degree of political participation of TCNs.

Our main normative source of inspiration was the convention on the participation of foreigners in public life at local level, which was opened for signature by the Member States of the Council of Europe on February 5, 1992. This convention hopes to stimulate states to allow foreign residents to participate in the affairs of their local community. One could, however, argue for the need to improve political inclusion of foreign residents beyond the local level and equally stimulate political integration on the supra-local level (the regional level) or even the nation-state level, in addition to improvement of access to state citizenship. For the purpose of MIPEX, we therefore have decided to not limit ourselves to the local level.

The convention on the participation of foreigners in public life at local level of the Council of Europe has not been very popular, one must admit. Only Cyprus, the Czech Republic, Denmark, Finland, Italy,[1] the Netherlands, Sweden and the United Kingdom have signed it among the EU Member States. Other signatories are Norway and Albania. In preparation of the convention different categories of measures have been put forward forming part of a step-by-step approach towards political inclusion of foreign residents on the local level. These include provisions of full information about civic rights and duties, mechanisms such as consultative committees to represent the views of foreign residents at the level of local authorities and the granting of voting rights to non-nationals.

Earlier recommendations of the Council of Europe for encouragement of participation of local life by foreign residents include (a) providing specific and active information policy, (b) ensuring account is taken as far as possible of their needs and wishes, (c) promoting the creation of local representative bodies for foreign residents to be consulted whenever appropriate, (d) taking steps to promote equal opportunities and good relation between all residents, whatever their nationality and (e) considering granting of voting rights.

The convention as such has three chapters. The first chapter (chapter A) deals with rights of freedom of expression, assembly and association. The second chapter (chapter B) deals with the creation of consultative bodies. The third chapter (chapter C) deals with the right to vote and stand as candidate in local elections. Moreover, the convention has the possibility built in of partial acceptance. States can decide to just accede to particular chapters. The focus of the convention is clearly on the local level. In the explanatory report it is stated:

> The convention concerns the participation of foreign residents at local level. For those living in a local community, numerous aspects of their daily life – such as housing, education, local amenities, public transport, cultural and sport facilities

[1] Italy did not sign chapter C which foresees in the right to vote in local authority elections.

> – are influenced by decisions taken by the local authority. Moreover, foreign residents participate actively in the life and prosperity of the local community. Therefore, for countries espousing the democratic principles of the Council of Europe it is fair to examine how a sometimes sizeable group of long-term local residents can contribute to the local decision-making process on matters which affect them.
>
> Similar considerations could be applied to some aspects of decision-making at central government level. Nevertheless, it is arguable that there is a closer link between possession of citizenship and participation in procedures for determining what may be conceived of as the 'national will', which would exclude participation of foreigners in national political life.[2]

With regard to voting rights, another justification can, however, equally be put forward for a limitation to the local and regional level (Jacobs, 1998). Political rights on the local and regional level are most often based on a logic of residence: one has the right to vote and to stand as a candidate because one lives in a particular location. For the national level, the rights are rather based on a logic of membership: being part of the 'club', constituting the national political community (or not being part of the 'club').

This being said, for the purpose of the citizenship index, we believe we should not limit the focus to the local or regional level but equally take into consideration possibilities for political integration on the national level. Interests of TCNs are, indeed, at stake on all political levels.

We constructed a set of indicators which can be grouped along four dimensions: electoral rights, political liberties, consultative bodies and implementation policies. Electoral rights are fairly straightforward: to what extent are TCNs given the right to vote and to stand as a candidate? With political liberties we refer to basic civic and political right such as the right to assembly and the right to association. The dimension related to consultative bodies assess to what extent immigrant representatives and/or immigrant organisations are consulted with regard to policy that directly concerns them and whether this is done in a structural, systematic way or on an *ad hoc* basis. Such forms of consultation are put forward as good practice by the Convention of the Council of Europe. The convention equally stresses the importance of foreigners being informed about their rights, an indicator which is part of our dimension focussing on "implementation policies." Under the umbrella of "implementation policies," we equally included the issue whether immigrant organisations are being funded to be able and play their part in consultative and advisory bodies. This is not part of the recommendations of the convention. We think, however, immigrant organisations should be allowed to develop the necessary skills and expertise in order to effectively be able to function in advisory and consultative bodies. In our opinion, weak and unprepared spokespersons of organisations can condemn

---

[2] *See* http://conventions.coe.int.

advisory bodies to be merely token institutions. In order to have substantive representation, governments can stimulate expertise building through financial support or support in kind. We therefore proposed to include this as an indicator.

Taking all the indicators together, one could formulate a best case scenario for political inclusion. This is a composite of the best policy practices from the MIPEX normative framework. Each of these practices was found, as of March 1, 2007, in at least one of the 28 countries. The best case scenario would look like this:

> A migrant has opportunities to participate in public life which conform to Europe's highest democratic principles. The state guarantees her political liberties to form an association, even a political one, to join political parties, and thus participate in civil society. As a legal resident, she can vote and stand for local elections, just like EU-nationals. She can also vote at the regional level. At local, regional, and national levels, migrants or migrant associations independently elect representatives to structural consultative bodies that discuss the policies that most affect them. The state implements policies that actively inform her of her political rights and offer migrant associations funding or in-kind support under the same conditions as other associations" (Niessen, Huddleston et alii, 2007).

In contrast, there is of course also the worst case scenario. This is a composite of the worst policy practices that MIPEX found, as of March 1, 2007, in at least one of the 28 countries. It looks like this:

> A migrant cannot contribute to the political decisions that affect his daily life. The state does not guarantee his political liberties to form an association or join and participate in a political party. As a resident, he may face more obligations than EU citizens living abroad in the same country, but he does not benefit from the same voting rights. Regardless of how long he lives there, he can never vote or stand for election to serve his community. Cities with the largest migrant populations have no consultative body to confer with them. Likewise, a migrant is excluded from contributing to decisions at regional and national levels. The state does nothing to implement policies to promote his political participation such as informing him of the opportunities that exist, or supporting migrant organisations (Niessen, Huddleston et alii, 2007).

We will refrain from commenting on the MIPEX results for political participation for all individual countries. Detailed information can be found in the MIPEX study and all the data can be checked on the website.[3] We would like to stress that this also gives the possibility to others to use the MIPEX data (and even add or drop certain indicators).[4] Let us just state that policies in Western Europe are on average slightly favourable, while those in Greece and Central and

[3] *See* http://www.integrationindex.eu.

[4] If one, for instance, does not agree with our choice to include funding for immigrant organisations, one can simple drop it. We now have simply calculated a non-weighted additive score

Eastern Europe are rather unfavourable. The 28 MIPEX countries diverge greatly on whether or not to grant electoral rights to non-EU residents. Five countries achieve best practice (the Nordic countries and Ireland), whilst 11 others grant no electoral rights; few fall between. Although full political liberties are granted to migrants in Western Europe, some are denied in the Czech Republic, Estonia, Latvia, Lithuania, Slovakia and Slovenia. The highest scores on consultative bodies belong to the Nordic countries, the Benelux, the Iberian Peninsula and Ireland. Critically unfavourable policies are found in ten countries.

In the upcoming paragraphs we will examine a number of general tendencies in the MIPEX results for political participation. In the next paragraph we will first look into the link between the scores for political participation in MIPEX and the scores on the strand for nationality acquisition.

E. *The Link Between the Scopes on Political Participation and Nationality Acquisition*

Nationality acquisition is one path towards full political rights. One could hence assume, as is often done in political debate (Jacobs, 1998), that there is a trade off between openness with regard to political rights for foreigners and openness with regard to nationality acquisition. If nationality has been acquired, one normally has full political rights. In systems with a liberal nationality legislation, this might be a reason not to grant political rights to foreigners, since they can make the choice to obtain national citizenship and, hence, political rights. In contrast, countries with a strict nationality legislation might want to compensate in extending political rights to non-nationals. Can we find such a pattern in our MIPEX data, comparing the strand scores for nationality acquisition[5] and the strand score for political participation?

There is no statistically significant correlation for the EU-25 between the overall policy score on nationality acquisition and the overall policy score for political participation (Spearman's rho=0.338, sign.=0.099).[6] Although the relationship is not significant from a statistical point of view,[7] the results seem to suggest there is a positive relation: the higher the score for nationality acquisition, the higher the score for political participation. Sweden and Portugal seem to be

for all indicators. One might consider developing a weight (for instance by letting immigrant groups evaluate the importance of each of the indicators).

[5] An additive score based on 28 indicators for access to nationality.

[6] Bulgaria and Romania are not included in the analysis since they only joined the EU in 2007.

[7] It should be noted that with only 25 cases, it is difficult to get statistically significant results. This could, in other words, be just a method effect.

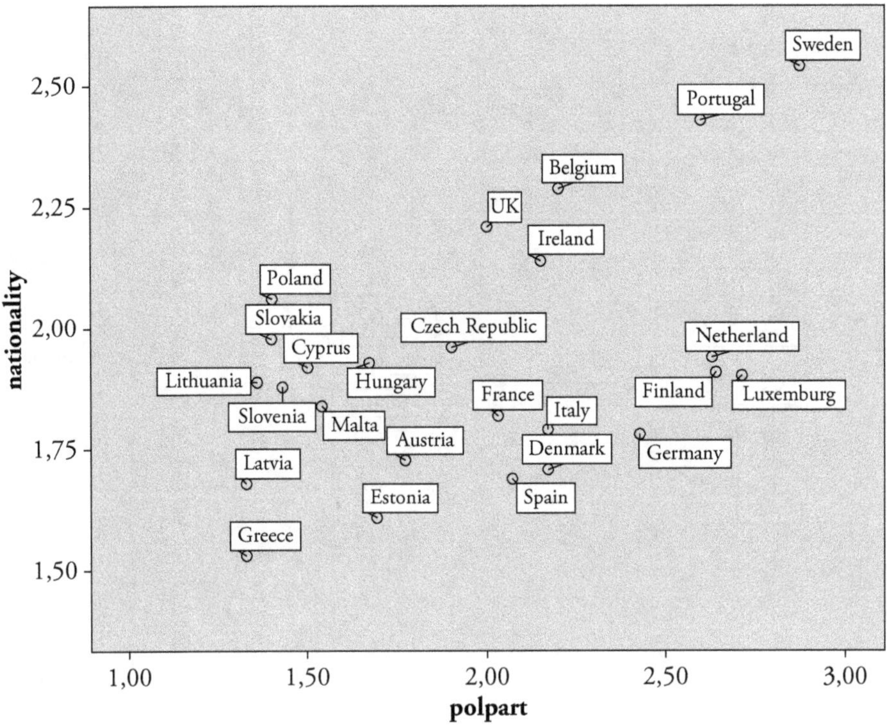

Figure 1: Scatterplot of index score for nationality acquisition and score for political participation

the two outliers[8] combining both a high score on nationality acquisition and a high score on political participation. For the other countries, there is quite some variation in combining either moderate scores on both or a high score on one indicator and a low score on another indicator (but this manifests itself in different combinations). There is clearly no negative relationship between political participation scores and access to nationality scores. There is, in other words, in any event no trade off effect, as can be seen in the scatter plot represented in figure 1.

But perhaps we should not focus on the overall score for political participation but just limit our attention to the issue of electoral rights. One could indeed argue that political liberties, for instance, are – at least should be – independent of access to nationality. The correlation between the policy score for nationality acquisition and the score for electoral rights comes very close to being statistically

[8] Indeed, if we leave Sweden and Portugal out of the analysis, the correlation becomes very clearly non significant (Spearman's rho=0.177, sign.=0.419).

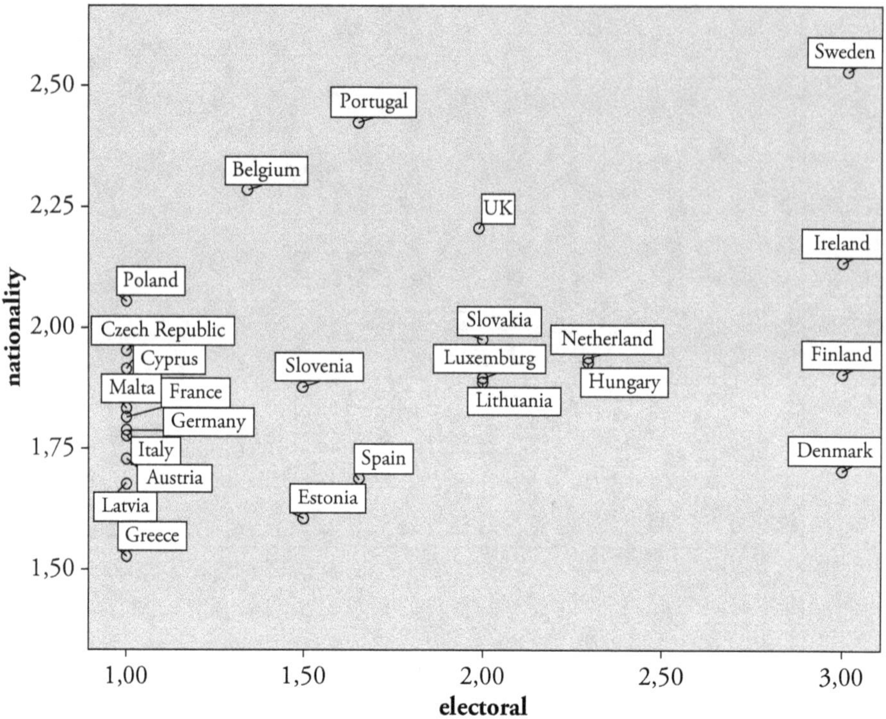

Figure 2: Scatterplot of index score for nationality acquisition and score for electoral rights

significant (Spearman's rho=0.391, sign.=0.054).[9] The relation is once more positive: the higher the score for nationality acquisition, the higher the score for electoral rights. Obviously, there is certainly no trade off between the two, as can be seen in the scatter plot in figure 2. It hence does not seem to be the case that either electoral rights are granted to TCNs "or" naturalisation is being facilitated in a mutually exclusive manner. We cannot claim either that both go hand in hand. The most valid interpretation seems to be that the two are unrelated. That in itself is an interesting finding since it is often argued in political debates that the enfranchisement of foreigners and easier access to nationality are contradictory and mutually exclusionary steps. This claim does in the EU not hold as an empirical fact.

Let us now focus on potential correlations between the different dimensions of the strand on political participation: electoral participation, political liberties, consultative bodies and implementation policies. We expect all four dimensions

[9] When we once again take Portugal and Sweden out of the calculation, the correlation becomes weaker in terms of strength and statistical significance: Spearman's rho=0.316, sign.=0.141.

to be co-varying, with the exception perhaps of the dimension of consultative bodies. The consultative bodies might possibly be used as an alternative form of political participation in order to compensate for the lack of electoral rights for foreigners – as was for instance the case in Belgium in the seventies and eighties (Jacobs, 1998). We will look into this in the next paragraph.

F. *The Link Between Different Strands for Political Participation*

As far as the sub-strands for political participation are concerned, there is a statistically significant correlation between political liberties and consultative provisions (Spearman's rho=0.417, sign.=0.038). The more political liberties there are, the more consultative provisions (and the less political liberties, the less consultation provisions), so it seems. The scatter plot in figure 3, however, shows the statistical effect is due to the position of a limited number of cases (those new Member States limiting access of foreigners to political associations) and should hence not lead to over-interpretation. We can, however, say the situation is problematic in Czech Republic, Estonia, Latvia, Lithuania, Slovakia and Slovenia as far as possibilities for political inclusion of TCNs is concerned.

A much clearer link is the very strong correlation between consultative provisions and implementation policies: the higher the score for consultative practices, the higher the score for implementation policies, mainly operationalised through state support for immigrant associations (Spearman's rho=0.738, sign.<0.001). It can be noted that outlier Denmark, a country with a high score on consultative bodies but a low score on implementation policies, used to have relatively generous subsidies for immigrant organisations not so long ago. In the early nineties the Danish government, however, decided to abolish most of this support for immigrant organisations (Goli & Shahamak, 2005).

Apart from the links highlighted above, there are no significant relations between the other sub strands for political participation. Contrary to our expectations, they do not seem to co-vary in a straightforward way. Furthermore, and substantially of more importance, there is no negative correlation between electoral rights and consultative policies. Advisory and consultative bodies do not seem to function systematically as alternative solutions for the lack of electoral rights for TCNs, across the board. There is no positive correlation either. Some countries with electoral rights for TCNs have well developed advisory and consultative bodies, while others have not.

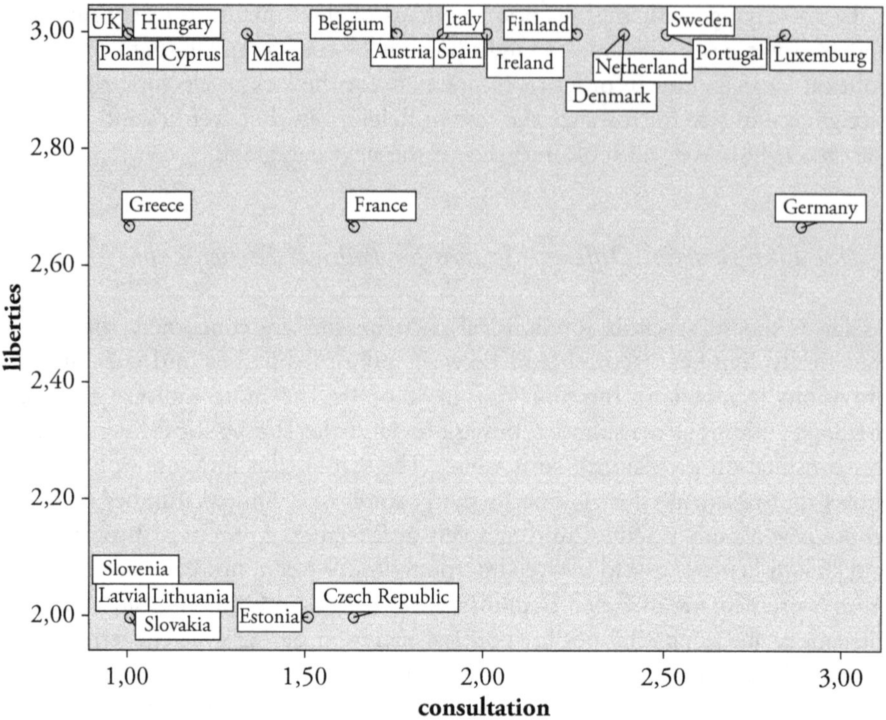

Figure 3: Scatterplot of index score for political liberties and consultative bodies

G. *The Support for More Ethnic Minority Politicians*

Unfortunately we have very limited cross European data with regard to the topic of public support for political inclusion of TCNs. Public opinion might function as an important trigger for the inclusion or non-inclusion of migrants in the political sphere. There is, however, one data source which might serve as a proxy for the measurement of public opinion with regard to this topic. Indeed, in the Special Eurobarometer on discrimination of 2006 one question surveyed support for descriptive representation on the basis of ethnicity: "Would you say that we need more members of parliament (MPs) of a different ethnic origin than the rest of the population?" Clearly, this question does not measure in a direct way the support for political inclusion of TCNs. Indeed, members of parliament in all countries have to be state citizens and can, hence, by definition not be TCNs. The question does survey, however, the degree of support for ethnic diversity in political representation in general.

In any event, there is a very clear association between the public support for more MPs of ethnic minority groups on the one hand and the openness of policy with regard to political inclusion of TCNs according to MIPEX on the

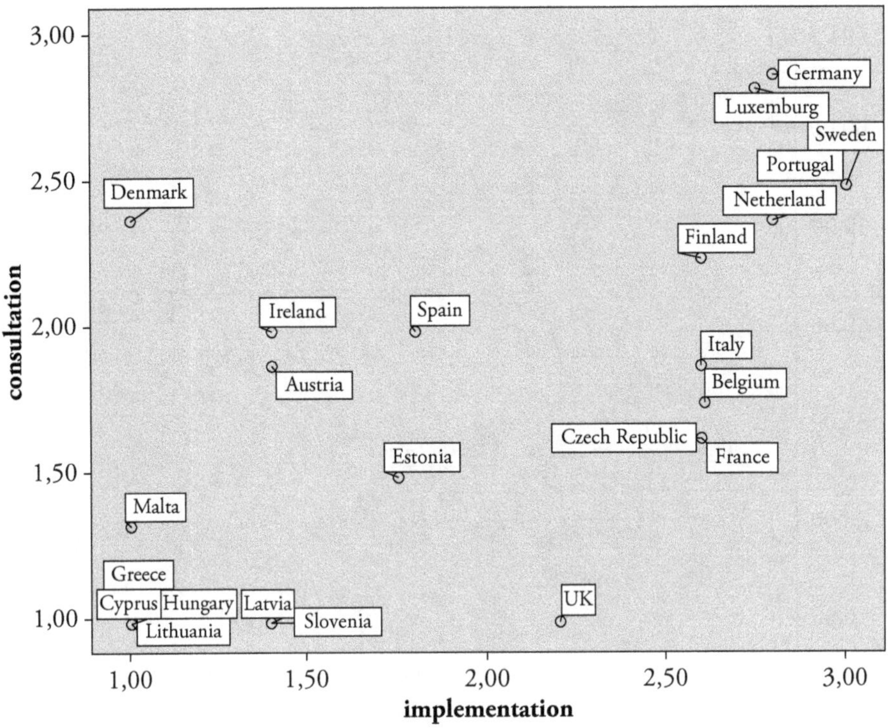

Figure 4: Scatterplot of index score for consultative bodies and implementation policies

other hand. Indeed, the proportion of inhabitants answering "yes, definitely" or "yes, probably" in the 25 EU Member States and all of the MIPEX indicators for political participation are highly correlated in positive way.[10] The opener the political opportunity structures for political inclusion of TCNs, the higher the support for the idea that there should be more MPs of a different ethnic origin.

The scatter plot in figure 5 shows the results for the overall political participation score. As one can notice, there is a strong positive relationship.

Apparently the existence of policies enabling political participation of TCNs (non-EU origin immigrants not holding state citizenship) does not have a negative

[10] Spearman's rho=0.752, sign.<0.001 for Political Participation, Spearman's rho=0.577, sign.<0.005 for Electoral Rights, Spearman's rho=0.464, sign.<0.05 for Political Liberties, Spearman's rho=0.605, sign.<0.005 for Consultative Bodies and Spearman's rho=0.592, sign.<0.005 for Implementation policies. All of these correlations remain significant after controlling for the percentage of foreigners in the country. The value of Spearman's rho=0.317, sign.=0.122 for Nationality Acquisition also seems to suggest a link with the wish to have more foreign origin MPs, although the result is strictly speaking not statistically significant.

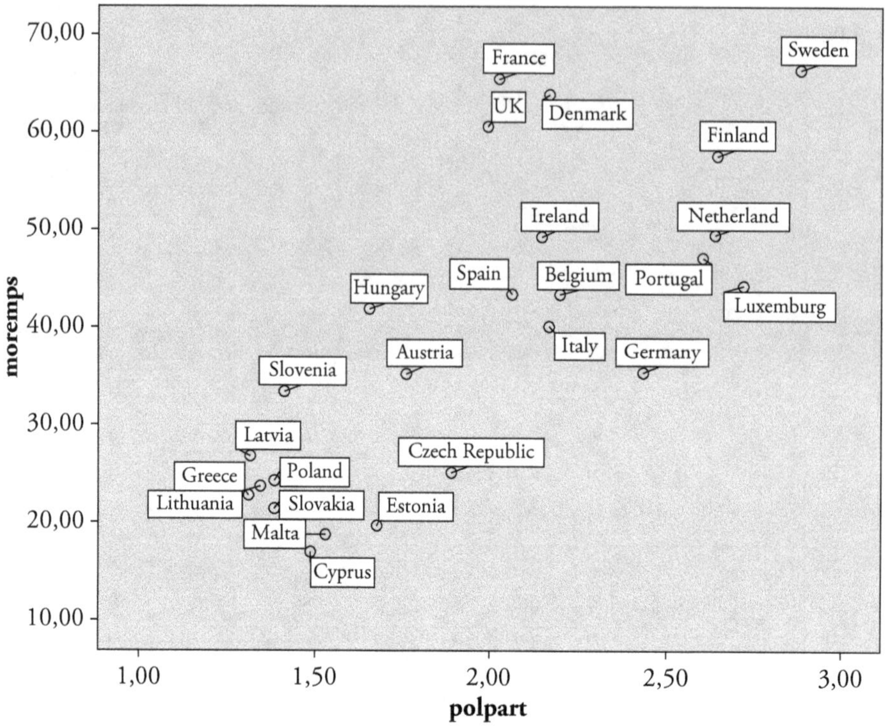

Figure 5: Scatterplot of index score political participation and the assessment that the country needs more MPs of a different ethnic origin (Eurobarometer 2006)

impact on the assessment whether there should be more foreign origin MPs in parliament, quite on the contrary. Remarkably, the effect holds after controlling for the number of foreign nationals living in the country.

We are not sure how to interpret this finding. One readily tends to assume that public opinion is a causal factor for policy change. Contrary to Freeman (1995), who thinks elite interests are the driving forces, authors like Lahav (2004) explicitly state that immigration and migrants' rights are policy areas in which public opinion matters. Political elites are heavily influenced by attitudes of the general public, she claims; "while national patterns vary, elites and the general publics embrace similar priorities and are driven by fears that converge considerably."[11] We could hence interpret the correlation in the following way; support by the public opinion for the idea of more ethnic diversity in the political arena is the motor behind more open political opportunity structures for TCNs. Resistance by the general public leads to a restrictive policy.

[11] Galya Lahav, *Immigration and politics in the New Europe. Reinventing borders*, 208 (Cambridge University Press, 2004).

There is, nevertheless, also an alternative interpretation. One might claim that the openness of political opportunity structures for political participation of foreigners from outside the EU increases awareness of (and support for) the normative ideal to have descriptive representation of foreign origin politicians in national parliament, reflecting ethnic diversity of society in the political arena at all levels. Policy change can, in other words, impact on public opinion. As an illustration we can cite the Dutch case of the 1980s, where a majority of public opinion opposing enfranchisement of foreign residents (before such a bill was passed) flipped over to a majority of supporters, once foreigners had been given voting rights (Jacobs, 1998b).

We should even consider the possibility of a feedback-effect in which both processes sequentially occur (public opinion impacting on policy making "and" policy making impacting on public opinion). We cannot assess this with our current data, but future editions of the policy index combined with more public opinion data might allow us to test a number of hypotheses in the upcoming years.

H. *Conclusion*

In this contribution we looked at the results of the MIPEX for the strand on political participation. Overall, it is safe to say there is still quite some room for improvement as far as policies towards political inclusion of TCNs are concerned. Most alarming is the conclusion that basic political liberties (for instance the right to association) for TCNs are still not assured in all EU Member States. Countries like the Czech Republic, Estonia, Latvia, Lithuania, Slovakia and Slovenia seriously lag behind on this point. Other countries not only assure political liberties but equally actively stimulate political inclusion through consultative bodies and electoral rights. Interestingly, there is no trade off between access to nationality and political rights for non-nationals, although this is often assumed. Even when nationality acquisition – a guarantee for full electoral rights on all levels – is facilitated in a considerable way, a number of countries still stimulate political inclusion of foreign residents, regardless of citizenship. Strikingly, there is a link between public opinion on diversity in politics and the openness of a state with regard to political participation of immigrants. Those countries which have a better score on the MIPEX strand for political participation have a larger part of public opinion which endorses the idea of more ethnic diversity among their political representatives. Probably it is public opinion which pushes policy in a certain direction (either more inclusive or less inclusive), but we cannot exclude it are changing political opportunity structures which have an impact on public attitudes. In fact, we suspect both processes are interlinked in a feedback process.

Annex 1: The Mipex Indicators for the Political Inclusion Strand

Dimension One: Access to Formal Political Rights for TCNs

Right to vote in national elections
a. equal rights as non-nationals after certain period of residence
b. reciprocity or other special conditions
c. no right

Right to vote in regional elections (sub-state entity or provincial level if not a federal state)
a. equal rights as non-nationals after certain period of residence
b. reciprocity, other special conditions, special registration procedure or only in some regions
c. no right

Right to vote in local elections
a. equal rights as EU-nationals
b. reciprocity, residence requirement, other special conditions or special registration procedure
c. no right

Right to stand for elections at local level
a. Unrestricted (as for EU-nationals)
b. Restricted to certain posts
c. No right or other restrictions apply

Dimension Two: Political Liberties

Right to association for foreign residents
a. No restrictions on creation of associations by foreigners, no restrictions regarding the composition of the board of such associations
b. A minimal number of national citizens should be on board
c. Other restrictions to associations for foreign residents apply

Membership of and participation to political parties
a. Equal access with nationals (no restrictions imposed by government)
b. Restricted access to internal elected positions
c. Other restrictions apply

Dimension Three: Consultation And Advice Bodies For TCN Groups

Consultation of foreign residents on national level

a. structural consultation through representative body (elected by foreign residents or members appointed by associations of foreign residents without special state intervention)
b. ad hoc consultation of immigrant organisations or token consultation (through non-representative state cooptation)
c. no consultation

Consultation of foreign residents on regional (sub-state entity or provincial) level

a. structural consultation through representative body (elected by foreign residents or members appointed by associations of foreign residents without state intervention)
b. ad hoc consultation of immigrant organisations, token consultation (through non-representative state cooptation), or structural consultation only present in some regional entities
c. no consultation

Consultation of foreign residents on local level

a. structural consultation through representative body (elected by foreign residents or members appointed by associations of foreign residents without state intervention) in local entities with significant numbers of foreign residents
b. ad hoc consultation of immigrant organisations, token consultation (through non-representative state cooptation) or structural consultation only present in some of the local entities with significant numbers of foreign residents
c. no consultation

Dimension Four: Implementation Policies

Active policy of information on political rights by national level (or by regional level in federal states)

a. policy of information targeted at foreign residents (or targeted at all) on individual basis
b. information campaigns (on a non-individual basis) towards foreign residents (or only individual campaigns in certain regions)
c. no active policy of information (or no political rights at any level to be informed about)

Funding of immigrant organisations on national level (or regional level in federal states)

a. support (in kind) or funding for immigrant organisations involved in consultation and advice at national or regional level without further conditions than being a partner in talks (or similar conditions as for non-immigrant organisations)
b. support or funding dependent on criteria set by the state (beyond being a partner in consultation and different than for non-immigrant groups), or only in some regions
c. no support or funding

Funding of immigrant organisations on local level

a. support (in kind) or funding for immigrant organisations involved in consultation and advice at local level without further conditions than being a partner in talks (or similar conditions as for non-immigrant organisations)
b. support or funding dependent on criteria set by the state (beyond being a partner in consultation and different than for non-immigrant groups), or only in some localities
c. no support or funding

List of References

CELIS, K. (2006) *De macht van het geslacht. Gender, politiek en beleid in België.* Leuven: Acco.

FENNEMA, M. (2001) *De Moderne Democratie. De Geschiedenis van een politieke theorie,* Amsterdam: Het Spinhuis.

FREEMAN, G. (1995) "Modes of Immigration Politics in Liberal Democratic States", *International Migration Review,* 29 (4): 881–908.

GAXIE, D. (1993) *Le cens caché. Inégalités culturelles et ségrégation politique.* Paris: Seuil.

GOLI, M. & R. SHAHAMAK (2005) *Active Civic Participation of Immigrants in Denmark,* Country Report prepared for the European research project POLITIS, Oldenburg. [http://www.uni-oldenburg.de/politis-europe]

HABERMAS, J. (1996) *Die Einbeziehung des Anderen. Studien zur politischen Theorie.* Frankfurt am Main: Suhrkamp Verlag.

HAMMAR, T. (1990) *Democracy and the Nation-State. Aliens, Denizens and Citizens in a World of International Migration.* Aldershot: Avebury.

JACOBS, D. (1998a) 'Les nouveaux venus dans la politique: réflexions sur la participation politique des étrangers', pp. 163–178 in *Engagements pour l'égalité, Rapport Annuel 1997 du Centre pour l'Egalité des Chances et la Lutte contre le Racisme.* Bruxelles: CECLR.

—— (1998b) *Nieuwkomers in de politiek.* Gent: Academia Press.

JACOBS, D., BOUSETTA, H., REA, A., MARTINIELLO, M. & SWYNGEDOUW, M. (2006) *Qui sont les candidats aux élections bruxelloises? Le profil des candidats à l'élection au parlement de la Région de Bruxelles Capitale du 13 Juin 2004,* Cahiers Migrations 37, Bruxelles: Academia Bruylant.

LAHAV, G. (2004) *Immigration and Politics in the New Europe. Reinventing Borders.* Cambridge: Cambridge University Press.

MANIN, B. (1996) *Principes du gouvernement représentatif.* Paris: Flammarion.

MARTINIELLO, M. (1997) 'Quelle participation politique?' in M. Coenen & Lewin, R. (red.) *La Belgique et ses Immigrés. Les politiques manquées.* Bruxelles: De Boeck Université.

NIESSEN, J., HUDDLESTON, T. & CITRON, L., in cooperation with GEDDES, A. & JACOBS, D. (2007) *Migrant Integration Policy Index.* Brussels: British Council and Migration Policy Group.

VERBA, S., SCHLOZMAN, K. & BRADY, H. (1995) *Voice and Equality. Civic voluntarism in American Politics.* Cambridge, Massachusetts: Harvard University Press.

Index

Immigration and Asylum Law and Policy in Europe

1. E. Guild and P. Minderhoud (eds.): *Security of Residence and Expulsion*. 2000 ISBN 90-411-1458-0
2. E. Guild: *Immigration Law in the European Community*. 2001 ISBN 90-411-1593-5
3. B. Melis: *Negotiating Europe's Immigration Frontiers*. 2001 ISBN 90-411-1614-1
4. R. Byrne, G. Noll and J. Vedsted-Hansen (eds.): *New Asylum Countries? Migration Control and Refugee Protection in an Enlarged European Union*. 2002 ISBN 90-411-1753-9
5. K. Groenendijk, E. Guild and P. Minderhoud (eds.): *In Search of Europe's Borders*. 2003 ISBN 90-411-1977-9
6. J. Niessen and I. Chopin (eds.): *The Development of Legal Instruments to Combat Racism in a Diverse Europe*. 2004 ISBN 90-04-13686-X
7. B. Bogusz, R. Cholewinski, A. Cygan and E. Szyszczak (eds.): *Irregular Migration and Human Rights: Theoretical, European and International Perspectives*. 2004 ISBN 90-04-14011-5
8. H. Battjes: *European Asylum Law and International Law*. 2006 ISBN 90-04-15087-0
9. Elspeth Guild and Paul Minderhoud (eds.): *Immigration and Criminal Law in the European Union: The Legal Measures and Social Consequences of Criminal Law in Member States on Trafficking and Smuggling in Human Beings*. 2006 ISBN 90-14-15064-1
10. Georgia Papagianni: *Institutional and Policy Dynamics of EU Migration Law*. 2006 ISBN 90-04-15279-2
11. Elspeth Guild and Anneliese Baldaccini (eds.): *Terrorism and the Foreigner: A Decade of Tension around the Rule of Law in Europe*. 2006 ISBN 90-04-015187-7
12. Steve Peers and Nicola Rogers (eds.): *EU Immigration and Asylum Law: Text and Commentary*. 2006 ISBN 90-04-15374-8
13. Prakash Shah (ed.): *Law and Ethnic Plurality: Socio-Legal Perspectives*. 2007 ISBN 978-90-04-16245-7
14. Bruno Nascimbene, Massimo Condinanzi and Alessandra Lang: *Citizenship of the Union and Free Movement of Persons*. 2008 ISBN 978-90-04-16300-3
15. Evelien Brouwer: *Digital Borders and Real Rights: Effective Remedies for Third-Country Nationals in the Schengen Information System*. 2008 ISBN 978-90-04-16503-8
16. Nils Coleman: *European Readmission Policy:Third Country Interests and Refugee Rights*. 2008 ISBN 978-90-04-16554-0
17. Sergio Carrera: *In Search of the Perfect Citizen? The Intersection between Integration, Immigration and Nationality in the EU*. 2009 ISBN 978-90-04-17509-9
18. Jan Niessen and Thomas Huddleston (eds.): *Legal Frameworks for the Integration of Third-Country Nationals*. 2009 ISBN 978-90-04-17069-8

Martinus Nijhoff Publishers – Leiden · Boston

www.ingramcontent.com/pod-product-compliance
Lightning Source LLC
LaVergne TN
LVHW080847300926
849162LV00003B/362